Volcanoes
and
Earthquakes

Other Books in the
DISCOVERING SCIENCE SERIES

VIOLENT STORMS (No. 2942)

This second book in the series deals with the atmospheric and climatic phenomena of Earth, as well as their effect on man and their influence on our planet.

MYSTERIOUS OCEANS (No. 3042)

The third volume in the series looks at the hydrologic phenomenon of Earth—its origin, purpose, mechanisms, and effect on life. The book concentrates on the oceans' role on our planet.

THE LIVING EARTH (No. 3142)

The fourth book in the series focuses on the biological phenomenon of Earth. It looks at the origins, history, and future of life, as well as the effects that the geologic, climatic, and hydrologic phenomena have on life.

EXPLORING EARTH FROM SPACE (No. 3242)

The final volume in the series deals with the technologic advances that enable us to view our planet from space. It covers the way man-made satellites can provide us with better information on the geologic, climatic, biologic, and hydrologic phenomena of our planet and enable us to better predict disasters, locate and monitor natural resources, and explore our Solar System.

Volcanoes
and
Earthquakes

Jon Erickson

TAB BOOKS Inc.
Blue Ridge Summit, PA

FIRST EDITION
SECOND PRINTING

Copyright © 1988 by TAB BOOKS Inc.
Printed in the United States of America

Library of Congress Cataloging in Publication Data

Erickson, Jon, 1948-
Volcanoes and earthquakes.

Bibliography: p.
Includes index.
1. Volcanoes. 2. Earthquakes. I. Title.
QE521.E75   1987   551.2'1   87-18030

ISBN 0-8306-1942-9
ISBN 0-8306-2842-8 (pbk.)

TAB BOOKS Inc. offers software for
sale. For information and a catalog,
please contact TAB Software Department,
Blue Ridge Summit, PA 17294-0850.

Questions regarding the content of this book
should be addressed to:

Reader Inquiry Branch
TAB BOOKS Inc.
Blue Ridge Summit, PA 17294-0214

Front cover photograph courtesy of United States Geological Survey.
Back cover photographs courtesy of National Oceanographic and
Atmospheric Administration

Contents

Acknowledgments

The following people and institutions are recognized for their help in obtaining photographs and editorial assistance: Carol Edwards and Joe McGregor (Geological Survey); Helen Bailey (National Oceanic and Atmospheric Administration); James Hughes and Jill Bauermeister (National Forest Service); Bill Graham, Maude Mosher, and Sally Murphy (Department of Energy, Grand Junction Office); Nina Cummings (Chicago Field Museum of Natural History); Nancy Green (Woods Hole Oceanographic Institution), Ruth Price (Department of Agriculture), the National Aeronautics and Space Administration; Kitt Peak National Observatory; family members; and friends.

Introduction

THE most fascinating subject of earth science is the dynamic processes that created the Earth. Earth science encompasses a wide range of fields, including geology, biology, oceanography, meteorology, and astronomy and combines them into one comprehensive study of the Earth. Earth science is an inadequate term though, because not all of natures forces are confined solely to the Earth. Every planet in our Solar System, and, indeed, every planet that exists in the wide expanse of space, obeys the same laws of nature. Therefore, it is expected that the Earth is not alone as far as the physical processes, such as volcanoes and earthquakes, are concerned. Whether life exists outside the Earth has not yet been proven. The search for a better understanding of the Earth and the universe might some day provide the answers to some of the most complexing questions that scholars and scientists alike have asked throughout man's short stay on this planet.

To learn how we got where we are, turn a telescope on the heavens and look at the beginning of time. The universe can be seen as though it were a vast nuclear explosion, infinitely larger than the weapons man has managed to create on Earth. The nuclear core of this bomb utilized almost all the matter in the universe, creating the largest explosion ever imagined. Matter was dispersed violently in all directions, and some sort of quirk of nature that scientists do not fully understand allowed it all to clump together into galaxies, stars, and planets. The most distant galaxies, far beyond the reach of the telescope, are moving away from each other at fantastic speeds. Either they will continue to fly apart, until all that is left is a thin veil of radiation, or gravity will pull them all back together into a dense cosmic soup whereupon the universe explodes again into new life.

The telescope zooms in on the Sun and its planets and shows how the Solar System formed out of intergalatic gases and dust particles, probably leftovers from a supernova exploding in the vicinity. The Sun continued to grow and caught fire when it reached a certain critical mass. Had Jupiter grown larger, Earth might be receiving light from two suns. Many stars are twins.

The sun is only one-third as old as the universe and is about halfway through its normal life span, after which it will puff up and become a red giant. Most likely, half the stars in our galaxy have planets, and, as yet, no one can be totally certain how many of these contain life.

It is fairly certain that only one planet in our Solar System can support living beings, which have been around in one form or another for three-quarters of Earth's history. The events of the first quarter of Earth's history can only be surmised because even the oldest rocks found on earth are not much older than life itself.

If you could turn the telescope backwards and use it to peer deep into the interior of the Earth, you would find a solid metallic core, surrounded by a liquid outer part, slowly rotating like a gigantic dynamo. The dynamo effect generates a magnetic field that helps navigators find their way and shields the Earth from harmful cosmic radiation. Above the core is the mantle that ever so imperceptibly churns over hot rocks in a vast firey cauldron. The mantle is heated by the same kind of energy used in nuclear power plants. The crust is nothing but a thin, cracked shell of solid rock consisting of plates of various sizes that are being shoved in what appears to be haphazard directions. The plates are constantly bumping into each other and form many of the land features of the Earth, including volcanoes and earthquakes. At one time, animals from Africa walked over to South America, Australia, and India — before great rifts split the land into new continents.

Taking the telescope into outer space and focusing it on the Earth, the oceans are colored a majestic blue, the land is tinged green, and whisps of white clouds float lazily by. The water and the atmosphere originally were sweated out of the mantle by erupting through the volcanic pores in the crust.

Sometime around the Earth's 4-billionth birthday, a precarious layer of ozone appeared in the upper layers of the atmosphere. This shielded out one of the most deadly radiations from the Sun, ultraviolet rays, which allowed the land to become teaming with life. This essentially is what makes the Earth unique among the planets of the Solar System. It is as though it were a living, breathing entity replete with all the right ingredients necessary to support all creatures great and small. The planet maintains a balance between the toxic elements and those that are beneficial to life. Regretably, man's activities in recent years has overloaded this living system with poisons.

If your telescope is taken back in time to the Pleistocene Epoch and aimed toward East Africa, a peculiar-looking animal could be seen walking across the desert floor. What sets this animal apart from all others is that he is nearly hairless and walks upright on his hind legs. Clutched firmly in one hand is a spear, carried in a determined manner, for this animal is stalking prey. Whether it is man or beast is not readily discerned. How this species we call Homo sapiens managed to survive his earliest ordeals probably had more to do with luck rather than braininess. Nevertheless, this animal's constant quest for knowledge about his surroundings has brought the world closer to an understanding of the Earth. Unfortunately, not all science is used for the betterment of the world. If Earth should turn out to be the only planet of its kind in the universe, it is our responsibility to see to it that it lives on to a ripe old age.

In the Beginning

SOMETIME between 13 and 18 billion years ago, the universe began with an explosion that created a shock front, traveling at near the speed of light. Behind this shock front were eddies of swirling matter from which galaxies were formed. Like an enormous nuclear fireball, the universe rapidly ballooned, creating matter out of pure energy as it continued its expansion. Within the first second of its life, the universe had a density equal to that of the Earth squeezed down to the size of a glass marble, and the temperature was 10 billion degrees centigrade, hotter than the interior of the largest stars. This primordial soup contained a plasma of elementary particles, consisting of 98 percent of all matter existing in the universe today. In the first three minutes of its life, the universe cooled to 1 billion degrees, and the density was less than that of water. Protons and neutrons began to form atomic nuclei composed of three-quarters hydrogen and one-quarter helium. After another half million years, the universe cooled to a few thousand degrees, near the temperature of the Sun's surface. At this temperature, electrons joined nuclei to form atoms. After 1 billion years, gravitational forces caused matter to clump together, forming a billion galaxies, each composed of 100 billion stars or more; the total number of which is equal to the number of atoms in a sugar cube.

EARLY THEORIES ON CREATION

The quest for understanding the universe began as far back as when man first raised his eyes to the night's sky and contemplated the myriad of stars overhead. Some thought that the Earth was flat and others considered the heavens the domain of the gods. Early religion and philosophy taught that the Earth was the center of the universe. Indeed, observation of the heavenly bodies seemed to bear this out.

By 350 B.C., Greek philosophers were beginning to believe that the Earth was a sphere and the universe was composed of an infinite number of worlds. Nearly nineteen centuries later, in 1522, Ferdinand Magellan proved that the Greeks were right by circumnavigating the globe. In 1543, the

Polish astronomer Nicolas Copernicus proposed that the Earth and the other planets revolved around the Sun. This radical notion ran counter to the Church, which believed that all bodies in the universe revolved around the Earth. In 1600, the Italian philospher Giordano Bruno was burned at the stake for heresy because he dared to suggest that there existed other inhabited worlds.

When Galileo Galilei invented (or reinvented) the telescope in 1608 and turned it on the night sky, a band of light known to the early Greeks as the galaxias, because of its milky appearance, was revealed to be a multitude of stars recognized today as the Milky Way galaxy (FIG. 1-1). Perhaps, Galileo is better known for his famous gravity experiment whereupon he dropped two different size balls from the Tower of Pisa to prove that the acceleration of gravity would cause them to hit the ground at the same time. The English physicist Isaac Newton, born in 1642, the same year that Galileo died, carried on where Galileo left off. Newton developed the laws of motion which precisely predicted the orbits of the planets (FIG. 1-2), and whose equations are used even today to launch objects into space. Like Galileo, he was interested in gravity, and proposed that gravity not only acts on the Earth but also affects the Moon, planets, and stars.

Newton was also responsible for discovering the solar spectrum. By passing sunlight through a prism, he was able to split the light into its separate band of colors. Different colors represent different wavelengths of visible light from red, the longest, to violet, the shortest. Astronomers are able to observe the spectrum of distant stars to determine their composition.

One of Newton's closest friends, the English astronomer Edmund Halley, whose namesake comet again passed by the Sun in early 1986 (FIG. 1-3), proposed one of the strangest paradoxes in astronomy. In 1720, Halley argued that if the universe was infinite the night sky would be saturated with starlight because a star would be seen in every point in the sky.

Over a hundred years later, in 1826, the idea was revived by the German astronomer Hinrich

Olbers, and today it is known as Olbers' Paradox. However, if the universe was expanding, not all the stars would be visible. Newton was also in favor of an infinite universe. He assumed that matter in the universe was evenly disbursed. And if the universe was finite, gravity would have caused all matter to collect in its center, and there would not be a multitude of individual stars but only a single huge luminous mass. Today, astronomers do not speak in terms of infinite or finite universe, but, instead, whether the universe is open or closed.

The English astronomer Thomas Wright suggested in 1750 that the known universe — at that time limited to the Milky Way galaxy due to the low power of early telescopes — was in the shape of a disk. Another English astronomer, Sir William Herschel, proposed in 1784 that the Milky Way was a lens-shaped cluster of stars with the Sun in the center. Herschel envisioned the Milky Way galaxy being composed of 300 million stars, 8000 light years across, and 1500 light years thick at the center. Today, astronomers estimate that our Galaxy consists of 100 billion stars, 100,000 light years across with a central bulge 8000 light years thick. The Sun lies in one of the three principal spiral arms about three-fifths the way out from the center of the Galaxy. It makes one complete revolution in about 200 million years, traveling at a speed of roughly 150 miles per second.

THE RED SHIFT

The Austrian mathematician Christian Johann Doppler pointed out in 1842 that sound and light waves shifted their frequency when the source was in motion relative to an outside observer. If the source was moving away, the frequency was lowered, and if the source was approaching, the frequency was raised (FIG. 1-4). The Doppler effect was later tested with a brass band playing a steady note on a fast moving train. As the train approached a listener, the sound waves were compressed in front of the train, giving the impression that the pitch was higher. When the train passed the listener, the sound waves became rarefied, and the pitch was lowered.

FIG. 1-1. The Milky Way Galaxy. (Courtesy of Kitt Peak National Observatory.)

Fig. 1-2. Orbits of the planets. (Courtesy of NASA.)

FIG. 1-3. Halley's Comet. (Courtesy of Kitt Peak National Observatory.)

When the Doppler effect was first applied to the stars within our Galaxy, it was found that the light from some stars was shifted to the red end of the spectrum, meaning they were receding from the Earth. Other stars were found to have their light shifted toward the blue end of the spectrum, indicating they were approaching the Earth.

It was not until the Doppler effect, or red shift, was applied to stars outside the Milky Way galaxy that confirmation of an expanding universe was found (FIG. 1-5). In 1923, using the new, 100-inch Mount Wilson telescope outside of Los Angeles, the American astronomer Edwin Hubble was able to resolve the Andromeda nebula (FIG. 1-6), our nearest galaxy, into individual stars — proving it was another spiral galaxy similar to our own Galaxy.

A nebula is a cloud of glowing gas and dust particles. Due to the poor resolution of the earlier telescopes, many galaxies were mistaken for nebulae because of their fuzzy appearance. The apparent luminosity of its stars was used to determine the distance to our closest galaxy, which is roughly

2 million light years away. Observations of the Doppler effect of Andromeda and other galaxies indicated that some were approaching our Galaxy, while others were receding from our Galaxy. Therefore, galaxies within our galactic cluster appeared to be moving in random directions relative to the Earth, while those outside appeared to be rushing away as though the universe was exploding.

In 1929, Hubble announced his discovery that the red shifts of distant galaxies increased proportional to their distance from the Earth. In other words, the greater the distance of the galaxies the faster they were rushing away, just as one would expect if the universe was exploding.

With knowledge of the velocities of the farthest visible galaxies, some of which are approaching the speed of light, the outer distance of the universe can be determined, and by reversing their tracks back to the very beginning, the age of the universe can be calculated. When Hubble first tried this method, he obtained a date of only 2 billion years. This could not possibly be correct because

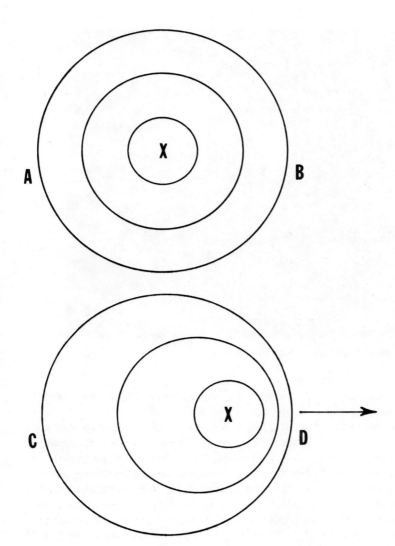

Fig. 1-4. The Doppler effect. Sound waves are compressed in front and rarefied behind as X moves from C to D.

the Earth is believed to be 4.6 billion years old. Modern calculation of the "Hubble age" is about 15 billion years, give or take a few billion years. This is the age accepted by most astronomers as the age of the universe. This would also give the universe a circumference of nearly a 100 billion light years.

THE BIG BANG THEORY

The first to predict that the universe was expanding was the Soviet mathematician Alex-ander Friedman, who realized in 1922 that the universe could exist in only one of two states. Either it had to be expanding or contracting at a steady rate. Also, if the mass of the universe was less than a certain critical value, the universe would continue to expand indefinitely. The Big Bang theory was originally proposed by the Belgian astrophysicist Georges Lemaitre who, unaware of Friedman's work, published a paper on the subject in 1927. Like Friedman, he was mostly ignored by the scientific community.

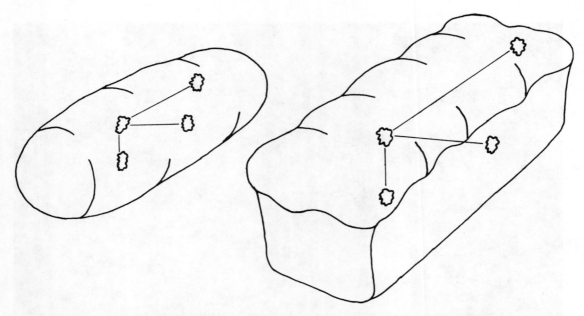

FIG. 1-5. The expanding universe is compared to raisins expanding in rising bread dough.

In 1933, Lemaitre proposed that the universe originally consisted of a primeval atom that contained all the matter that would later become the universe. He envisioned this matter flying apart like splitting atoms in a nuclear explosion. Lemaitre assumed that if the universe was expanding, it must have once existed in a very condensed state.

One of Friedman's former students, a physicist named George Gamow who, after emigrating to the United States, modernized Lemaitre's theory and coined the term Big Bang. In his theory, the early universe was composed of neutrons packed tightly together in a fireball of tremendous temperature, so hot that there was more energy than matter.

After the universe expanded and cooled, about half of the free neutrons decayed into protons, electrons, and neutrinos (little neutrons), providing the basic building blocks for hydrogen and helium — the major elements in the universe. But the universe could not have started out with free neutrons alone, and something else had to be responsi-ble for the heavier elements, or metals (see TABLE 1-1).

The chief rival to the Big Bang theory was the steady-state theory proposed in 1948 by Hermann Bondi, Thomas Gold, and Fred Hoyle. According to this theory, the universe appears to be expanding as shown by the red shifts of the distant galaxies, but the space vacated by galaxies receding from each other is filled by newly created matter which formed new galaxies. In other words, matter is all the time being created at the precise rate required to fill the voids caused by the expansion of the universe. This implies that the universe had no beginning and, also, has no end. Although this theory might be philosophically and emotionally appealing, it was little more than scientific hocus-pocus.

One of the major problems with the theory was where did all this new matter come from? Proponents of the theory suggested that positive matter could be created out of negative energy without breaking any of the laws of physics. Some adherents proposed the idea of special centers of

FIG. 1-6. The Andromeda Galaxy. (Courtesy of Kitt Peak National Observatory.)

TABLE 1-1. Abundance of Chemical Elements in the Universe

Name	Symbol	Atomic Number	Atomic Weight	Relative Abundance
Hydrogen	H	1	1	1.0×10^{12}
Helium	He	2	4	8.5×10^{10}
Lithium	Li	3	7	1000
Berylium	Be	4	9	15
Boron	B	5	11	200
Carbon	C	6	12	4.8×10^{8}
Nitrogen	N	7	14	8.5×10^{7}
Oxygen	O	8	16	8.0×10^{8}
Fluorine	F	9	19	3.4×10^{4}
Neon	Ne	10	20	1.0×10^{8}
Sodium	Na	11	23	2.1×10^{6}
Magnesium	Mg	12	24	3.9×10^{7}
Aluminum	Al	13	27	3.1×10^{6}
Silicon	Si	14	28	3.7×10^{7}
Phosphorous	P	15	31	3.5×10^{5}
Sulfur	S	16	32	1.7×10^{7}
Chlorine	Cl	17	36	1.7×10^{5}
Argon	Ar	18	40	3.3×10^{6}
Potassium	K	19	39	1.3×10^{5}
Calcium	Ca	20	40	2.3×10^{6}
Scandium	Sc	21	45	1.3×10^{3}
Titanium	Ti	22	48	1.0×10^{5}
Vanadium	V	23	51	1.0×10^{4}
Chromium	Cr	24	52	4.8×10^{5}
Manganese	Mn	25	55	2.9×10^{5}
Iron	Fe	26	56	3.3×10^{7}
Cobalt	Co	27	59	7.8×10^{4}
Nickel	Ni	28	59	7.8×10^{4}
Copper	Cu	29	64	1.9×10^{4}
Zinc	Zn	30	65	5.0×10^{4}
Gallium	Ga	31	70	1800
Germanium	Ge	32	73	4300
Arsenic	As	33	75	240
Selenium	Se	34	79	2500
Bromine	Br	35	80	520
Krypton	Kr	36	84	1700
Rubidium	Rb	37	85	220
Strontium	Sr	38	88	1000
Yttrium	Y	39	89	185
Zirconium	Zr	40	91	1000
Niobium	Nb	41	93	52
Molybdenum	Mo	42	96	150
Technetium	Tc	43	99	—

TABLE 1-1. **Abundance of Chemical Elements in the Universe**

NAME	SYMBOL	ATOMIC NUMBER	ATOMIC WEIGHT	RELATIVE ABUNDANCE
Ruthenium	Ru	44	101	70
Rhodium	Rh	45	103	15
Palladium	Pd	46	106	48
Silver	Ag	47	108	17
Cadmium	Cd	48	112	56
Indium	In	49	115	7.4
Tin	Sn	50	119	130
Antimony	Sb	51	122	11
Tellurium	Te	52	128	240
Iodine	I	53	127	41
Xenon	Xe	54	131	200
Cesium	Cs	55	133	15
Barium	Ba	56	137	180
Lanthanum	La	57	139	15
Cerium	Ce	58	140	44
Praesodymium	Pr	59	141	5.5
Neodymium	Nd	60	144	30
Promethium	Pm	61	147	—
Samarium	Sm	62	150	7.4
Europium	Eu	63	152	3.0
Gadolinium	Gd	64	157	11
Terbium	Tb	65	159	1.8
Dysprosium	Dy	66	163	13
Holmium	Ho	67	165	3.0
Erbium	Er	68	167	7.4
Thulium	Tm	69	169	1.3
Ytterbium	Yb	70	173	8.1
Lutetium	Lu	71	175	1.5
Halfnium	Hf	72	178	7.8
Tantalum	Ta	73	181	0.7
Tungsten	W	74	184	5.9
Rhenium	Re	75	186	1.8
Osmium	Os	76	190	28
Iridium	Ir	77	192	27
Platinum	Pt	78	195	52
Gold	Au	79	197	7.4
Mercury	Hg	80	201	15
Thallium	Tl	81	204	7.0
Lead	Pb	82	207	111
Bismuth	Bi	83	209	5.2
Polonium	Po	84	210	
Astatine	At	85	211	
Radon	Rn	86	222	

TABLE 1-1. Abundance of Chemical Elements in the Universe

NAME	SYMBOL	ATOMIC NUMBER	ATOMIC WEIGHT	RELATIVE ABUNDANCE
Francium	Fr	87	223	
Radium	Ra	88	226	
Actinium	Ac	89	227	
Thorium	Th	90	232	1.8
Protactinium	Pa	91	231	
Uranium	U	92	238	1.1
Neptunium	Np	93	237	
Plutonium	Pu	94	242	
Americium	Am	95	243	
Curium	Cm	96	243	
Berkelium	Bk	97	245	
Californium	Ca	98	246	
Einsteinium	Es	99	253	
Fermium	Fm	100	254	
Mendelevium	Mv	101	254	
Nobelium	No	102		
Lawrencium	Lw	103		

creation where huge amounts of matter gushed violently into space. Heated debates over which of the two creational theories were correct erupted throughout the decade of the 1950s, with the steady-state theory finally falling from grace in the 1960s.

THE COSMIC NOISE

In order to prove the Big Bang theory, there had to be direct evidence that the universe did indeed have a beginning. According to the theory, the universe in its early stages was very hot, on the order of billions of degrees centigrade. All objects above absolute zero (−273 degrees centigrade or 0 degrees Kelvin) radiate energy.

For instance, a light bulb gives off light in the visible spectrum by virtue of its white-hot filament. When the lamp is turned off, it continues to radiate invisible infrared energy. Physicists have calculated that at present, 15 billion years after the Big Bang, the leftover energy of the fireball should have cooled to 3 degrees above absolute zero, or 3 degrees Kelvin. It so happens that this tempera-

ture represents the microwave region of the electromagnetic spectrum, between radio and infrared wavelengths; the very same energy used to cook food in microwave ovens (FIG. 1-7).

A search for this leftover radiation from the Big Bang began in 1965 when the American physicist Robert Dicke, a pioneer in radio astronomy, and his coworkers set up a small microwave antenna on the roof of the physics laboratory at Princeton University. At the same time, two Bell Telephone scientists, Arno Penzias and Robert Wilson, were working on a satellite communication system at the Bell laboratory in Holmdel, New Jersey. Satellite communications was in its infancy, and experiments were conducted to test the ability of satellites to return radio signals to Earth. The Bell scientists built a 20-foot, horn-shaped radio telescope that was capable of being directed toward a satellite in any direction.

Signals received from a distant satellite would be extremely weak. Therefore, any noise generated internally by receiver circuits and externally by the antenna and surrounding medium had to be eliminated. When the radio receiver was tuned to a

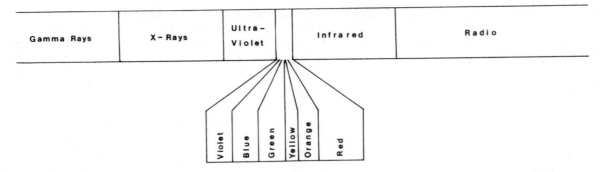

FIG. 1-7. The electromagnetic spectrum.

frequency of about 4000 megahertz, a hissing noise, like static from a transistor radio, was picked up in all directions. Penzias and Wilson, certain that the noise was coming from the antenna, disassembled, cleaned, and rebuilt it—to no avail. The annoying hiss remained.

Word about the perplexing noises that plagued the two Bell scientists reached their colleagues at Princeton through the scientists' grapevine. Apparently, the noise they were receiving was not from any terrestrial source, but cosmic microwave background radiation originating from deep space. The signal was not really noise after all, but microwave radiation that is a direct consequence of the Big Bang. This microwave background should not be mistaken for the average temperature of the universe because it is not recently emitted by bodies with temperatures of 3 degrees Kelvin. Instead, it has been traveling around the universe since the very beginning. For stumbling across what might well be the greatest scientific discovery in this century, Penzias and Wilson were awarded the Nobel Prize in physics in 1978.

Another puzzling question about the universe concerns why there is so much helium. Helium is observed on the surface of the Sun, and it was discovered on the Sun even before it was found on Earth. Helium exists in the stars of our own Galaxy, the stars of other galaxies, and in interstellar space. It is estimated that the universe is composed of 25 percent helium, 75 percent hydrogen, and minor amounts of other elements. The nuclear fusion reactions that power the stars and convert hydrogen into helium can only account for a few percent of the helium. Therefore, the bulk of the helium must have come from the Big Bang.

The early universe was composed of half protons and half neutrons, as opposed to all neutrons in the Gamow theory. Under extreme temperatures and pressures, collisions between protons and neutrons formed nuclei of deuterium (one proton, one neutron), tritium (one proton, two neutrons), and helium (two protons, two neutrons). All free neutrons not captured by nuclei, swiftly decayed into protons, electrons, and neutrinos until the universe was almost entirely composed of protons, helium nuclei, free electrons, and neutrinos.

After about a half billion years, the universe cooled to the point where electrons were captured by nuclei, forming our present day ratio of hydrogen and helium.

THE OPEN UNIVERSE CONCEPT

With strong evidence confirming the Big Bang theory, the question that was on scientists' minds was whether the universe was open or closed. Scientists and philosophers alike tend to get a little jittery when dealing with the infinite, and a closed universe seems easier to grasp and the mathematics are more tidy than in an open one. An open universe keeps on expanding until all the stars burn out, and the available intergalactic hydrogen gas, from which new stars are created, runs out. A closed universe, on the other hand, would be cyclical; therefore, it could live on forever. Successive collapses and re-explosions, called the "Big Bounce," could rejuvenate the universe every 100 billion years or so. This seems to be more philosophically satisfying, partly because it is in human nature to want the universe to live on indefinitely.

By the mid 1970s, evidence began mounting in favor of an open universe. Given the average mass density of the universe, there is just not enough matter for gravity to pull it all back together again; therefore, the universe would continue to fly apart. In other words, a rapidly expanding universe would not be dense enough for a collapse to occur. There is also too much primordial deuterium leftover from the Big Bang for the universe to be closed.

Rapid expansion of the infant universe caused matter to remained closely packed for only a short time, allowing deuterium to escape into space. Otherwise, if the expansion was slower, which would be the case if the universe was closed, most of the deuterium would have broken up. Also, in a closed universe, the fireball is allowed to cook longer; therefore, more helium should be produced than what is observed, indicating the universe is rapidly receding and thus open.

GALAXY FORMATION

Part of the problem of deciding whether the universe is open or closed stems from the fact that scientists do not fully understand the mechanics of galaxy formation. The force of the Big Bang explosion should be such that would make it impossible for the formation of galaxies, since matter was hurled outward at such fantastic velocities. Any clumping of matter resulting from currents and eddies in the plasma would rapidly break up like ripples in a flowing stream. Radiation pressure would also see to it that atoms would remain apart, just as an automobile tire remains inflated by air molecules bouncing off its rubber sides. Also, it takes too long for a collection of atoms to build up to galactic size. Therefore, rapid aggregation of matter must take place. Otherwise, expansion will

carry the material out of reach, and galaxies could not possibly form.

The universe could also have been created with matter already clumped together. If the Big Bang started out lumpy, like lumps in a bowl of cream of wheat, then there still remains the question of where did these lumps come from. Somehow, condensations would have had to occur very early in the life of the universe. Otherwise, matter would have been too widespread, and gravity would have had no chance to pull it all together into lumps of matter. Currents and eddies in the primordial soup can not satisfactorily account for the compression of matter into galaxies either. In another idea, the birth of the universe was not a single big bang, but a multitude of "little bangs" that forced matter to compress into galaxies. The universe could have erupted frothlike, similar to opening a shaken bottle of beer. The galaxies could have formed where the bubbles made contact with each other. According to another theory, magnetic fields produced the lumps. Also, if the universe was closed, the lumps could have come from melted down galaxies during the Big Bounce. Unfortunately, not even the whole of human existence up to now is enough time to observe the formation of a new galaxy.

THE MISSING MASS PROBLEM

The inability to observe a new galaxy coming into being provides a major stumbling block in determining certain qualities about our universe. For without knowledge of the formation of galaxies, scientists cannot know how much matter is in the form of galaxies, and how much is interstellar gas and dust. This makes it difficult to determine the actual amount of mass in the universe which will determine whether the universe is open or closed.

In other words, by just the observation of the visible matter in the universe, scientists can draw the conclusion that the universe is open. But it is the matter which cannot be seen — including galaxies beyond the reach of our telescopes and invisible hydrogen, helium, and dust particles — that might tip the scales in favor of a closed universe. This is called the "missing mass" problem.

Not all the mass in the galaxies is accounted for by visible mass alone. There must be an additional mass that allows mutual gravitational attraction between galaxies in large clusters. Because about 70 percent of all galaxies are bound up in clusters that are themselves clustered in even larger groups called superclusters, this so-called missing mass can be quite large.

If the Milky Way galaxy can be considered average in size, with some 100 billion stars, and the observable universe has over a billion galaxies, then star counting alone can not account for all the mass in the universe. It was found that dark galactic haloes, composed of hydrogen, neutrinos, and possibly remnants of dead stars or stars that never ignited, contained much more mass than the galaxies themselves. Some invisible mass is also bound up in black holes. These are regions in space and the centers of galaxies composed of very massive collapsed stars that gobble up matter; even light can not escape such powerful gravitational attraction.

A black hole has also been described as a miniature closed universe where nothing can get out. Letting the imagination run wild, one could envision our universe as a black hole within another universe, which is itself another black hole within another universe, ad infinitum.

Throughout the decade of the 1970s, arguments continued to rage whether or not there was enough matter to close the universe. Then in the early 1980s, new discoveries were made indicating that most of the mass of the universe could be in a form other than matter. Neutrinos, or little neutrons, are leftovers from the Big Bang and are also produced in nuclear reactions in stars and nuclear power plants on Earth. They have been described as the nearest thing next to nothing ever conceived by physicists, and exist in a ratio of several billion for every atom of ordinary matter. Although neutrinos might appear to be good candidates for the missing mass, they seem to have no appreciable rest mass and could not contribute significantly to the overall mass of the universe.

In recent years, there has been a profusion of discoveries of elementary particles, from various baryons (proton and neutron class) to leptons (electron class). Also, every particle should have a mirror image of itself or antiparticle that is opposite in all respects. This condition was once thought to play havoc with the Big Bang theory.

During the instant of creation, there should have been an equal amount of matter and antimatter. When two opposite particles collide, they annihilate each other — producing energy. If this is the case, then scientists have a difficult time explaining why there seems to be a predominance of matter in the universe. Matter and antimatter could have segregated into two hemispheres; one containing matter, the other containing antimatter. At the matter-antimatter interface, there should be mutual annihilation and subsequent photon and gamma radiation. But astronomers are unable to detect what should obviously be a clear demarcation in the universe. For whatever reason, nature favored matter over antimatter. Perhaps the universe is left-handed for similar reasons that DNA molecules exist in only left-handed spirals.

If it can be proved that the neutrino did indeed have even a tiny mass, their overwhelming numbers could easily make up for the missing mass in the universe, and a number of outstanding problems could be cleared up. Soviet physicists at the Institute of Theoretical and Experimental Physics in Moscow reported they had detected a neutrino mass. Western scientists who had yet to catch the elusive particle, which can penetrate the Earth without slowing down, refuted the Soviet's findings. Nevertheless, if neutrinos do have mass, they could be responsible for the galactic haloes and most of the mass in the galaxies. It could also be that neutrinos were responsible for galaxy formation in the first place by increasing their gravitational attraction. In other words, the galaxies could have first began with lumps of neutrinos that existed before atoms were created. Neutrinos concentrated in the galactic haloes, however, cannot account for all the missing mass; therefore, they alone cannot close the universe.

THE BIG CRUNCH

If the universe is closed, then in about another 40 billion years it will cease its expansion. As a ball tossed into the air stops for a moment before returning earthwards, so will all the galaxies in the universe reverse their courses and return to their point of origin. This is what is known as the "Big Crunch." Instead of light from the distant galaxies being red-shifted, as it is now, it will become blue-shifted as galaxies approach each other.

By the time the universe again reaches its present size, it will be 80 billion years older, and most of the stars, including the Sun, will have long past died. Galaxies will be less luminous, with a greater proportion of white dwarfs, neutron stars, and other faint objects. As the universe contracts to one-thousandth of its present size, space will pervade with brightness. Interstellar matter will begin to disassociate itself into nuclei and electrons. Eventually, the stars and their planets will melt down into a universal melting pot. The universe will continue to compress down to the original state of the Big Bang, whence it will rebound in a new Big Bang.

If this prospect for the future is unsatisfactory, there is always the open universe concept. All matter in the universe will be like air molecules in an atmosphere that is constantly getting thinner. Stars will burn out, and galaxies will get dimmer. The densely packed stars in the galactic cores will coalesce into black holes which, in turn, will gobble up the remaining stars in the galaxies. Stars on the very fringes of galaxies will simply evaporate. Eventually, all matter will become unstable and decay until all that is left of the universe is radiation. As the expansion of the universe continues, even radiation will become so diffuse that for all practical purposes there is nothing left but empty space.

A Star Is Born

As NOTED in Chapter 1, the mechanics of galaxy formation are not well understood. But because the Sun is in our own celestial backyard, as compared with the distant galaxies, it is a little easier to study. Also, astronomers are able to witness the birth and death of stars within our own Galaxy and can surmise some of the physical changes taking place. For instance, seventeenth century astronomers noted a cloudy patch in the constellation Taurus that was later identified as the Crab nebula (Fig. 2-1). Closer examination showed that the Crab nebula was a massive explosion, caught in mid-stride. Research through ancient Oriental records showed that in 1054, Chinese astronomers reported what is now called a supernova in the same position as the Crab nebula. What was perhaps the brightest object in the night sky in recorded history, turned out to be the explosion of a giant star — 4500 light years away.

THE SOLAR SYSTEM

Our Sun is an insignificant star in terms of its size and brilliance. It is located in one of the three spiral arms of the Milky Way galaxy, between 23,000 and 33,000 light years from the center. The Sun is accompanied by nine planets (Fig. 2-2), their satellites, and other orbiting bodies such as comets. Early religions were based on Sun worship that gave the Sun a special significance because of its role in the sustenance of life.

The early Greeks dismissed this exalted throne for the Sun, and along with the six known planets of that time, the Sun was thought to circle the Earth. It was only a few hundred years ago that the Sun was thought to be just an ordinary star. Even Copernicus and Kepler held the view that stars were points of light engraved on an ethereal sphere and the Sun held a special place in the cosmos. The famous English astronomer Sir William Herschel, who discovered the planet Uranus in 1781, placed the Sun in the center of our galaxy. Even as late as 1900, some astronomers still maintained the Sun was in the center of our galactic system.

The first suggestion that the Sun and planets existed in a heliocentric system (helios being Greek for Sun) came from the Greek philosopher Aristar-

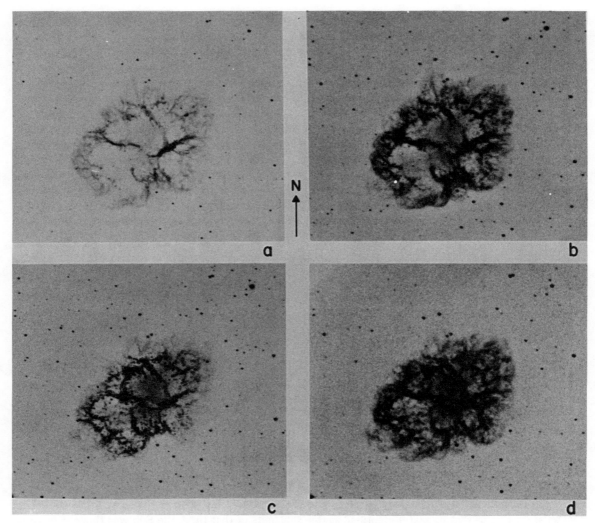

FIG. 2-1. The Crab Nebula. (Courtesy of Kitt Peak National Observatory.)

chus about 300 B.C. This notion that the Sun was in the center was discarded in favor of the Ptolemaic system, named after the second century A.D. Egyptian astronomer Ptolemy. The Ptolemaic system places the Earth in the center with the Sun being nothing more than an exceptionally bright planet. It was not until 1543 that things were set right again.

Nicholas Copernicus proposed a solar system (Sol being Latin for Sun) with the Sun once again in the center. This Copernican system was slow to gain acceptance. Because it provided more accurate calculations for planetary positions, most astronomers began using it. However, planetary orbits of perfect circles did not satisfy observations, and a new, more accurate model was advanced by the German astronomer Johannes Kepler in 1609. He reasoned that the only geometric figure that would fit the observations was an ellipse with the Sun at one focus of the planetary

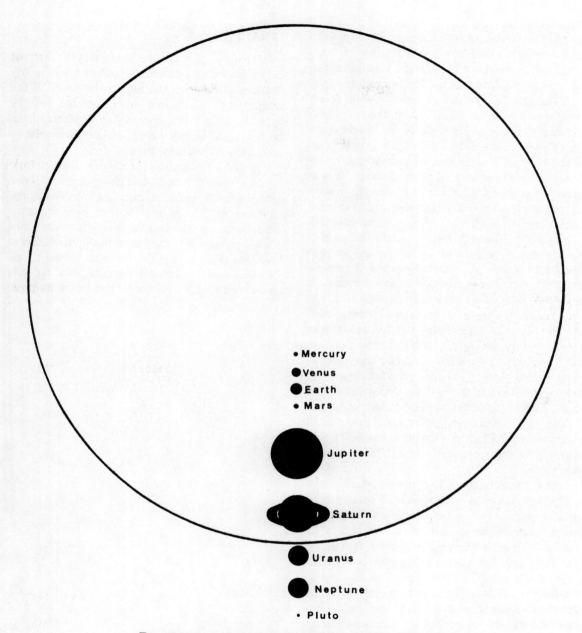

FIG. 2-2. Approximate relative sizes of the sun and planets.

orbits. This system allowed astronomers to accurately fix the orbits of planets relative to each other, but it could not provide the actual distance each planet was from each other or from the Sun.

The English scientist Sir Isaac Newton developed the law of universal gravitation in 1684, which states that every body in the universe attracts every other body with a force proportional to the product of their masses and inversely proportional to the square of their distance. It also explained Kepler's solar model in straightforward mathematical terms. This allowed orbital calculations, even if only a portion of the orbit is observed.

In 1704, Newton's young friend Edmund Halley was able to take advantage of the new gravitational calculations to predict the orbits of comets, those ice-like visitors from outer space with such elongated orbits that they take several tens and even hundreds of years to make one circuit around the Sun. They swing close by the Sun at fantastic speeds and fly out again, many going in all directions and even beyond the orbit of Pluto, the farthest known planet. The most famous comet was first reported in 240 B.C. and has since returned 29 times. This is the comet named in honor of Halley. Taking the comets and other small undetected planets beyond Pluto into account, the Solar System is quite vast, reaching several billions of miles into space.

One curiosity about Kepler's planetary model is that, according to calculations, there should be another planet orbiting between Mars and Jupiter. Instead, astronomers found an asteroid belt in the precise orbit of this nonexistent planet. It could be that long ago, this planet disintegrated, torn between the gravitational pull of the Sun on one side and the alignment of Jupiter and the other planets on the other side in what is now termed the Jupiter effect. Being able to predict the orbits of planets could aid in the discovery of other planets. Some astronomers predict there lies another planet between Mercury and the Sun but, because the Sun is so bright, it cannot be seen. They are so confident their theory is correct, they even gave the yet-to-be-discovered planet a name — Vulcan, the Roman god of fire.

PARALLAX

During Kepler's time, Saturn was the farthest known planet, and its relative position was nearly 10 times as far from the Sun as the Earth. If the distance of the Earth from any one planet could be determined, then the distances of all planets from the Sun could be calculated because their relative positions were already known.

Actually, calculating the Earth's distance from the Sun was not that difficult of a task. Two-sighted animals, including man, are capable of judging distances. This is because their eyes are separated by a certain length, and when they are focused on an object, they point in slightly different directions (FIG. 2-3). This allows an animal to unconsciously determine, for instance, how far it is necessary to jump in order to pounce on its prey.

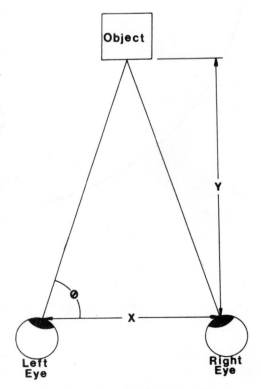

FIG. 2-3. The principle of parallax.

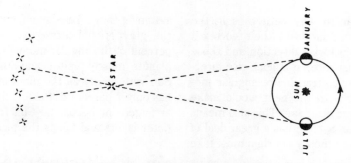

FIG. 2-4. The parallax method of determining the distance to the stars.

This phenomenon is known as parallax (FIG. 2-4), and it was first successfully used to determine the distance to the Moon.

By using two observatories stationed several hundred miles apart as the eyes, the distance to the Moon could be triangulated. The observatories see the Moon at two different angles compared with the stars in the background. This forms a triangle with one leg and two angles known. Simple trigonometry can compute one of the other legs of the triangle which gives a distance of roughly 240,000 miles. This figure was in complete agreement with the early Greeks who used the curvature of the Earth's shadow as it fell across the Moon's surface during a lunar eclipse to calculate the distance.

The Sun's parallax could not be accurately determined in this manner because no fixed points on its blinding surface could be found accurately. Instead, French astronomers measured the distance to Mars, the next closest planet to the Earth, and used Kepler's planetary model to determine the distance to the Sun. The first measurement was taken in 1671 and gave the Earth's distance from the Sun of 87 million miles. This missed the mark by about 6 million miles, but the measurement was astonishingly accurate for those times.

One hundred years later, a more accurate determination of the parallax of Venus was made as it passed between the Earth and the Sun. The invention of radar during World War II supplied another highly accurate method of measuring objects in space. In 1961, microwave beams were bounced off Venus, giving a calculated average distance from the Earth to the Sun of nearly 93 million miles or eight light minutes. With knowledge of the distance to the Sun, it was an easy step to determine its diameter by using simple geometry. It turns out that the Sun's diameter is little over 100 times that of the Earth, or 864,000 miles.

THE NEBULAR HYPOTHESIS

The German philosopher Immanuel Kant speculated in 1755 that the Solar System had a common origin. Kant thought that a rotating nebula might have condensed to form the sun and planets with the planets circling the sun in the same direction as the original nebula was rotating. This would also account for all the major planets lying in nearly the same plane.

The difficulty with Kant's theory is that the main part of the condensed nebula, the Sun, should be rotating very rapidly similar to the way an ice skater increases her spin by closing her outstretched arms. This is what is known as conservation of angular momentum, the quality of a spinning body in which motion can never be created or destroyed, but can only be transferred from one body to another. Instead, the Sun is rotating rather slowly—once every 27 days.

Most of the bodies of the Solar System rotate in the same direction as the Sun. If they are viewed high above the Earth's North Pole, they would be rotating in a counterclockwise direction. The reason for this is similar to why bath tubs in the Northern Hemisphere drain with their vortexes turning in a counterclockwise direction and those in the Southern Hemisphere, in a clockwise direction. In other words, the transfer of angular momentum from one body to the next would make them rotate in the same direction. This also means that, because the Solar System has a great deal of angular momentum, any theory of origin must take this into account.

The French mathematician Pierre Simon de Laplace later refined Kant's theory to include the notion that rings of matter would have broken off the condensing nebula by centrifugal force, as it contracted and spun with increasing speed. The rings would coalesce into planets of nearly circular orbits. This was called the "nebular hypothesis" (FIG. 2-5) because it would have a similar appearance to spiral nebulae such as the Andromeda nebula that Laplace thought was the formation of a planetary system, (whereas Kant predicted it was a galaxy similar to our own). The nebular hypothesis was very popular among astronomers throughout the nineteenth century. Shortly after the turn of the twentieth century, a parallax determination reported the Andromeda nebula was 2 million light years away, much too far to be an evolving planetary system, and proving Kant was right.

If the nebular hypothesis was a true picture of the evolution of the Solar System, then the oldest planet would be the outermost and the youngest planet would be the innermost, with the Sun the youngest of them all. If the age of the Earth is taken to be 4.6 billion years, then it follows that the Sun would be some what younger than that. Scientists now know that this can not be so, and the Sun is the same age or slightly older than the Earth. But the real downfall of the theory was its inability to account for the angular momentum of the Solar System.

If a vast quantity of gas and dust started out with a certain angular momentum, then as the cloud condensed, it would have to spin ever so much faster until most of the angular momentum would be in the main body, the Sun, and very little is left for the planets. The planets would in turn, assuming they formed at all, fall into the Sun due to the gravitational attraction. As it turns out, 99 percent of the angular momentum resides with the planets (mostly Jupiter) and other bodies, while the Sun with nearly all the mass of the Solar System, has only 1 percent of the angular momentum. This arrangement keeps the Sun from spinning off its outer layers and keeps the planets in their orbits.

THE PLANETESIMAL HYPOTHESIS

For the nebular hypothesis to work at all, some plausible method had to be found to shift nearly all the angular momentum from the center to the planetary matter. Because no internal mechanism could be found, perhaps the angular momentum came from an outside source. This is the theory suggested, in 1906, by two Americans, geologist Thomas Chamberlin and astronomer Forest Moulton.

Assuming the Sun condensed from a nebula to begin with, it had to do so without liberating shells of matter and become just another lone star. Now suppose another star approached the Sun close enough for gravitational forces to cause huge tidal bulges to form on both stars. Perhaps material was pulled out of both stars to form a temporary bridge between them (FIG. 2-6). As the stars rapidly passed each other, the bridge would separate and begin to swing rapidly around the Sun, gaining angular momentum at the Sun's expense. The bridge would eventually coalesce into planets and take most of the angular momentum of the system.

The Chamberlin-Moulton theory was a tidy way of clearing up some of the major problems of the nebular hypothesis. It accounted for the slow rotation of the Sun and the condensation of matter into small, solid bodies, known as planetesimals, that would coalesce into the planets. The planetesimal hypothesis, as it was called, rapidly gained popularity and was undisputed for nearly 40 years.

Variations of the same theme, known as encounter theories, including a direct collision between the Sun and another star, have also been put forward. Two English astronomers, James Jeans and Harold Jeffreys, later improved on the planete-

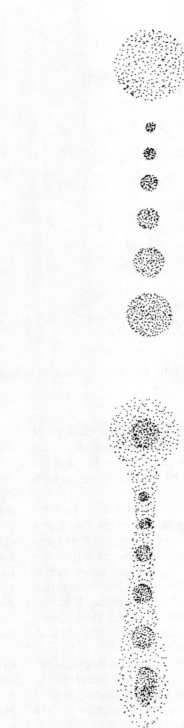

FIG. 2-5. Evolution of the Solar system from the solar nebula.

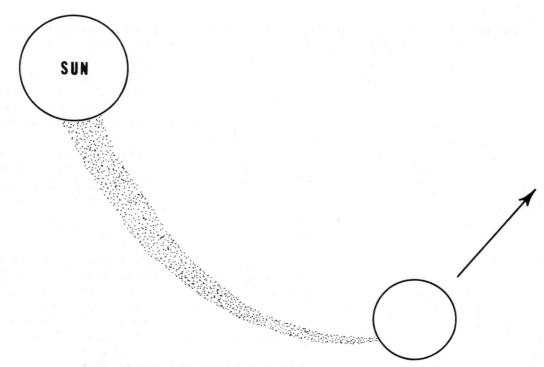

FIG. 2-6. The planetesimal hypothesis of planetary evolution.

simal hypothesis by suggestion that a filament of matter pulled out of the Sun would be cigar-shaped, accounting for the large planets of Jupiter and Saturn in the middle and the smaller planets on each end.

One intriguing theory put forth by Ramond Lyttleton in 1936 suggested that the Sun had a companion star. Such binary star systems are quite common, accounting for more than half of the stars in our Galaxy. Binary stars occur when matter retains its angular momentum and forms ring structures in which two stars condense. If matter and angular momentum is separated, then planets are formed instead. If this is the case, then all single stars should have planets.

Lyttleton envisioned a collision between the Sun's twin sister and another star. Some of the debris from the collision was left rotating around the Sun while the colliding stars bounced off into space like two billiard balls. The problem with this theory is that the debris would orbit around the Sun in all directions instead of mostly in one plane.

The main objection to the encounter theories is that the probability of a chance encounter with two stars is astronomical. The distances between stars is so great that two galaxies can merge into each other without a single star collision. Besides a collision or near collision being highly improbable, the choreography between the two stars would have to be so precise that the chances of a planetary system forming by this method are very slim. Also, the encounter theories do not adequately account for the heavy elements in the planets and their moons.

The Sun is composed of roughly 80 percent hydrogen and 20 percent helium, with a very minor constituent of other elements. The Sun, because of its small size, is incapable of producing the heavy elements on its own. It would have to sweep them up out of the nebula during its formation. The origin of the heavy elements in the nebula was probably galactic debris, perhaps from a supernova residing in the vicinity.

By the 1940s, it appeared the encounter theories were on their way out. No adequate mechanism was suggested for how solid planets could have formed out of hot gases pulled out of the Sun. Calculations showed that such condensations were possible only if the matter were a few thousand degrees centigrade, such as that which exists on the surface of the Sun. But instead, matter torn from the Sun would come from deep within, and it would be several million degrees. Upon breaking the surface of the Sun, this super-hot matter would simply explode and form a gaseous nebula around the Sun, which could not possibly condense into planets.

Even if matter could be drawn out of the Sun, its trajectory would be such that 99 percent of it would fall back into the Sun. Also, the abundant deuterium in the Earth's oceans could not have come from the Sun because the Sun would have burned it all up early in its history. These major flaws necessitated a return to the nebular hypothesis, but this time with a few new twists.

The German astronomer Carl von Weizacker suggested in 1943 that the nebula that formed the Solar System did not revolve as a unit, but instead was highly turbulent. Matter would gyrate wildly in whirlpools. Where adjacent whirlpools met there would be collisions of particles and coalescence of larger and larger particles into planets (FIG. 2-7). This theory neatly explained the spacing of the planets and the distribution of angular momentum.

Although the theory was enthusiastically received, not everyone was satisfied with the mechanism for transferring the angular momentum of the Sun to the planets. One of the more promising ideas was presented by two astronomers, Hanns Alfven and Fred Hoyle, in which the Sun's magnetic field transferred the angular momentum.

The solar wind, which is subatomic particle radiation responsible for the tails of comets, has also been proposed as a means for slowing down the Sun's rotation. It might also aid in planetary formation by driving outward the condensing nebular material. The solar wind could be responsible for the general decrease in densities of planets going outward from the Sun.

The four inner terrestrial planets are composed of heavy matter. Jupiter and Saturn are gaseous planets similar to the Sun in composition, while Uranus and Neptune are mainly composed of ice and rock fragments.

Regardless of which mechanism is correct, the formation of a planetary system should be the natural consequence of star formation; therefore, most single stars would be expected to have planets.

THE ENERGY OF THE SUN

A corollary to the law of conservation of angular momentum was proposed in the late 1840s by the German physicist Hermann von Helmholtz. This was known as the law of conservation of energy in which energy, like momentum, can be neither created nor destroyed, but can only be transferred from one place to another. This law became a vital link in trying to determine the energy of the Sun.

Helmholtz pondered over the fact that the energy output of the Sun had to be enormous, for only a minuscule amount (1/2,000,000,000) of it ever reached the Earth. If the Sun was made of coal, the major fuel resource of that day, then it would burn, at most, for only a couple thousand years. Therefore, an alternative source of energy had to be found. Rejecting the notion that meteor bombardment could heat the Sun because this would perceptually increased the Sun's mass, Helmholtz turned to the Sun's own gravitational contraction.

As the outer layers fell inward toward the center of the Sun, the compression would heat the core, which would radiate energy without any change in mass and with only an insignificant amount of shrinkage. Helmholtz was correct assuming that, as the Sun formed out of the nebula, its increasing mass and gravitational contraction would heat up the core, but this was only the beginning.

Near the turn of the twentieth century, scien-

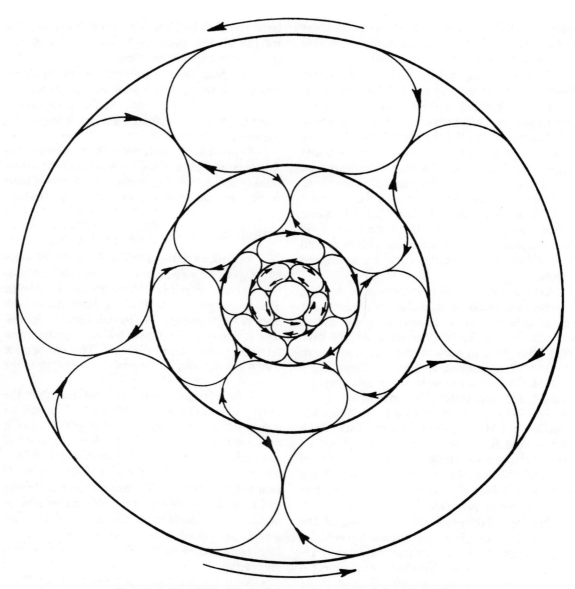

Fig. 2-7. Van Weizsacker's theory of formation of the solar system.

tists were uncovering the secrets of the atom. The French physicist Henri Becquerel discovered in 1896 that uranium spontaneously gave off radiation, called gamma rays. In 1897, J.J. Thomson identified the electron as the negative charged particle orbiting the atom. In 1898, Ernest Rutherford discovered alpha and beta particles, and that same year, Pierre and Marie Curie isolated many radioactive elements. In 1905, Albert Einstein published his theory of Special Relativity, whereby mass is converted into energy, and expressed in his famous equation $E = mc^2$, or energy equals mass times the speed of light squared. Light travels 186,000 miles, or 300,000 kilometers, per second. Multiplied by itself, the speed of light produces an extremely large number. Therefore, a tiny amount of mass can produce a tremendous amount of energy. For instance, an ounce of matter might contain the nuclear energy equivalent of a train load of coal. Now the energy locked up in the Sun seemed almost limitless.

As the Sun was condensing out of the nebula, it continued to build up a large gravitational attraction that brought in more matter, mostly composed of hydrogen. At some point, during the gravitational contraction, the core — which is several thousands of miles across — reached the ignition temperature (20 million degrees C) for the fusion of hydrogen into helium, releasing copious amounts of energy (FIG. 2-8).

To maintain the temperature on the surface of the Sun at a constant 6000 degrees, the Sun must be continually losing heat at a steady rate. Therefore, the gravitational contraction must be perfectly balanced by hot expanding gases. Otherwise, the Sun would collapse upon itself. The rate at which energy is produced is determined by the temperature of the core. If the core becomes too hot, then the excess energy causes the Sun to expand, providing a larger surface area for which to radiate the excess energy. If the core becomes too cool, then the loss of energy compresses the Sun, which heats up the core.

The remarkable feature about the Sun is its stability for most of its lifetime. Otherwise, life on Earth would never have a chance of gaining a foothold, or hang on for as long as it has. Even minor variations in the solar output could be responsible for disastrous changes in climate, causing massive dying of species and periods of glaciation.

SOLAR ACTIVITY

Despite its seemingly changelessness, the Sun is anything but quiescent. The surface of the Sun is furiously boiling and globules of white hot gas rise to the surface, cool, and descend again. This boiling layer of the Sun can extend as far as one-third of the way toward the center and can reach temperatures of several millions of degrees. This is still not hot enough to support nuclear reactions which occur only in the core.

Sunspots (FIG. 2-9) periodically (every eleven years) mar the Sun's surface and play havoc with radio communications here on Earth. Sunspots are large patches of relatively cool gas associated with magnetic vortices and energetic solar flares, hence the radio disturbances. Galileo first used them to determine the rate of the Sun's rotation, because they are the only landmarks on an otherwise barren surface. The Sun possesses an atmosphere, or chromosphere, that can be seen during a total eclipse. It is a reddish glowing layer of gas, thousands of miles thick, and surrounded by an intensely hot halo, called the corona, that extends millions of miles into space. Jets of gas can be seen spurting millions of miles high, arching over, and falling back to the surface again.

When in its youth, the Sun was a very different star than what we see today. The young Sun was only 70 percent as bright as it is now. To compensate for its lack of virility, it periodically puffed itself up and threw angry tantrums, consisting of powerful flares and strong solar winds. These might have been responsible for stripping away the volatiles of the inner planets and depositing them further out in the solar system, giving the larger planets their gaseous composition. Any life attempting to form on Earth would be immediately snuffed out as jets of hot gases swept across the planet.

The early Sun spun much more rapidly, completing one rotation in only a few days; now it takes 27 days. The greater rotational speed also caused a larger magnetic field, such as a fast-turning dynamo generates more electricity than a slow one. Sometime around its 1 billionth birthday, the Sun, shorn of its adolescent pranks, settled down to a more respectable adult life. It is this stability that allowed life to form on Earth; otherwise, life would be subject to the fickle whims of the Sun and not have any chance to grow.

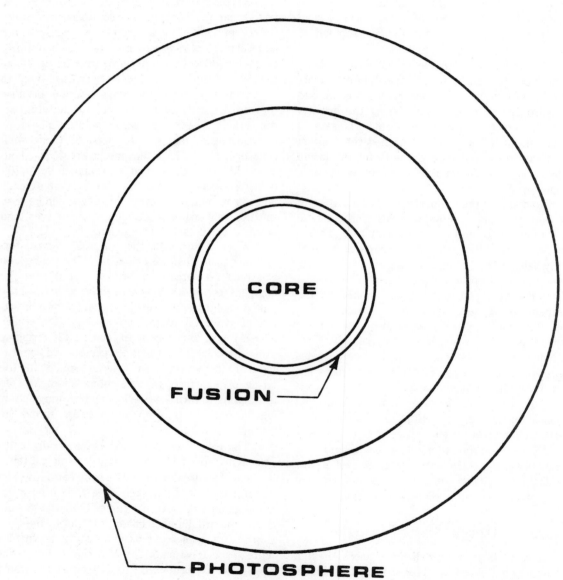

FIG. 2-8. The layering of the sun.

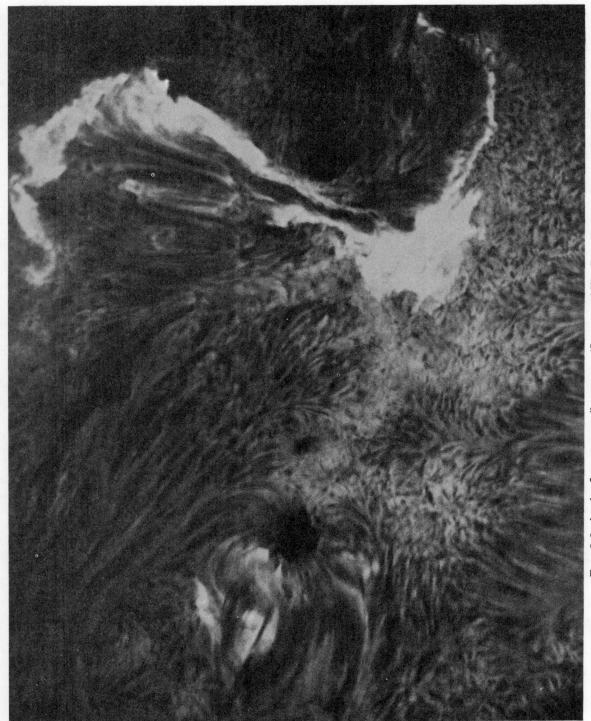

FIG. 2-9. A solar flare near small sunspots. (Courtesy of Kitt Peak National Observatory.)

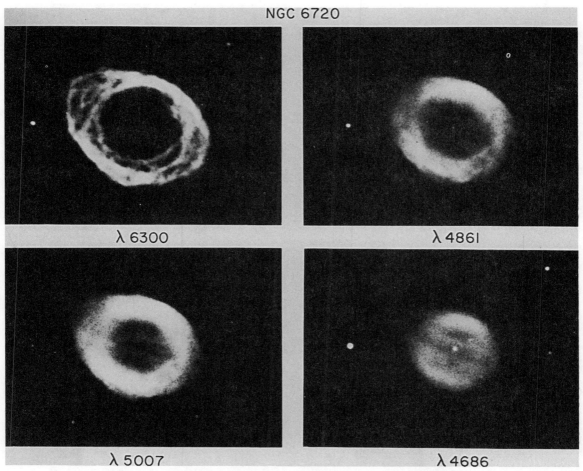

NGC 6720

λ 6300

λ 4861

λ 5007

λ 4686

FIG. 2-10. A ring nebula in Lyra. (Courtesy of Kitt Peak National Observatory.)

THE FUTURE OF THE SUN

The Sun can be expected to continue shining the way it does for another 5 billion years. The solar wind is now so feeble that the Sun's rotation rate will decrease only slightly. Violent activities, such as solar flares, will probably become less pronounced. As time goes on, the Sun will continue to get hotter as it depletes its hydrogen fuel and the core becomes polluted with helium "ash." About 1.5 billion years from now, the sun's luminosity, or brightness, will be 15 percent greater than at present. On earth, the ice caps will have melted,

causing massive flooding, and Canada will be as hot as a desert. Life forms, in order to stay alive, will have had to evolve mechanisms to compensate for the higher temperatures. If man is still around, he will have to modify his environment to deal with the heat. Perhaps his cities will be covered with air-conditioned domes, like present-day football stadiums.

By the time the Sun is 10 billion years old, the nuclear fires will burn virtually all the hydrogen in its core to helium and begin to die out. In its last dying breaths, the Sun will balloon to a radius 40 percent greater than present, and it will be about twice as bright. Life on earth will have long since vanished, and if man has not left to colonize some other planet in another Solar System, he too will be extinct.

In another 1.5 billion years, as the last of the hydrogen fuel is used up, the core will gradually contract because there is not enough pressure to resist the weight of the overlying layers. Increased gravitational contraction will increase the temperature of the core, eventually igniting the hydrogen fuel in the overlying regions. As this fuel is burned, the Sun will continue expanding until it reaches the present orbit of Mercury and becomes a red giant with a surface temperature of only half of what it is now, but with a luminosity of 500 times its present value.

The Sun will live a comparatively short life as a red giant, only 250 million years. After this time, the core will begin to fuse helium into carbon and oxygen. The burning will be so rapid that it will become an explosive event known as a "helium flash." The outer layers will be blown off, taking away a significant part of the Sun's mass. Afterwards, the Sun will contract to about 10 times its present diameter and will settle down to a steady burning of helium.

As the Sun again gradually grows, successive outer layers will be blown off by the intense solar wind until the core is finally exposed. The result will be what is known as a ring nebula, with debris surrounding a very hot stellar remnant in the center (FIG. 2-10). Eventually, the debris will clear away, resulting in a lone hot star with only about half its present mass, but compressed down to the size of the Earth. Its extreme heat will cause it to glow white hot, hence its name white dwarf. The Sun will live on in this manner for perhaps another 15 billion years. Then it will gradually cool down to end its days as a cold black dwarf.

3

Enters the Earth

ALMOST everywhere primitive man looked the ground was level and the sky appeared as though it was a dome-shaped cover. This observation led early man to believe the Earth was flat. Yet, if the Earth was flat, it would have to end somewhere. The oceans would pour off on all sides, and any ship caught on the edge would fall off. This was still feared by some as late as the time of Columbus, who set sail for India in 1492 to prove the world was round; only to have his way barred by America. This notion of a flat Earth also troubled the early Greeks. If one traveled northward, some stars sank beyond the southern horizon while new stars appeared in the northern horizon. If the Earth was flat, the same stars should be visible everywhere. Ships on the high seas disappeared hull-down, below the horizon, no matter which direction they sailed. It was like watching someone climb a hill and disappear legs first down the other side. Therefore, the early Greeks reasoned that the Earth was curved in all directions, and the only geometric figure that meets this criteria is a sphere. Also, by observing the eclipse of the Moon, Greek astronomers noticed that the Earth's shadow projected across the Moon's face was always curved, no matter which part of the sky the Moon was in, indicating that the Earth had to be a sphere.

MEASURING THE EARTH

After determining the shape of the Earth, the early Greeks set out to measure it. The Earth had to be large but not too large; otherwise the curvature would be too slight. The Greeks had traveled from the Strait of Gibralter to India, without doubling back, so the circumference of the Earth had to be greater than 6000 miles. Around 240 B.C., the Greek astronomer Eratosthenes, near the present site of Aswan, Egypt, discovered that when he planted a stick upright in the ground, during the summer solstice on June 21, the stick cast no shadow at noon time. When the same experiment was conducted 500 miles north at Alexandria, the stick cast a short shadow, indicating the Earth was indeed curved (FIG. 3-1). Otherwise, if the Earth was flat, the sticks should point in the same direction and neither would cast a shadow. This meant that the Sun at Alexandria was 7 degrees lower on the horizon. Eratosthenes, using simple geometry, proved that if 7 degrees represents 500 miles of travel, then in the same proportion, 360 degrees, the number of degrees in a circle, would calculate out to be roughly 25,000 miles. If the circumference of the Earth was 25,000 miles, dividing by pi (3.14), gave a diameter of about 8000 miles. Modern measurements, nearly 22 centuries later, give a circumference at the equator of 24,902 miles and an average diameter of 7918 miles, slightly greater at the equator than at the poles. Eratosthenes was remarkably close considering the crude instruments used in his time.

THE AGE OF THE EARTH

Perhaps, the first to speculate on the age of the Earth was the sixth century B.C. Greek philosopher Xenophanes. He knew that seashells embedded in rocks in the mountains were evidence that the mountains at one time were below sea level. His deduction was that either the Earth was extremely old with time enough to allow the imperceptible growth of mountains, or some enormous catastrophe pushed the mountains high above the sea in the not-too-distant past.

Faith in catastrophic events was common in ancient legends and religions. The early Christians took the fossils as evidence of a biblical flood that covered the entire world and killed all life, save one family who escaped in an ark full of animals. The Archbishup James Ussher of Ireland in 1658 went so far as to pick the exact time and date the Earth was created by counting all generations following the Biblical Adam and Eve. His date for the creation of the Earth was 9:00 A.M. on October 26, 4004 B.C., giving the Earth an age of roughly 6000 years.

This date was unacceptable to the French naturalist Georges de Buffon, who in 1778 suggested the Earth took at least 75,000 years to cool down to its present state. Buffon envisioned the Earth being created by a comet colliding with the Sun and tearing off a piece of it. The Earth thus in a molten state slowly solidified with a slight bulge at the equator due to the Earth's rotation. He speculated that the solid crust of the Earth then wrinkled into mountains like the skin of a baked apple. As the Earth cooled, water vapor condensed out of the atmosphere and rained down to form the oceans.

Buffon believed that sea life formed about

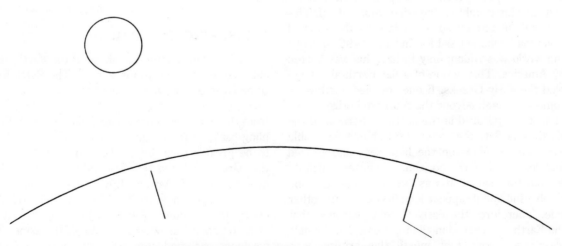

FIG. 3-1. Measuring the circumference of the earth.

40,000 years ago, and some were trapped in the mud, becoming fossils. Dry land was exposed as the water on the continents drained away through cracks into the Earth's interior. Animals appeared on the dry land and eventually man came along. Buffon's theories of the Earth's development and evolution of life, based on degeneration where apes evolved from man, greatly offended the church, and he was forced to retract his views.

Various methods of scientifically determining the age of the Earth were tried. One of these involved the salinity of the oceans. It was assumed that in the early development of the Earth, the oceans consisted of fresh water. By estimating the amount of salt carried yearly by the rivers emptying into the oceans, the time it takes for the ocean to reach its present salinity could be calculated. In 1899, John Joly made his calculation using this method and came up with an age of 90 million years.

The problems with Joly's estimate was that he could not have known the amount of salt lost in sediments such as salt beds. He could not have known the original salt content of juvenile waters because waters of present day geysers and volcanoes are quite salty, indicating that they are largely recycled seawater. Also, if erosion rates in the past were faster or slower than they are presently, then salt would be transported to the oceans at a different rate.

Some geologists reasoned that if they could determine the average rate of sedimentation per year, then measuring the total thickness of the geologic record would produce the age of the Earth. Unfortunately, sedimentation rates vary according to type of sediment, location, and climate. Also, the geologic record varies according to region and whether there are gaps, or unconformities, from periods of erosion or non-deposition. Nevertheless, one calculation gave an age of 1.5 billion years. This pushed the age of the Earth way beyond anything imaginable at that time. Generally though, most geologists accepted an average age of 100 million years.

Even physicists, like Lord Kelvin, got in the act and tried to calculate the Earth's age from a thermodynamics point of view. Like Buffon, Kelvin assumed the Earth was once molten and cooled to its present condition. Applying his heat-flow calculations, Kelvin arrived at a date of somewhere between 20 and 40 million years. This date was unacceptable by both geologists and biologists who believed the Earth had to be older in order for changes to occur in the Earth's crust and in living organisms. Unfortunately, Kelvin was unaware at that time that radioactivy was responsible for stoking the fires of the Earth, and so his calculations were meaningless.

UNIFORMITARIANISM

The Scottish geologist James Hutton known as the "father of geology" put forward his theory of uniformitarianism in 1785. This theory with a long name simply means the present is the key to the past. In other words, the forces that shaped the Earth are uniform and operated in the past the same way and at the same rate as they do today. Therefore, the events taking place today, such as seashells being buried in the mud on the shore, have their counterparts in the rocks of mountains and canyons laid down a very long time ago. Hutton envisioned that the prime mover causing these slow changes was the Earth's own internal heat. Geologists had long ago recognized that rocks were molten in the Earth's interior and manifested themselves in volcanoes. Also, temperatures in deep mines increased with greater depths, indicating that the Earth grew hotter toward the center. This great heat engine, as Hutton called it, was apparently a leftover from the time the Earth was originally in a molten state. The British geologist Sir Charles Lyell, born in 1797, the same year Hutton died, took up where Hutton left off. Because of his excellent work, *The Principles of Geology*, uniformitarianism began to gain world-wide acceptance.

Still some geologists felt the theory of uniformitarianism was a little oversimplified, and there might have been events in the past that were not slowly evolving, but happened rather suddenly. This is the theory of catastrophism, a throwback

FIG. 3-2. A sandstone block containing a large fossil palm leaf. It was found in a coal mine near Newcastle, Colorado. (Courtesy of H.S. Gale, USGS.)

from earlier philosophies of the Earth's creation. Its adherents pointed out gaps in the geologic record and the dying out of a large number of species. This could only be explained through some catastrophic event. It was thought that the Earth underwent periods of catastrophic death of all life on Earth, after which everything started anew. This would explain the abundance of fossils at certain stages in the geologic record. But more importantly, the theory coincided with religious belief and postulated that one final dying out occurred 6000 years in the past; whereupon, the Earth was created as it is now according to biblical testament.

Modern geologists do not speak in strict terms of uniformitarianism or catastrophism, but use a bit of both. The Soviet geologists take the general view of catastrophism from observing features on their continent, while Americans favor uniformitarianism because of the nature by which rocks formed on the North American continent.

GEOLOGIC TIME

Geologists measure relative time by tracing fossils through the rock strata and noticing the greater change with depth of the strata, with respect to present-day organisms. Therefore, it stood to reason that the older rocks were toward the bottom and the younger ones were toward the top. Like a layer cake, the bottom layer had to be laid down first.

The British geologists William Smith (1769–1839) took this idea one step further with his law of faunal succession. Fossil-bearing strata could be followed horizontally over great distances because a specific fossil bed could be identified in another locality with respect to those above and below. These became marker beds and were used for identifying geologic formations and helped in such things as exploration for coal. Because coal-bearing seams are generally the same age and were laid down during times of abundant plant life, geologists could determine where to mine coal by studying fossil-bearing formations.

The English naturalist Charles Darwin, returning from his adventures around the world on board the *HMS Beagle,* published his book *The Origin of Species* in 1859. Darwin considered how various species had evolved from observations of plants and animals during his voyage. It became apparent to him that a lot of time was needed for these changes to take place. Most changes would be very minute as species adapted to their constantly changing environment.

The term survival of the fittest suggested that the members of a particular species that can best utilize their environment have the best chance of producing offspring that take on the attributes of their parents. Natural selection favored those best adapted to their environment at the expense of weaker species. This was a highly controversial subject (and still is) and ran directly against the teachings of the church. But geologists embraced the theory. A clear understanding of morphological changes in fossils was now at hand. Geologist were able to date certain events by studying the evolutionary changes having taken place in certain fossils (FIG. 3-2).

FIG. 3-3. The Wolf Creek meteorite from western Australia. (Courtesy of USGS.)

Radioactive elements, such as uranium, thorium, and potassium, exist in minor amounts in the Earth's crust and interior. They have the unusual quality of spontaneously decaying and radiating energy. This property was first discovered by Henri Becquerel near the turn of the twentieth century. Each atom gives off an infinitesimal amount of heat when it decays. Taking into account all the radioactive atoms in the Earth, there are a sufficient number to supply the Earth's heat in the past and for a long time into the future. Therefore, it can be said that the Earth derrives its heat from nuclear energy.

Another property of radioactive elements is that they decay at a statistically steady rate, unaffected by outside forces which exist on the Earth. In other words, each atom is like a tiny clock, ticking away, independent of physical and chemical processes found on Earth.

In 1907, the American chemist B. B. Bolt-wood found that uranium eventually decayed into lead. Knowing how long it takes for the transformation of uranium into lead and the ratio of uranium to lead in a rock, its absolute age could be calculated. This technique is known as radiometric dating. Uranium's half-life, the time it takes for one-half the atoms to decay into lead, happens to be 4.5 billion years (or approximately the age of the Earth).

If the ratio of uranium to lead in a rock sample was 1:1, then that rock would be 4.5 billion years old. The oldest rocks found on Earth were shy of this date by about one billion years (the reason for this is covered in Chapter four), but meteorites have been dated at 4.5 billion years and slightly older (FIG. 3-3). If the Earth is contemporaneous with the rest of the Solar System, then it too must be as old as the meteorites. Also, when men first visited the Moon in 1969 and brought back Moon rocks, they were found to be 4.2 to 4.6 billion

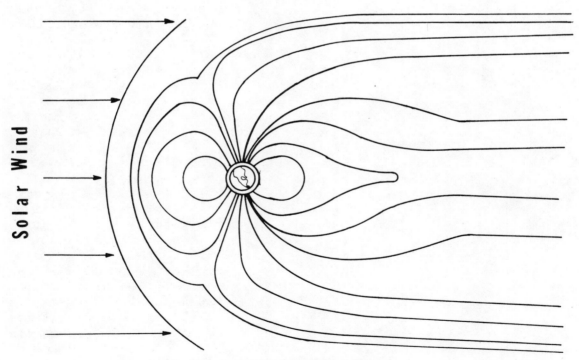

FIG. 3-4. The earth's magnetic field.

years old, which was also in agreement with the range of dates for the Earth.

THE EARTH'S MOON

The Moon's creation remains one of the unsolved mysteries of our universe. The early Greeks were the first to measure the distance to the Moon, the second brightest object in the sky. Based on its relative motion compared with the stars and planets, the Moon was judged to be the closest of all the celestial bodies. The Greek astronomer Hipparchus in the second century B.C., upon observing the shadow of the Earth across the Moon during a lunar eclipse, came to the conclusion that the distance to the Moon was 30 times the diameter of the Earth. If Eratosthenes' figure for the Earth's diameter of 8000 miles was correct, then the moon must be 240,000 miles away. This was amazingly close to the mark, considering the state of the art in those days. Modern measurements using radar and laser beams give an average distance, center to center, of 238,857 miles. The Moon does not orbit the Earth in a perfect circle; therefore, its closest approach is roughly 221,000 miles and the farthest it gets from Earth is about 253,000 miles.

By knowing the distance to the Moon, it is a simple procedure to determine its diameter because imaginary lines drawn to the edges of the Moon form a triangle with two sides and one angle known. This gives a diameter of 2160 miles and multiplying by pi (3.14), produces a circumference of 6800 miles. This means the Moon is roughly 1/50th the size of the Earth and could fit within the continental United States with room to spare.

Before Copernicus straightened out the Solar System in 1543, it was thought that the Sun and all the planets (the Moon was considered a planet then) orbited the Earth. When Copernicus was finished, only the Moon was left orbiting the Earth, and the Moon did so once every 28 days.

One aspect of the Moon, which was noticed when Galileo turned his telescope on its beaming face, was that only one side points toward the Earth. In other words, it is gravitationally locked into the Earth, rotating on its axis exactly the same rate that it orbits the Earth.

The Moon was at one time much closer to the Earth. About 370 million years ago, the Earth was spinning faster and a day was only 22 hours long. The Moon's tidal drag continuously slowed down the Earth's rotation, giving our present day of 24 hours. Angular momentum was transferred from the Earth to the Moon, forcing it to move further from the Earth at a rate of 2 inches per year.

In 1871, George Darwin, son of Charles Darwin, speculated that the Moon was plucked out of the Earth in its early molten state by the tidal pull of the Sun. At that time, the day was only a few hours long, and the Moon orbited the Earth in a matter of hours. As the Earth's rotation gradually slowed down, the Moon's orbit grew outward. According to the theory, creation of the Moon in this manner would leave a great gash in the Earth that might have been responsible for the Pacific basin (more on this in Chapter 4). Geophysicists tell us that if such an event took place, it is doubtful that either the Earth or the Moon could survive.

Another suggestion was that the Moon might have been captured by the Earth. However, if the Earth captured the Moon, the increased angular momentum of the Earth-Moon system would have heated the Earth, probably to its melting point, and no evidence of such melting is indicated anywhere in the geologic record. The Moon could also have started out as a seed and grew by accretion from the bombardment of asteroids and meteoroids. The face of the Moon is pock-marked with numerous craters, attesting to this occurence. The Moon has no appreciable magnetic field, which suggests it does not have a liquid iron-nickel core as does the Earth. The Moon is only 60 percent as dense as the Earth, making it 80 times lighter. If the Earth and Moon formed at the same time out of a common dust cloud, then they should have much the same composition. Moon rocks taken back from the Apollo missions are of different composition than those on the Earth's surface and are more closely related to those found in the Earth's mantle.

THE GEOSPHERE

Assuming the Earth and Moon formed out of the same debris, they probably started out relatively cool and homogeneous. The Earth, being considerably more massive than the Moon, contracted and began heating. Radioactive material was more abundant in the beginning and this added substantially to the heating process. Also, like the Moon, the Earth was bombarded by meteors that produced heat on contact with the Earth's surface.

Unlike the Moon, however, weathering processes operating on the Earth erased the craters — except those of the most recent origin. As the Earth began to melt, gravitational forces differentiated the Earth into the core, mantle, and crust. The heavier materials like iron and nickel settled toward the center while the lighter rock-forming materials moved outward. This formed an insulating blanket around the core that allowed it to retain its heat and remain liquid. This makes the Earth's magnetic field possible and this field helps shield the Earth from cosmic radiation (FIG. 3-4).

An alternative theory put foreward by two geologists at the University of California, Gustaf Arrhenius and Hannes Alfven, held that the Earth formed early on as a product of its initial aggregation from the planetary nebula and not from any subsequent processes. The core was formed first from the accumulation of iron and nickel-rich particles some 4.6 billion years ago. This was followed by a slower accumulation of the mantle that repeatedly remelted, forcing gravitational segregation of infalling materials in the order of increasing density. The crust was formed by whatever scum floated to the surface, like slag forming on top of molten iron ore.

Arrhenius and Alfven believed that some of the water vapor and gases sweated out of the mantle by volcanism as it was being heated, but most was derived on impact of solid particles. Also, the surface temperature would be below the boiling point of water to allow oceans to form early on. This would mean that sedimentary processes would have began very early in the Earth's history. However, the nature of sedimentary rocks, composed of detritus from older rock material, makes them difficult to date accurately, and so the theory can not be fully tested in this manner.

In 1909, the Yugoslavian seismologist Andrija Mohorovicic first discovered the division between the mantle and the crust, called the Mohorovicic discontinuity or simply Moho. By studying pressure (P) and shear (S) waves generated by earthquakes, seizmologists were able to determine certain properties of the inner earth. The P waves can travel through solids as well as liquids while S waves can travel in solids only (FIG. 3-5).

By analyzing P and S waves on seizmometers on opposite ends of the globe following an earthquake, seizmologists were able to prove that the core was in a liquid state and composed of iron and silicates. The core is about half the diameter of the Earth, or 4300 miles, and has a crystalline inner core that is composed of iron and nickel, roughly 1600 miles in diameter. The core is surround by a solid mantle, 1800 miles thick, which itself is surrounded by the crust that in most places is between 5 and 25 miles thick (FIG. 3-6).

The Earth's axis is tilted 23.5 degrees from the perpendicular of the plane of the Earth's orbit around the Sun. This defines the north and south geographic poles and is responsible for the change in seasons. The magnetic poles do not coincide with the geographic poles. The magnetic north pole lies just north of Canada and the magnetic south pole is 180 degrees opposite on the edge of Antarctica. The Earth's axis presently points towards Polaris, the north star, but this was not always so.

The Moon exerts a force on the spinning Earth, called nutation (FIG. 3-7) and, like a toy top, the Earth's axis wobbles or precesses. The Earth's axis resembles a cone as it precesses in the opposite direction of the Earth's spin. The Earth's axis precesses quite slowly, taking about 26,000 years for one complete cycle. This means that around the year 12,000 B.C., if primitive man cared to notice such things, he would see Vega as the north star. Summer and winter would have been reversed and those constellations presently seen only in the Southern Hemisphere, would be seen in the Northern Hemisphere.

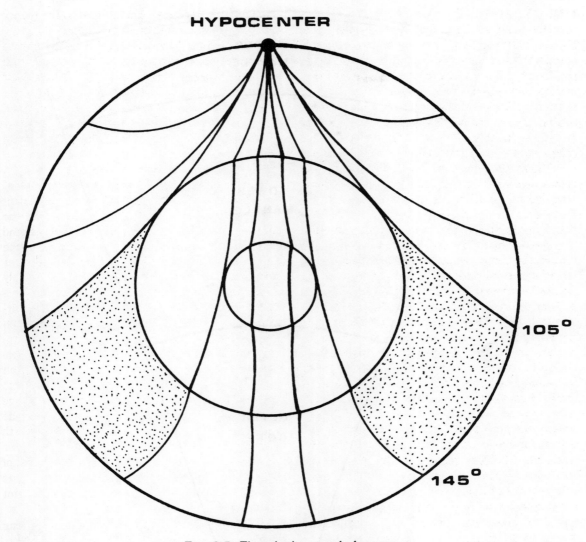

FIG. 3-5. The seismic wave shadow zone.

THE HYDROSPHERE

The oceans were believed to be formed from early volcanic emanations during the segregation of the mantle. The main volatile in magma is water that escapes from volcanoes as steam (FIG. 3-8). Therefore, the early atmosphere contained a great deal of steam until the Earth cooled down sufficiently to allow precipitation. The Earth was still very hot and condensing water vapor immediately returned to steam as it landed on the Earth's surface, forming a continuous cloud shrouding the Earth. As the Earth further cooled, water was allowed to gather in the ocean basins. Some of the water could also have come from the bombardment of the Earth by icy meteors.

The oceans cover 70 percent of the surface of the Earth. If the Earth was a smooth, perfect

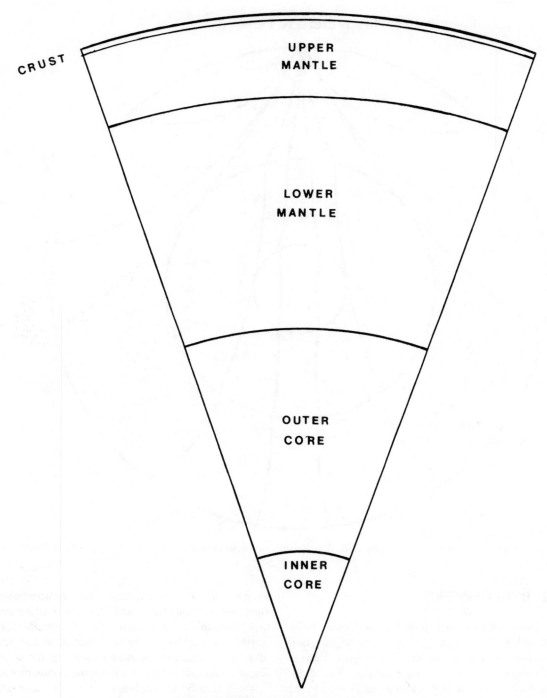

FIG. 3-6. The layering of the earth.

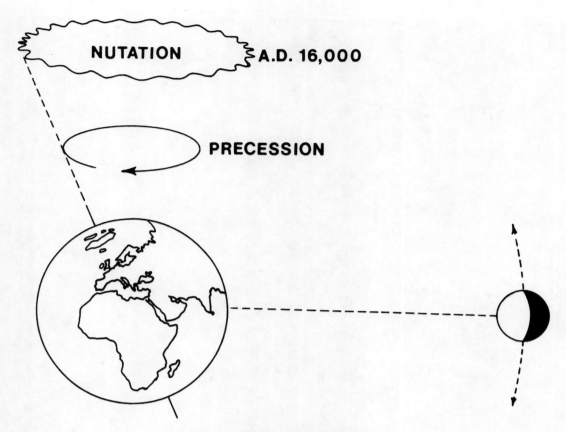

FIG. 3-7. Precession of the earth.

THE ATMOSPHERE

sphere, there would be enough water to cover the entire surface 2 miles deep. It appears that no other planet in our Solar System has as much water as the Earth. The deepest regions of the ocean are in the Pacific basin, with depths of nearly seven miles. If Mount Everest, the tallest mountain, was placed here, water would still extend a mile above it. The ocean floor is made up of vast mountain ranges, some of which break the surface, and their peaks become islands. Underwater volcanoes rise from the ocean floor to create new islands. There are canyons in the ocean floor that rival even the Grand Canyon (FIG. 3-9).

Between the time the Earth was formed and when life first appeared, 3.5 billion years ago, several changes occurred that gave us our present-day world. In the beginning, the Earth had an original atmosphere of hydrogen and helium that vanished either due to the intense solar wind or the heat from the melting of the Earth, which drove off the light gases. The "neon argument" supports the theory of loss or lack of an original atmosphere. Neon gas is relatively abundant in the universe (refer to TABLE 1-1), yet our atmosphere has only

FIG. 3-8. The 1980 eruption of Mount St. Helens. (Courtesy of Austin Post, USGS.)

a trivial fraction of neon, much less than that expected in an original atmosphere.

As the crust began to solidify, numerous volcanoes spewed their contents over the landscape. Large amounts of water vapor, nitrogen, carbon dioxide, and other gases belched from the cones in what geologists call the "big burp." Volatiles such as water and gases under high pressure make up a significant part of the magma. When they reach the surface of the Earth, the reduction in pressure forces the volatiles to be liberated explosively.

Two American chemists, Stanly Miller and Harold Urey, at the University of Chicago, proposed in 1953, that the Earth's early atmosphere was composed of methane, ammonia, and water vapor. They boiled these ingredients in a special

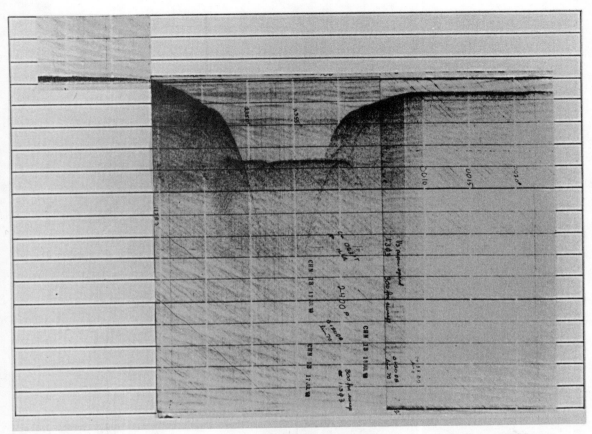

FIG. 3-9. The Mid-Ocean Canyon in Newfoundland Basin. (Courtesy of R.M. Pratt, USGS.)

apparatus (FIG. 3-10) that passed the gases over an electric spark to simulate lightning or ultraviolet radiation that could easily penetrate the oxygen-free atmosphere of the early Earth.

After several days, they obtained a dark soup containing complex amino acids, the building blocks of proteins. Since that time, chemists have been able to synthesize nearly every major constituent of living organisms from various combinations of volatiles, including nitrogen and carbon dioxide. This suggested that the Earth's early atmosphere contained the right combination of chemicals and energy to form life, if given enough time.

Life could not have taken place in an atmosphere initially composed of free oxygen for the simple reason that organic molecules cannot form in the presence of free oxygen, and oxygen in the form of ozone would block the ultraviolet light. Any free oxygen liberated during the formation of the early atmosphere would have to be locked up with other chemical elements such as iron.

The oldest known fossils are of a blue-green class of algae found in northwestern Australia, dated about 3.5 billion years old. Plant life has the unique property of being able to convert sunlight and carbon dioxide into proteins, which allows them to grow while at the same time liberating oxygen. It is thought that the original atmosphere had only a very minor constituent of oxygen, some of which probably came from the disassociation of water.

As the number of algae and other evolving plants propagated, so did the amount of oxygen in the atmosphere, until it reached its present value.

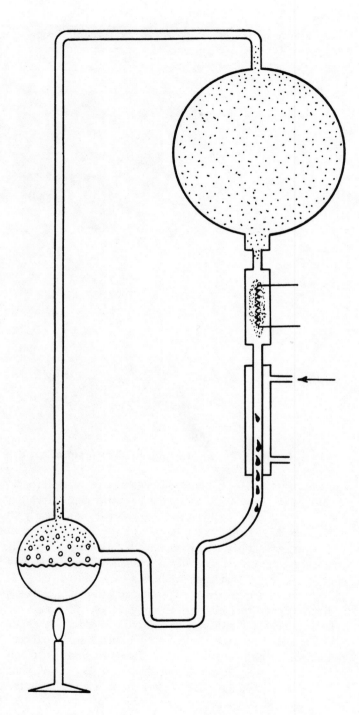

FIG. 3-10. The Miller-Urey experiment.

Today's atmosphere is composed of 78 percent nitrogen from the original atmosphere, 21 percent oxygen created by plant photosynthesis, and about 1 percent other gases, mostly carbon dioxide. Besides plants having since evolved to live on the land, most of the Earth's oxygen still comes from the ocean.

The Land Appears

VIEWING the Earth from outer space (FIG. 4-1), the first thing astronauts notice is the majestic blue color of the oceans and a greenish tinge on continents composed of mountains, deserts, and plains. The outlines of the ocean shores and the inland seas and lakes are clearly visible. The poles are white with snow and ice, and white whisps of clouds sail by below. The Earth appears to be unique among the other planets in the solar system, almost as though it is a living entity constantly in motion.

Men and women who have seen the Earth from their space capsules have regarded it with tremendous respect and reverence, as they witness the beauty and wonder of it all. In February 1962, John Glenn—the first American astronaut to orbit the Earth—a hundred miles up in space described the magnificent sights he encountered as the Earth passed beneath him.

It is no wonder that men of science want to protect and preserve what might well be the only living planet in the universe. And for all practical purposes, it is the only one. Communication with another intelligent species on another planet similar to Earth is riddled with ridicule and doubt. Are the radio antennas pointed in the right direction? How long would it take the radio waves to reach them? Will a technological society be listening in at the right time and on the right wavelength when the signal arrives? If the extremely weak signal is received by an intelligent species, the two-way trip through space might take a million years or more. If so, will there be someone on this end to receive the call? Also, it is feared that by advertising our presence, an unscrupulous space-warrior civilization might home in on the signal and invade the Earth.

THE CRUST OF THE EARTH

Early in the Earth's history, a crust of lighter materials floated to the top of the mantle and solidified, becoming something like an egg with a solid shell and liquid interior. Granite, an aluminum-sili-

FIG. 4-1. Earth-rise over the lunar horizon. (Courtesy of USGS.)

cate rock, makes up most of the continents. Basalt, a heavier, iron and magnesium-rich rock, makes up the ocean floor (FIG. 4-2). The crust of the continents is generally 25 to 30 miles thick, with the Himalayan mountain system and its deep roots about 45 miles thick. Like an iceberg, only the tip of the crust shows above sea level. The majority of the crust is out of sight below the surface (FIG. 4-3). In a few select areas on the ocean floor, the crust is only a few miles thick. Over 4 billion years of history is accumulated in the Earth's crust and only 3.7 billion of those years are accounted for in the rocks. The rocks of the ocean floor are among the youngest, no more than 200 million years old.

THE OLDEST ROCKS

The oldest rocks are exposed in broad, low-lying geologic stable areas of the interior of continents called shields (FIG. 4-4). The shields are named for their rounded, shield like appearance. The southwestern tip of Greenland has the most ancient rocks, dating about 3.7 billion years old, yet to be discovered.

The shields that formed the nuclei from which the present continents grew are thought to be remnants of the original crust. They initially comprised considerably less area, probably no more than 10 percent of the present continents. The

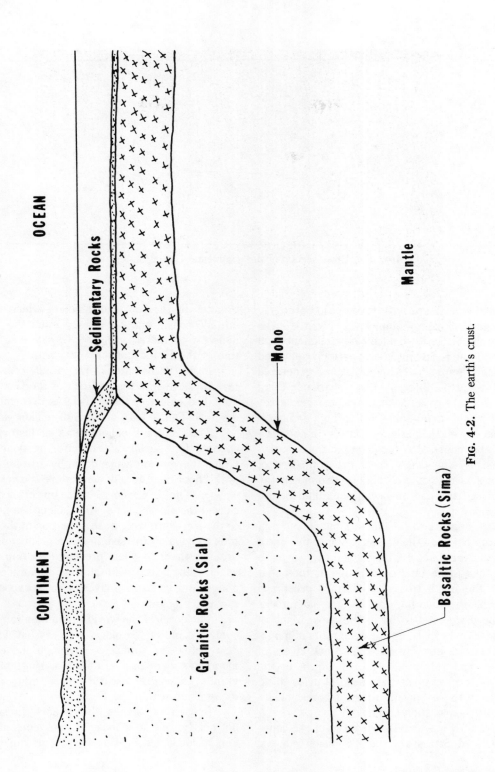

FIG. 4-2. The earth's crust.

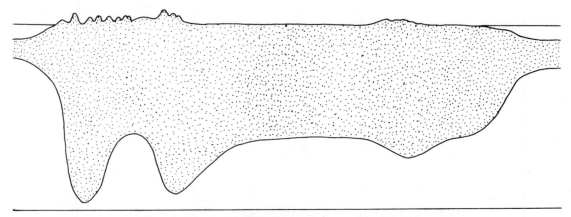

FIG. 4-3. Cross-section of the continental United States.

continental shields are mostly composed of highly altered granitic and metamorphic rocks. These metamorphic rocks were once older sediments and lava flows that were buried and partially remelted by the high temperatures and pressures generated within the Earth's interior. The remarkable thing about the shield rocks is that, besides their great age and having been subjected to high temperatures and stress, they are very similar in composition to the younger rocks being formed today. Also, because the oldest rocks are composed of metamorphosed marine sediments, this means the Earth must have had an ocean sometime before their formation.

There appears to be almost a billion years of lost history between the condensation of the Earth from the solar nebula, 4.6 billion years ago, and the oldest rocks found on Earth. Either it took that long for the Earth to cool to form a crust and ocean, which is doubtful, or there are older rocks yet to be discovered to fill in the gaps. Many of these older rocks make up the deep roots of mountains. They are also buried under thick layers of sediments and volcanics, some of which, in the interior of the continents, are several miles thick. This makes these ancient rocks unaccessible to present-day exploration technology.

Some of the oldest known rocks in the continental United States are the 2.5 billion-year-old

granites of the Canadian shield—which extends into Wisconsin and Minnesota—and the 1.8 billion-year-old metamorphic rocks that lie at the bottom of the Grand Canyon (FIG. 4-5).

In northern Arizona, over a mile of sedimentary rocks overlie the bedrock of the Grand Canyon. The oldest of these rocks is Precambrian in age (see TABLE 4-4), about 800 million years old.

This leaves a billion years of history unaccounted for, during which time the floor of the Grand Canyon was worn down by erosion. On top of this floor, marine sediments were laid down very slowly. The continuous build up of sediments caused the subsidence of the ancient sea floor due to the increased weight. In a fraction of the time it took to build up the sediments, a gradual upheaval brought them to their present elevation, during which time, the swift flowing Colorado River gouged out layer upon layer of rock, exposing the raw earth below.

The cores of the world's mountain ranges also contain some of the oldest rocks. What was once deep below the surface is now high above as the mountains were pushed upwards. Huge blocks of granite, called cratons, were thrust up by tectonic forces deep within the Earth.

In the early stages, the relief of the land was not nearly what it is today. It took eons of mountain building and erosion to give us our present

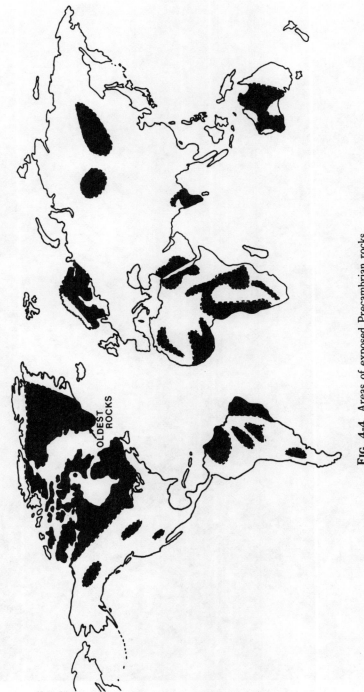

FIG. 4-4. Areas of exposed Precambrian rocks.

FIG. 4-5. The Grand Canyon. (Courtesy of USGS.)

TABLE 4-1. Classification of the Earth's Crust

ENVIRONMENT	CRUST TYPE	TECTONIC CHARACTER	CRUSTAL THICKNESS	GEOLOGIC FEATURES
Continental crust overlying stable mantle	Shield Midcontinent	Very stable Stable	22 miles 24 miles	Little or no sediment, exposed Precambrian rocks
Continental crust overlying unstable mantle	Basin-range	Very unstable	20 miles	Recent normal faulting, volcanism, and intrusion; high mean elevation
	Alpine	Very unstable	34 miles	Rapid recent uplift, relatively recent intrusion; high mean elevation
	Island arc	Very unstable	20 miles	High volcanism, intense folding and faulting
Oceanic crust overlying stable mantle	Ocean basin	Very stable	7 miles	Very thin sediments overlying basalts, no thick Palaeozoic sediments
Oceanic crust overlying unstable mantle	Ocean ridge	Unstable	6 miles	Active basaltic volcanism, little or no sediment

landscape of high mountains and deep valleys. Mount Everest is the tallest peak, 29,000 feet above sea level, and Death Valley, California is 280 feet below sea level. Before the spread of plant life on the continents, soil eroded easily without plant roots to hold it in place. Therefore, erosion rates in the early history of the crust could have been much greater than they are today.

One of the first to recognize the building and erosion of land forms was the Greek historian Hirodotus (484–425 B.C.). During his exploration of Egypt, Hirodotus noticed how new land was created as the Nile River emptied into the Mediterranean Sea. He could see that the land for over a hundred miles up the river was once under water. Sediments brought down by the river gradually built up, turning marshes into dry land. He proved that the soil washed down by the river extended far into the sea by observing how sailors would bring up river mud that clung to their lead lines as they were taking soundings of the seafloor. Hirodotus reasoned that the seacoast was at one time at the inland hills because he found fossils of seashells embedded in the rocks, indicating the hills too were once underwater.

THE PROTEROZOIC ERA

The protocontinents, from which the continental shields are the only remnants, provided the seeds for our present continents. Small land masses were assembled into successively larger ones. These smaller protocontinents were probably thin and moved about freely on a sea of plastic rock called the asthenosphere (the mechanics of crustal movement is discussed in more detail in Chapter 6).

TABLE 4-2. Composition of the Earth's Crust

CRUST TYPE	SHELL	AVERAGE THICKNESS IN MILES	PERCENT COMPOSITION OF OXIDES						
			SILICA	ALUM	IRON	MAGN	CALC	SODI	POTAS
Continental	Sedimentary	2.1	50	13	6	3	12	2	2
	Granitic	12.5	64	15	5	2	4	3	3
	Basaltic	12.5	58	16	8	4	6	3	3
Total		27.1							
Subcontinental	Sedimentary	1.8	50	13	6	3	12	2	2
	Granitic	5.6	64	15	5	2	4	3	3
	Basaltic	7.3	58	16	8	4	6	3	3
Total		14.7							
Oceanic	Sedimentary	0.3	41	11	6	3	17	1	2
	Volcanic	0.7	46	14	7	5	14	2	1
	Basaltic sediment	3.5	50	17	8	7	12	3	<1
Total		4.5							
Average		15.4	52	14	7	4	11	2	2

TABLE 4-3. Crustal Abundance of Rock Types and Minerals

ROCK TYPE	PERCENT VOLUME	MINERALS	PERCENT VOLUME
Sandstone	1.7	Quartz	12.0
Clays and shales	4.2	Potassium feldspar	12.0
Carbonates	2.0	Plagioclase	39.0
Granites	10.4	Micas	5.0
Grandiorite		Amphiboles	5.0
Quartz diorite	11.2	Pyroxenes	11.0
Syenites	0.4	Olivine	3.0
Basalts		Sheet silicates	4.6
Gabbros		Calcite	1.5
Amphibolites		Dolomite	0.5
Granulites	42.5	Magnetite	1.5
Ultramafics	0.2	Other	4.9
Gneisses	21.4		
Schists	5.1		
Marbles	0.9		

TABLE 4-4. Geologic Time Scale

ERA	PERIOD	EPOCH	AGE IN MILLIONS OF YEARS	FIRST LIFE FORMS
Cenozoic	Quaternary	Holocene	.01	
		Pleistocene	2	Man
		Pliocene	10	Mastodons
		Miocene	25	Saber-tooth tigers
	Tertiary	Oligocene	40	
		Eocene	60	Whales
		Paleocene	65	Horses Alligators
Mesozoic	Cretaceous		135	
	Jurassic		180	Birds Mammals Dinosaurs
	Triassic		230	
Paleozoic	Permian		280	Reptiles
	Pennsylvanian		310	Trees
	Mississippian		345	Amphibians Insects
	Devonian		405	Sharks
	Silurian		425	Land plants
	Ordovician		500	Fish
	Cambrian		570	Sea plants
Precambrian	Proterozoic		3300	Invertebrates Oldest rocks
	Archaean		4600	Meteorites

About 2.5 billion years ago, during Proterozoic time, all the material that now constitutes the continents and their associative islands were assembled into one large coherent land mass or supercontinent, called Pangaea, meaning all-land (FIG. 4-6). The Proterozoic era, which lasted until the beginning of the Cambrian period, 570 million years ago, was a time of large-scale metamorphism, differentiation, and recycling of rocks. Rocks rich in iron and magnesium were replaced with silica-rich varieties.

Precipitates, such as limestones and dolomites became abundant, and the continents began to thicken with the accretion of lighter materials. Silica-rich magmatic fluids worked their way upward and became incorporated in the lighter sandstones and siltstones, becoming intrusive rocks from which mineral ores are mined today.

It was during the Proterozoic that the first highly evolved animals appeared. These were worm like creatures with a separate head, a nervous system with sense organs, an ability to take in

Fig. 4-6. Pangaea.

and digest food, and excrete wastes, along with a primitive means of locomotion. Before, there was no sharp division between plants and animals and one shared some features of the other.

Because these early worms were soft-bodied, they left no fossil record of their existence, except for their sinuous trails and burrows in the mud that later solidified into rock. Fossils of early single-cell animals, similar to present-day protozoans, were found at the bottom of the Grand Canyon and were dated at about 750 million years old. Even fossils of

ancestral jellyfish, which date late Precambrian, have been found in Australia.

Ever since there was water in the oceans and precipitation, either in the form of rain or snow, there have been ice ages. The first ice age ever recorded in geologic history took place around 2 billion years ago. It was followed by a second ice age very late in the Proterozoic, and it appeared to be even more widespread.

Glacial rock deposits, called glacial moraines, are composed mostly of boulders and gravels scooped up by the glaciers and deposited in large heaps when the glaciers melted. These rocks have been found and dated at very early ages on every continent except Antarctica. It might be that this latter ice age was perhaps the greatest the Earth has ever experienced, ending about 700 million years ago. With all ice ages, including an ice age some experts suggest we will be entering into in the not too distant future (FIG. 4-7), there is no clear-cut explanation for their occurrence. Various forces, including loss of solar energy or volcanic activity causing less sunlight to strike the Earth, could be responsible for the general cooling of the climate and bringing on an ice age.

In the western United States, there is a preponderance of red rocks exposed in the mountains and canyons. These sedimentary rocks contain a small amount of iron that had been oxidized, in a form of rust, into the mineral hematite named so because of its blood-red color. Many of these rocks formed late in geologic history, but other rocks of an earlier age, called redbeds, formed on dry land during the Proterozoic and are clear evidence that the Earth's atmosphere contained oxygen during that period. The oxygen combined with iron to form a red iron oxide that stained the grains of sand. This also corresponds with the time the first animals appeared in the oceans.

THE PALEOZOIC ERA

At the boundary between the Precambrian and Cambrian periods, about 570 million years ago, there appears to be an explosion of animal life (FIG. 4-8). The evidence is indicated by numerous fossil skeletons and shells of various species embedded in the rocks.

Prior to this time, the lands were relatively high, with localized mountains, and the oceans were well confined within their basins. With the melting of the glaciers due to the warmer climate, the ocean levels rose and this, coupled with the erosion of the continents, brought the level of the land down to the level of the ocean, causing extensive flooding along with a proliferation of marine animal life. There was in existence, by the Paleozoic Era, 570 to 230 million years ago, two supercontinents called Gondwanaland—present-day Africa, South America, Australia, India, and Antarctica (FIG. 4-9)—and Laurasia, the remaining continents of the Northern Hemisphere. The supercontinents were separated by what geologists called the Tethys Seaway, and Europe and North America were separated by a proto-Atlantic ocean.

These ancient seas narrowed in the late Paleozioc as the continents rejoined in a great continental collision. Many of the worlds mountain

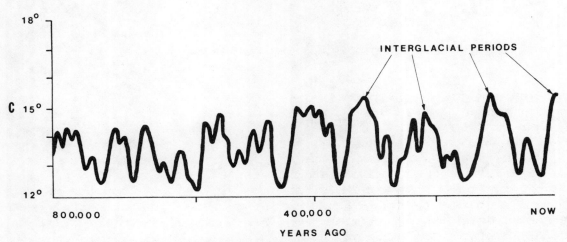

FIG. 4-7. Warming trends throughout civilization.

Fig. 4-8. Sea life in the Paleozoic Era. (Courtesy of Field Museum of Natural History, Chicago.)

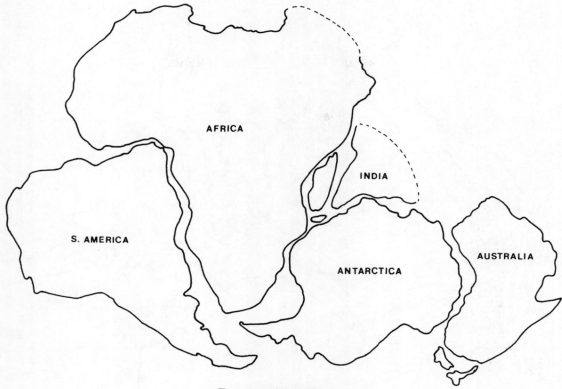

FIG. 4-9. Gonwanaland.

ranges had their origin as a result of these late Paleozioc continental collisions (FIG. 4-10). The Appalachians and the Ouachitas began forming when North America and Africa slammed into each other. The Ural Mountains were first created out of a collision between the Siberian and Russian shields. The Alps were initially formed when Africa collided with southern Europe. And the Himalayans first rose up when India broke off of Gondwanaland and rammed into Asia.

Plant life first appeared on the continents during the Paleozoic era. It is amazing that it took this long because life had been around for at least 3 billion years prior to this time. One possible explanation for this is that the ozone layer of the upper atmosphere had not yet formed. The ozone layer is composed of complex molecules of oxygen and it filters out ultraviolet radiation that is deadly to

plants as well as animals. Prior to this time, plants existed partly shielded in shallow water. The first land plants probably sprouted from these shallow-water seaweed like varieties as the ozone layer became thick enough to provide adequate protection.

The earliest known land plants were small, lacking roots and leaves, and were fertilized by the use of spores at the ends of simple branching limbs. Trees evolved from a fern like plant and developed a strong stem, a root system, leaves, and seeds that replaced spores. These earlier plants lived along coastal areas in lowlands and swamps and later adapted to survive in the drier inland areas.

In the animal kingdom, the first vertebrates, with an internal skeleton, appeared in the Cambrian period and began to flourish by the middle of the Paleozoic. Before this time, animals, called in-

FIG. 4-10. Paleozoic mountain belts.

vertebrates, had to support their bodies with external skeletons made of calcite or chiten which, in some cases, must be shed, placing it in grave danger to predators, as the animal grows. The advantages of an internal skeleton is its lightness and strength, a vast increase in flexibility, a more efficient attachment for muscles, and the skeleton grows as the animal grows. The first fish were small mud-grubbers and sea squirts that lacked jaws and teeth. Despite their obscure beginnings, fish were destined to become the masters of the sea, with the shark reigning supreme as king of the deep.

The ocean was teeming with sea life, including sponges, coelenterates, cephalopods, brachiopods, arthropods, and a large variety of shelled animals. Unfortunately, as the Paleozoic was brought to a close, there was a massive extermination of many species of invertebrates. The climate might have been unusually cool, possibly caused by a long period of intense volcanic activity that also might have altered the chemistry of the oceans. Whatever was the mechanism for the destruction, half the known families of animals disappeared by the end of the Permian period.

Land animals did not make their appearance until mid- to late Paleozoic, about 350 million years ago. These were the first amphibians. They were fish with lobe-fins, having internal radial bones, that were modified into walking limbs, and lungs adapted for air breathing. These animals, looking somewhat like modern tadpoles, probably did not stay on land indefinitely because their primitive legs and feet could not support their weight very long, forcing them to return to the water.

What might have attracted these animals to the land was an abundance of food swept up on the beaches by the tides. This was a period of rapid growth and fierce competition in the ocean. The land offered an incentive for animals to leave the ocean, even if just for a short while.

As their limbs strengthen from digging in the sand for food and shelter, some amphibians were enticed to wander further inland in search of crustaceans and insects. This was also a time of abundant plant life, especially in the great swamps which were particularly attractive to the amphibians. These swamps belonged to a period called the Carboniferous, and were responsible for much of our present coal deposites. With an abundance of prey, the amphibians rapidly became the dominant land animals until the arrival of the reptiles.

As the Paleozoic came to a close, the land began to dry out and the temperature became cooler. This started the decline of the amphibians and the rise of the reptiles, which evolved from the amphibians about 320 million years ago. The major disadvantage of the amphibians was its weak, clumsy legs. It took quite a lot of effort for them to raise their heavy bodies off the ground. Rapid locomotion was out of the question. The amphibians were happy as long as there was plenty of water around, but water was becoming more confined to watercourses in the now dry regions. Reptiles, on the other hand, were totally suited to a continuous life on land. Their bodies were less clumsy and their legs were much stronger, allowing them to scurry across the land at great speed. Reptiles also laid eggs that could be hatched out of water. These characteristic are what essentially separates the reptiles from their amphibian cousins.

THE MESOZOIC ERA

The Mesozoic era is called the time of middle life and spans from the end of the Paleozoic to the beginning of the Cenozoic, 230 to 65 million years ago. All the land was joined together in one crescent-shaped aggregation stretching almost from pole to pole. Near the middle of the Mesozoic, the continents began to drift apart.

By the end of the Mesozoic, three new bodies of water were formed, the Atlantic, Arctic, and Indian Oceans. The climate appears to have been less extreme compared to the previous era. In the warmer regions, lime-secreting organisms flourished, producing great reefs and massive beds of chalk, limestone, and dolomite. The Tethys Seaway accumulated layer upon layer of sediments in a vast geosyncline, a huge bulge in the Earth's crust.

Before the Mesozoic ended, these deposits were uplifted to form many great mountain ranges of Europe and North Africa, including the Alps, Apennines, Atlas, Pyrenees, and others.

The Mesozoic is known for its erosion of previously formed mountain ranges, such as the Appalachians, that were planed off, leaving only stumps. Large inland lakes formed and the seas invaded the interior of most continents. Much of Russia, western Siberia, and Asia was under water; so were portions of western North America and parts of South America. Large amounts of sediments accumulated in the inundated areas, and the central seas were crowded out by these deposits.

By the end of the Mesozoic, salt lakes and swamps were formed by the receding waters. The Mesozoic was also noted for its widespread basalt lava flows, with the most extensive activity in the Southern Hemisphere. The lava flows were accompanied by large-scale intrusions of igneous rocks. The Mesozoic is responsible for much of our oil and gas, coal, and ore production.

Life in the mesozoic was in a period of transition. Toward the end of the era, plants had changed drastically and bore little similarity to those at the beginning of the era and were more closely related to those of the present. On land, a vastly improved means of fertilization came about with the evolution of the flower bearing plants and the concurrent development of pollinaters such as insects and birds.

The flowers attracted the pollinaters either by color, smell, or promise of sweet nectar. Pollen grains were deposited on the unwary intruder and carried to the next plant it visited, whereupon that plant became fertilized. Plants devised ingenious methods for dispersing their seeds such as floating them on water, flying them on air currents, or disguising them as tasteful seed cases or fruit that passed through the animal and planted some distance away. Cone-bearing trees, called conifers, are highly adaptable to cooler dryer climates, and they dominated the landscape. Toward the end of the era, deciduous trees and other seasonal plants such as grasses, shrubs, and herbs also formed in response to the cooler climate.

During the Mesozoic, life in the ocean saw many advancements. Many invertebrates that escaped extinction at the end of the Paleozoic became quite different from their ancestors and were closer to species of the present (FIG. 4-11). The invertebrates went on to recover lost ground from

FIG. 4-11. Sea life in the Mesozoic Era. (Courtesy of Field Museum of National History, Chicago.)

the last die-out and began to flourish toward the end of the Mesozoic. It seems that those species that developed greater intelligence, keener senses, and a sophisticated means of locomotion had the best chance of survival and growth. The cephalopods were particularly spectacular during this time. Their ability to swim or crawl provided them their independence from ocean bottom conditions. Similarly, the crustaceans perfected their mobility and lived their lives near the shores. Those species that were stationary and anchored to the ocean floor generally declined, probably due to competition by their more mobile rivals for a common food source.

The Mesozoic is more popularly known as the "age of the dinosaurs" (FIG. 4-12). Reptiles were at this time the most successful land animals — they dominated the surface of the Earth — and even reentered the ocean to compete with the fish. A relatively stable warm climate and an abundant food supply might have had some bearing on giantism among certain reptilian species. These reptiles never ceased growing entirely, but continued growing slowly until age, accidental death, or disease took their lives.

Heated debates continue among paleontologists whether the dinosaurs were warm-blooded, like mammals and birds, or cold blooded, like other reptiles. There is no clear cut evidence pointing in either direction. The most remarkable feature about some dinosaurs, besides their huge size, was their ability to permanently stand and travel bird-like on their hind legs. This was important because it freed the forelimbs for other functions such as foraging for food. Part of the reason dinosaurs flourished all over the world was that they had no natural predators except for carnivorous dinosaurs.

THE CENOZOIC ERA

Sixty-five million years ago, the earth witnessed a rapid, mass die-out of species both on land and in the water. This brought to a close the Mesozoic Era and opened the Cenozoic era, or time of modern life (FIG. 4-13).

According to the American physicist Luis Alvarez the Earth could have been struck by a large asteroid, perhaps as much as six miles across, with the subsequent spewing of enormous quantities of dust into the atmosphere. This darkening of the sky would have blocked the Sun's rays from striking the Earth's surface and bring on a rapid, short-term, geologically speaking, cooling of the climate. Lack of sunlight would also adversely affect plant growth and disrupt the food chain.

Evidence for such an event at the Mesozoic-Cenozoic boundary can be found worldwide in a thin layer of clay composed of an unusual concentration of the rare element iridium that was thought to have come from an extraterrestrial source.

Actually, the occurrence of large meteorites is not unusual even for fairly recent times. Meteor Crater (FIG. 4-14) near Winslow, Arizona, is 4000 feet in diameter and 600 feet deep, and it is estimated to be only 25,000 years old. In 1908, trees in a remote forest in northern Siberia were leveled for 40 miles, as though by an atomic blast, and this might have been caused by an explosion of a large meteorite or comet.

An alternative explanation suggests the iridium could have come from terrestrial volcanics. Nevertheless, if dinosaurs were indeed cold blooded, their great size would be responsible for a large amount of body heat loss in a colder climate, and they would not be long for this world.

The demise of the dinosaurs and other reptiles paved the way for the mammals. The first mammals were small rodentlike creatures, and it is perhaps due to their small size — along with the capability to regulate their body temperature — that saved them from extinction.

The Cenozoic, 65 million years to the present, is regarded as the "age of the mammals" because mammals have dominated the Earth during this era. At the beginning of the era, the breakup of the supercontinent was near complete, and continents were well on their way toward their present positions. The Cenozoic is noted for intensive mountain building, including the Alps, other European ranges, the Rocky Mountains of North America,

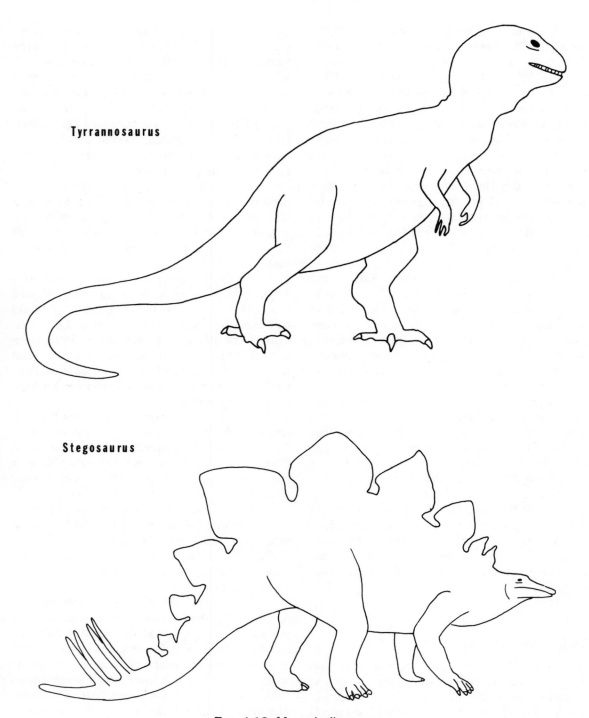

FIG. 4-12. Mesozoic dinosaurs.

Brontosaurus

Triceratops

and the Andes of South America. Chains of islands, called island arcs, fringed great stretches of the Pacific Ocean. The era is also known for worldwide Tertiary volcanic activity, but perhaps it is best known for the Pleistocene Ice Age.

More than any other interval of the Earth's history, the Cenozoic was an age of constant change. This brought about a large diversity of species trying to adapt to a variety of living conditions—from hot desert to cold arctic and everything else in between. The separation of the continents would be largely responsible for the divergence of species.

The evolution of brainy mammals offered more variety as species lived by their wits, competing with each other for a scarce food supply. Grasslands replaced huge forests with the subsequent proliferation of hoofed grazing mammals.

FIG. 4-13. Geologic time spiral. (Courtesy of USGS.)

FIG. 4-14. Meteor Crater, Arizona. (Courtesy of USGS.)

The great die-out at the end of the Mesozoic left the oceans of the Cenozoic devoid of many earlier species.

Sometime toward the beginning of the Quaternary Period, about 2 million years ago, an unusual looking primate walked out of Olduvai Gorge of ancient Tanzania. What set this particular mammal apart from all the rest was that he was highly inquisitive, loudly vocal, walked upright, and was nearly hairless. He was setting out on a journey, an adventure that would eventually lead him to rediscover his planet from outer space.

5

Continents Adrift

EARLY explorers of the world drew maps of the newly discovered lands, but these charts were crudely drawn and inaccurate. The sixteenth century Flemish geographer Gerhardus Mercator, for which our present day Mercator projections were named, greatly refined the art of mapmaking. Early cartographers must have puzzled over the way the bulge on the east coast of South America fitted easily into the cleft on the west coast of Africa, as though they were pieces of a gigantic jigsaw puzzle.

In 1620, the English philosopher Sir Francis Bacon could not help but notice how similar the New World was with the Old World. Bacon thought that was no accident. Isthmuses and capes looked much the same, and both continents were broad and extended toward the north but narrow and pointed toward the south. Likewise, the French naturalist Georges de Buffon suggested in 1750 that Europe and North America had once been joined because of the similarities of their present plants and animals. Many men of science were cautious about expounding on these new ideas be-cause religion still dominated men's thinking about the creation of the Earth.

THE DIVIDED LAND

Seventeenth and eighteenth century geologists still spoke in terms of the biblical flood and argued that the flood was so devastating that it broke up the old continents and created entirely new ones. Taking this idea one step further, the nineteenth century German naturalist-explorer Alexander von Humboldt, for which the Pacific Humboldt Current is named, thought that a huge tidal wave surged across the globe and carved out the Atlantic Ocean like a giant river valley, leaving the continents divided with opposing shorelines.

The American writer Antonio Snider suggested, in 1858, that as the Earth cooled and crystallized, most of the continental material gathered on one side, making the Earth lopsided and unbalanced. This created such internal stresses and strains that the single continent cracked wide open

TABLE 5-1. The Drifting of the Continents

AGE IN MILLIONS OF YEARS		GONDWANALAND	LAURASIA
Quaternary	3		Opening of Gulf of California
Pliocene	11	Begin spreading near Galapagos Islands	Change spreading directions in eastern Pacific
		Opening of the Gulf of Aden	Birth of Iceland
Miocene	25	Opening of Red Sea	
Oligocene	40	Collision of India with Eurasia	Begin spreading in Arctic Basin
Eocene	60	Separation of Australia from Antarctica	Separation of Greenland from Norway
Paleocene	65		
		Separation of New Zealand from Antarctica	Opening of the Labrador Sea
		Separation of Africa from Madagascar and South America	Opening of the bay of Biscay
			Major rifting of North America from Eurasia
Cretaceous	135	Separation of Africa from India, Australia, New Zealand, and Antarctica	
Jurassic	180		
			Begin separation of North America from Africa
Triassic	230		
Permian	280		

and hot lavas bled through the fissures. At the same time, the rains came, and for 40 days and 40 nights, the raging waters pushed apart the segments of the broken continent to their present positions. Snider pointed to evidence of a single, large land mass by the fact that coal beds of Africa and South America were of similar age with similar fossils, dating back to the Carboniferous period.

Playing on George Darwin's theory for the origin of the Moon, (see Chapter 3), the American scientist Osmond Fisher in 1882 published a paper in which he suggested that the Moon left a great rent when it was torn out of the Earth. This cavity formed the Pacific basin, which began to fill with molten rock from the Earth's interior. As the upper fluid layers flowed into the cavity, the cooling solid crust, which floated on top, was broken up and part of it was pulled toward the cavity like a raft riding on the current of a river.

Scientists now know the Moon could not have formed in the manner suggested by Darwin, and that it had to evolve separately out of the solar nebula from which the Earth came. Nevertheless, Fisher's mechanism for transporting the continents on a sea of molten rock was close to the truth.

One of the major concerns of biologists and geologists near the turn of the twentieth century was the similarity between fossils and some living plants and animals of the Old World and the New. One explanation was that the continents did not actually move laterally, but that ocean basins developed from the sinking of the land that linked the present continents. Many thought the Earth was contracting, and as the interior cooled and shrank, blocks of crust fell inward to fill the empty spaces left behind, thereby creating the ocean basins.

This also explained the lost continent of Atlantis which, according to legend, disappeared somewhere in the Atlantic Ocean. The theory also allowed life forms a convenient method of moving from one continent to another. Unfortunately, it placed severe limits on the age of the Earth, implying that it formed only tens of millions instead of billions of years ago.

The Austrian geologist Edward Suess made the first serious investigation into the fitting together of the continents and in 1885, he published a four-part volume called *The Face of the Earth*. In his works, Suess showed how the continents of the Southern Hemisphere could come together into a composite land mass he called Gondwanaland, after a province in India. Suess called the northern land mass Laurasia, which he named for the Laurentian province of Canada, and Asia (FIG. 5-1). The belief that the Earth had to be shrinking in order to maintain its internal temperature was soon discarded with the discovery that radioactive decay could supply the energy to keep the Earth's interior hot. Many geologists then did a complete turn around and suggested that the Earth was expanding in order to get rid of excess heat.

One interesting feature about the Earth's crust that geologists found quite by accident was that Scandinavia and parts of Canada were slowly rising, on the order of about two-fifths of an inch per year. Over the centuries, mooring rings on the harbor walls in the Baltic seaports have risen so far above the water that they could no longer be used to tie up ships.

A gravity survey in South America showed the pull of gravity on top of the Andes Mountains was less than at sea level. One explanation was that the granites in the mountains were lighter or less dense than the rocks below and exerted a lesser gravitational tug on the instruments.

Geologists concluded that the continents were composed of lighter granitelike materials they called sial, from the words silica and aluminum, and the ocean floor was composed of heavier basaltlike substances they called sima, from the words silica and magnesium. The weight difference between the two materials would make the continents buoyant, which in geology is called isostasy a Greek word meaning "equal standing." Therefore, the lighter continents floated on a sea of heavier rocks. During the last ice age, which ended about 10,000 years ago, the northern land masses were covered with a sheet of ice several miles thick. Under the weight of ice, North America and Scandinavia began to sink like an overloaded ship. When the ice melted, the regions became lighter and began to rise again (FIG. 5-2).

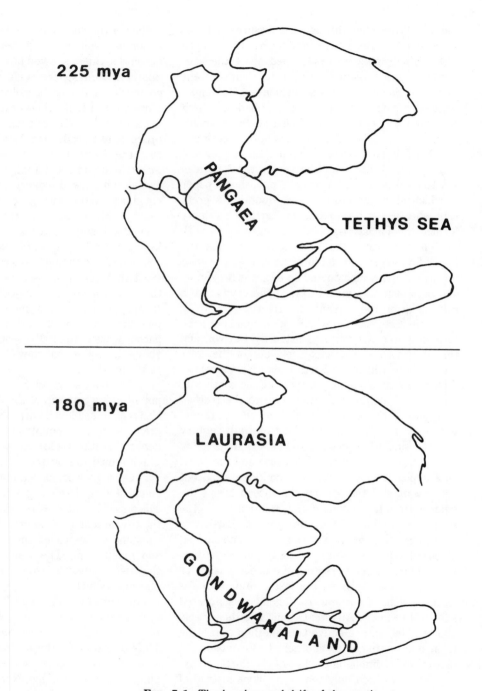

225 mya

PANGAEA

TETHYS SEA

180 mya

LAURASIA

GONDWANALAND

FIG. 5-1. The breakup and drift of the continents.

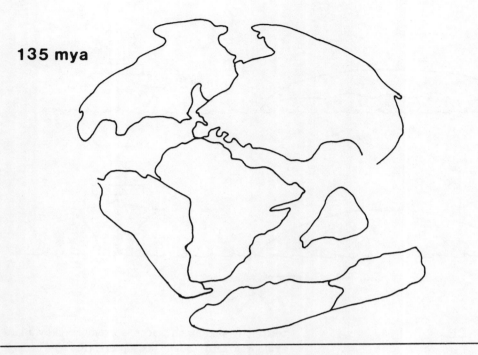

135 mya

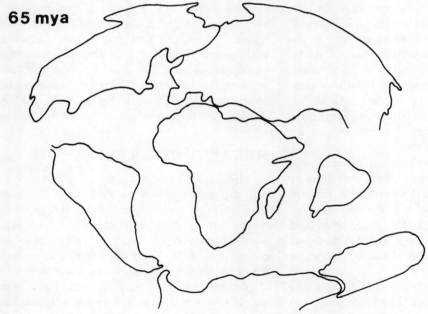

65 mya

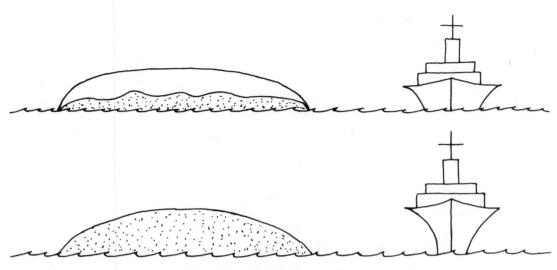

FIG. 5-2. The principle of isostacy.

FOSSIL EVIDENCE

The basic flaw in early theories regarding the separation of the continents was that the phenomenon is purported to have commenced early in the Earth's history. Thus, scientists had to devise other complex theories to account for the similarity among plant and animal fossils that have been separated by oceans for eons. It seemed unlikely that such a variety of species could have evolved along parallel lines in such diverse environments as, for example, India and Antarctica.

Plant seeds could have been carried over large distances by water or wind currents, or even by birds, but transporting land animals is a different matter entirely. Fossils of a 250-million-year-old reptile, called Mesosaurus (FIG. 5-3), have been found in both Brazil and South Africa. This 2-foot long reptile spent its time in shallow, fresh-water lakes.

It is doubtful Mesosaurus could swim the 2000-mile distance between the two continents in a saltwater ocean. It seems even more remote that animals, especially large dinosaurs, drifted across the oceans on rafts of vegetation that would have to stay afloat for long periods. The fact that life is distinctly alike in all places is exemplified by a late Paleozoic fern, called Glossopteris (FIG. 5-4) which is found everywhere in the Southern Hemisphere but is suspiciously missing in the Northern Hemisphere. Instead, the Northern Hemisphere was itself distinct, blanketed with luxuriant forests of tropical vegetation. This could be proof that there were, at one time, one large land mass in the south and one in the north, separated by a sea, and their breakup was relatively late in the Earth's history.

SIMILARITY OF ROCKS

Geologists could not ignore the fact that not only did plant and animal life on the continents seem to have common ancestors, but the older rocks were remarkably alike as well and there were matches in the rocks of certain mountain ranges (FIG. 5-5). The Cape Mountains in South Africa connected with the Sierra Mountains, south of Buenos Aires, Argentina, and there were matches between mountains in Canada, Scotland, and Norway. Not only were the rock strata of the same type, but they were also laid down in the same order.

South Africa, South America, Australia, India,

FIG. 5-3. Mesosaurus

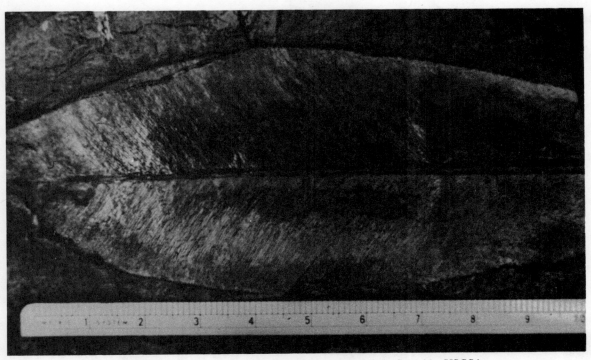

FIG. 5-4. Fossil Glossopteris leaf. (Courtesy of D.L. Schmidt, USGS.)

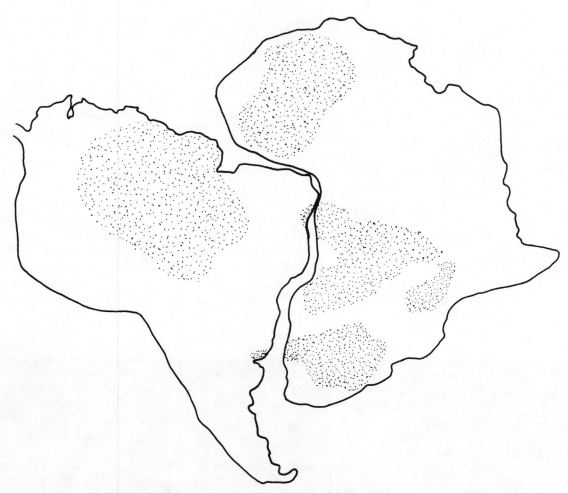

FIG. 5-5. The match of geological provinces of Africa and South America.

and Antarctica all show evidence of contemporaneous glaciation in the upper paleozoic, about 280 million years ago, as indicated by deposits of glacial till and scratches in ancient rocks caused by boulders embedded in slowly moving masses of ice. The lines of ice flow are away from the equator and toward the poles. This is just the opposite of what would be expected if the continents were situated as they are now. The continents must have been joined so that the ice moved across a single land mass. In some cases, boulders were composed of rock types not found elsewhere on the continent, but matched well with rocks on the opposite continent.

The glacial deposits were followed by a thick sequence of terrestrial deposits, which were themselves followed by massive outpourings of basalt lava flows. On top of all this, there are coal deposits with similar fossilized plant material. It stands to reason that, up to the time of the lower Mesozoic — about 200 million years ago — the continents must have had a common heritage and therefore were linked together. Geologists have also found glacial deposits in the equatorial areas, which at one time must have been much colder, and coral reefs and coal deposits in the north polar regions that indicate a tropical climate must have existed there at one time. Also, in the arctic regions, there are salt deposits that are indicative of desert climates. Either the climate in the past changed dramatically or the continental areas changed position with respect to the poles.

THE CONTINENTAL DRIFT THEORY

Even in the early years of the twentieth century, scientists still held to the theory that a narrow land bridge spanned the distance between continents. Their belief was that the continents had always remained fixed and that the land bridges rose up from the ocean floor. Then, in the not too distant past, such bridges sank out of sight beneath the surface of the sea. A search for evidence of the land bridges by sampling the ocean floor failed to turn up even a trace of drowned land.

In 1908, two obscure American geologists, Frank Taylor and Howard Baker, working independently suggested alternative explanations based on continental movements. Taylor went so far as to suggest that two great land masses, located at the poles, slowly crept toward the equator. Unfortunately, neither scientist could offer an explanation for the process of continental movements. As a result, they were not very persuasive nor taken very seriously, and consequently, their ideas fell by the wayside.

A German meteorologist and arctic explorer named Alfred Wegener was impressed with the geology of Greenland, the world's largest island, during his expeditions there. On his journies, he probably noticed the rifting and drifting of sea ice and came to the conclusion that the continents were constantly in motion.

Like others before him, Wegener noticed the high degree of correspondence between the shapes of continental coastlines on either side of the Atlantic Ocean. By 1910, a seed of an idea germinated in his mind. After reading accounts of the similarity of fossils in South America and Africa to support the theory of a land bridge, Wegener thought the facts were interpreted totally wrong. A land bridge was impossible. The continents stand higher than the sea floor for the simple reason that they are composed of light granitic rocks that float on the denser basaltic rocks of the upper mantle in an isostatic relationship. He maintained that it was inconceivable for lighter rocks to sink into heavier ones (they can but under different circumstances), and it was more likely that the two continents were once one and drifted apart.

Wegener then conceived the theory of continental drift and, in 1915, he published a book called *The Origin of Continents and Oceans*. He believed that 200 million years ago, all the land masses existed in one large continent he named Pangaea, and the rest of the world was nothing but an ocean he called Panthalassa or "universal sea." Then Pangaea began to break up and drift apart to open up the Atlantic Ocean and the Indian Ocean as the continents separated. He supported his hypothesis with an impressive collection of facts, including the geometric fit of continental margins, matching mountain chains on opposite continents, corresponding rock successions, similar ancient climatic conditions, and identical life forms on continents now widely separated by ocean. The continents were likened to torn pieces of newspaper. The edges match when fitted together and so do the printed words.

Before Wegener came along, there was not a good explanation for the building of mountain ranges. Geologists just assumed that the mountains formed when the molten crust solidifed and shriveled up. After making more extensive studies of mountain ranges, geologists were forced to conclude that the folding of mountain rock layers was much too intense (FIG. 5-6). This would have required considerably more rapid cooling and contraction than the Earth could possibly have undergone.

Wegener's theory was convincing because of its elegance and simplicity. As the continents pushed through the ocean floor following their break up, they encountered increasing resistance that caused the leading edges to crumble, fold back, and thrust upward. Wegener pointed to the

FIG. 5-6. Folded Cambrian rocks of Scapegoat Mountain. (Courtesy of M.R. Mudge, USGS.)

long sinuous Rocky Mountains (FIG. 5-7) and Andes Mountains on the western coast of the Americas as classic examples.

OPPOSITION TO DRIFT

Continental drift drew furious fire from most of the scientific community and many opponents attempted to justify their opposition by contending that Wegener's theories were simply preposterous. How could the soft, light rocks of the continents penetrate the hard, dense rocks of the ocean floor? Why did the break up occur so late in the Earth's history? They also insisted that matching coastlines was no more than a coincidence. According to geophysicists, Wegener also failed to supply an adequate mechanism for moving the continents around.

Wegener looked to the Earth's own rotation to provide the necessary force. As the Earth spins on its axis, centrifugal force tends to make the outer layers fly outward, pushing them away from the poles and causing a bulge at the equator. To account for the westerly drift of the continents, Wegener proposed that the gravitational pull of the Sun and Moon acted on the land similar to the way they caused the ebb and flow of ocean tides.

But geophysicists were not satisfied with Wegener's ideas and calculated that these external forces were much too weak to account for the movements of continents in many directions for such a short period of time. The energy involved would have to be tremendous and no power on heaven or Earth was enough to budge the continents. Studies of deep earthquakes at the ocean-continent boundaries, especially around the Pacific, demonstrated the very deep structure of the continents with their roots well embedded in the mantle.

Also, calculations of the Earth's heat flow suggested the continents were formed from the mantle beneath them. If drift occurred, there would be — yet to be found — uneven patterns of heat flow. This placed severe restrictions on continental drift, for the continents were much thicker and therefore less mobile than it was at first realized.

One of the chief protagonists of continental drift was Harold Jefferes of Cambridge University. In the 1920s, he dealt with Wagener's theory in his classic book, *The Earth*. He picked on minor details, and when these failed the acid test, the whole theory was swepted aside. Geologists resisted continental drift for fear of having to give up years of painstaking research, their pet theories, or their university careers. Wegener was made an outcast mainly because he was not a brethren geologist, and also, because of this, he was unable to obtain a suitable university posting.

Some scientists did try to keep Wegener's theory alive, making new discoveries and even modifying the way in which the continents moved about. Unfortunately, their arguments fell on deaf ears. Wegener worked so hard to prove his theory that he tended to exaggerate, seeing evidence

FIG. 5-7. The Colorado Rockies. (Courtesy of W. Cross, USGS.)

where none existed. His calculation for Greenland's drift was an amazing 40 yards per year and, at that highly improbable rate, it would completely circle the Earth once every million years. In 1930, on his last heroic expedition to his beloved Greenland, where he hoped to find more definitive proof for his theory, Wegener died at the age of 50, from exhaustion, on his return from his lonely outpost on top of the world. With its champion gone, continental drift, for three decades, died along with him.

The death of continental drift was a prime example of prejudice in science. Geologists were caught in the middle of a scientific revolution and a crisis of contradiction where hard evidence was simply ignored. All too often scientists are placed in a position of either publish or perish and, as a result, some of what was published was scientific drivel. If the continental drift theory was ever spoken of at all, it was held to ridicule and contempt and considered a classic scientific blunder. Not since Charles Darwin's theory of evolution had a theory received so much opposition. Perhaps this is so because it is human nature to think of the world as being permanent and unchanging.

By the late 1940s, Wegener's theory was so discredited in scientific circles (mostly in the Northern Hemisphere; geologists in the Southern Hemisphere were too overwhelmed with evidence to the contrary) that any geologist who argued for it risked ridicule by his collegues, and more importantly, loss of those things scientists covet the most — fame and recognition. As it was, the revival of continental drift came from a totally unexpected quarter.

PALEOMAGNETISM

When the first sailors took to the seas in ships, they stayed close to the coastline for fear of losing sight of land and drifting aimlessly into oblivion. The ancient Chinese and Greeks discovered that if a lodestone, a magnetic rock, was suspended from a string, or floated on a piece of wood in a bowl of water, it always pointed north. This became the first compass and sailors were no longer fearful of sailing around in circles.

The reason the rocks always pointed north was believed to be caused by the pull of the north star. It was not until the sixteenth century English physician-physicist William Gilbert began experimenting with magnets that the secret was revealed. Gilbert correctly guessed that the Earth acted like a huge magnet and this is what pulled the compass needle north. The mechanism for the Earth's magnetism was beyond Gilbert's comprehension, although others thought that a rich vein of magnetite existed near the North Pole. Scientists now believe that the magnetism is generated in the Earth's core and works similarly to a giant dynamo.

The earth's magnetic field might have originated from electric currents in the core. An electric current will generate magnetism and conversely, a current is generated when a conductor is moving through a magnetic field. Electrical currents in the core could be generated by any number of means, such as through the battery action caused by the chemical differences between various layers. Once these currents are started, they could be amplified by the dynamo action of the core as it spins.

Because the core is composed of iron and nickel, both good electrical conductors, the electrical currents passing through it set up a weak magnetic field within the core. The motion of the core generates more current which, in turn, generates a greater magnetic field. The motion of the core, which could come from convection currents, does not have to be very much to sustain the dynamo effect because of the core's great size.

Because the Earth is rotating, this tends to keep the magnetic field aligned in one direction. Apparently the Earth's magnetic field remains stable for long periods of time, and then, for some unknown reason, the electrical currents fail and the magnetic field collapses altogether, later to be regenerated with opposite poles.

For over a century, scientists have known that when basalt lava, which is normally iron rich, cools down the iron molecules line up with the Earth's magnetic field like miniature bar magnets and become a sort of fossilized compass pointing in whatever direction north happens to be at that time.

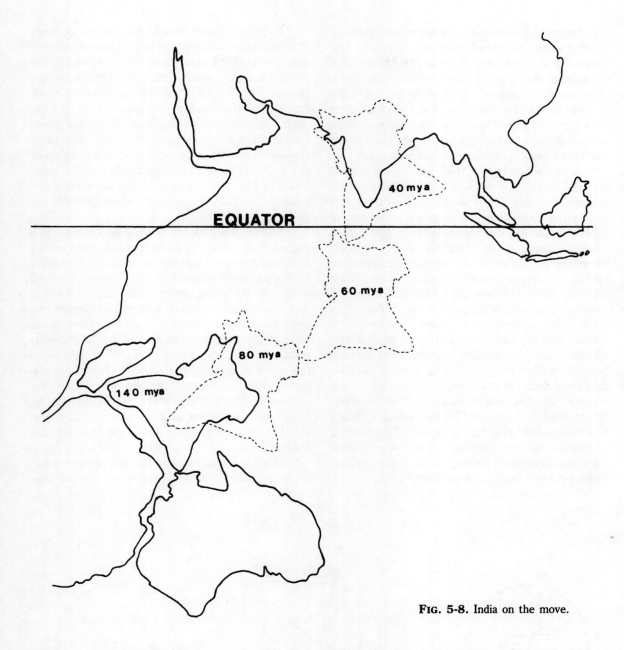

EQUATOR

40 mya

60 mya

80 mya

140 mya

Fig. 5-8. India on the move.

However, instruments in those days were not sensitive enough to detect the faint fossil magnetism.

In the early 1950s, the British Nobel laureate in physics P. M. S. Blakett invented the magnetometer, which could detect extremely weak magnetic fields. When the new instruments were first taken to the field, scientists in England obtained strange results. Rocks formed 200 million years ago showed a magnetic inclination of 30 degrees north.

Magnetic inclination is the downward pointing of the needle of a vertically held compass. The inclination is almost 0 degrees at the equator and 90 degrees at the poles. What bothered the scientists was that England's present inclination is 65 degrees north. The only conclusion that could be drawn from the data was that England must have at one time been further south. Wegener must have been reeling in his grave with laughter.

As a further test of their astounding discovery, the scientists took their instruments to India, the opposite side of the world. Rocks dating 150 million years old showed a magnetic inclination of 64 degrees south. Cretaceous rocks of 100 million years in age decreased slightly to 60 degrees. Rocks, 50 million years old, indicated a inclination of only 26 degrees south. Even more surprising was that 25-million-year-old rocks did a complete reversal, with an inclination of 17 degrees north. In other words, India at one time was in the Southern Hemisphere and had crossed over the equator into the Northern Hemisphere to its present location below Asia (FIG. 5-8). Now there seemed to be no doubt that India, at one time, was nestled between Africa, Australia, and Antarctica. Unfortunately, this method was only good for measuring distances in a north-south direction (latitude). Therefore, a continent could be anywhere along an east-west direction (longitude), making it extremely difficult for reconstructions of the continents.

Skeptics refused to acknowledge the findings of paleomagnetism, pointing out that the same phenomenon could be brought about by shifting of the Earth's magnetic poles (FIG. 5-9). This phenomenon was first suggested as early as the seventeenth century by the English physicist Robert Hooke. Such polar wandering would have altered the direction of the Earth's magnetic field and records of these changes would be permanently locked up in the rocks. Therefore, rocks formed at different times in England and India would have been imprinted with different inclinations without moving an inch.

The evidence for the drifting land masses was turned against itself to prove that it was the North Pole that had wandered around on top of the world over millions of years. But the scheme backfired when similar experiments with magnetometers were conducted in North America. Although the polar paths, derived from data on both continents, were much the same shape and had a common point of origin, the curves gradually veered away from each other (FIG. 5-10). Only by hypothetically joining the continents together would the two curves overlap. In their efforts to disprove continental drift, scientists inadvertently provided one of the strongest pieces of evidence for its existence.

Even this was not enough to convince most scientists, and there were still many dyed-in-the-

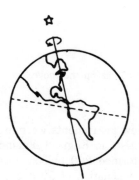 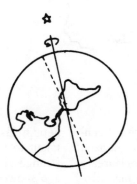 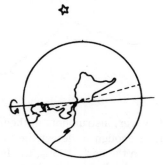

FIG. 5-9. Possible varieties of polar wandering.

FIG. 5-10. Polar wandering curves.

wool adversaries who had discredited continental drift for so long that it could not possibly be resurrected overnight. For one thing the science of paleomagnetism was in its infancy, and the scientists themselves were the first to admit that their readings were subject to error.

Alternative explanations were sought including the idea that there might have been multiple poles in the earth's past. It was too early then for scientists to go dashing off with new theories on continental drift. Nevertheless, magnetic fossil hunters doggedly kept up their search. By the late 1950s, so much data had been accumulated in its favor that continental drift was once again becoming a serious topic of scientific discussion. Alfred Wegener, the unsung hero of continental drift, was well on his way to becoming vindicated.

6

Worlds In Collision

DURING an Antarctic expedition in the summer of 1969–70, American fieldworkers discovered, in the frigid cliffs of the Trans-Antarctic Mountains, a fossilized jawbone and canine tooth belonging to lystrosaurus (FIG. 6-1). This unusual-looking, 2-foot-long reptile with large down-pointing tusks lived around 160 million years ago. The only other known fossils of lystrosaurus were found in China, India, and southern Africa. It is very unlikely that this fresh-water reptile swam across the salty oceans that now separate the southern continents. Instead, its discovery on the frozen wastes of Antarctica was hailed as final proof for the existence of Gondwanaland.

Marsupials are mammals with pouched bellies, like opossums and kangaroos, and only exist today in the Americas and Australia. In 1985, a small fossil opossum tooth, dated 37 million years old, was discovered in central Siberia. Opossums have been known to exist from the late Cretaceous, about 85 million years ago, to the present. The animal could have taken the northern route to Aus-

tralia by going through Asia or the direct southern route (FIG. 6-2). Recently a fossil of a South American marsupial was found in Antarctica, and it seemed to support the theory of a southern route with Antarctica acting as a bridge between the southern tip of South America and Australia. Here was further support for the existence of Gondwanaland. Although the Asian tooth seemed to support the theory for the northern route, it is the same age as the oldest known fossils of Australian marsupials; therefore, the Asian marsupials were too late. Also, there are no similar species found in Australia, and they appeared to have died out in Asia without leaving any descendants.

By the mid-1960s, computers were coming into their own, aiding scientists in making new discoveries and proving their theories. Computer-aided drawings of the reconstruction of the continents were enthusiastically received by the scientific community. Decades before, almost identical drawings by Wegener and others were nearly entirely rejected. If the oceans were drained down

Fig. 6-1. Lystrosaurus.

below the level of the continental shelves, which are shallow-water areas extending a short distance beyond the coastlines, then the true edges of the continents would appear. At these edges, the sea floor plunges steeply down to the deep-sea platform. It seems reasonable to conclude that if the continents broke apart, then this edge marks the break. With this added continental material, the true shapes of the continents are revealed and the pieces of the global jigsaw puzzle now fit together remarkably well.

MID-OCEAN RIDGES

Proof that the continents were once together forming a supercontinent abound while theories which attempt to prove the continents have always been apart are not so well supported. Although more than reasonable evidence existed to support continental drift, it was not until new discoveries made in the 1960s paved the way to explaining the process of crustal movement. Before this time, scientists who wanted to believe in continental drift, despite the overwhelming evidence supporting the theory, could not conscientiously do so until a viable method was found to move solid land across a solid ocean floor.

Scientists attempting to find clues to support continental drift were looking in the only places accessible to them at the time — the dry land. Because three-quarters of the Earth is covered by ocean, a huge repository of information was being neglected. The ocean bottom was once considered barren and featureless, covered with thick, muddy sediments and therefore uninteresting.

During the mid-1800s, soundings made in preparations for laying the first transcontinental telegraph cables told of hills and valleys and a mid-Atlantic rise, later named Telegraph Plateau, where the ocean was supposed to be the deepest. Scientists began to realize that the ocean floor was much more complicated and intriguing than they had at first thought.

Since World War II, ships at sea have carried on-board sonar depth finders that trace the contour of the ocean bottom on a strip chart recorder. This data was used by scientists to draw a clear picture of the ocean floor. What they produced was a startling map showing strange mountain ranges and deep canyons that even rival those found on the Earth's surface.

The ocean was once thought to be a vast dumping ground for sediments, debris of dead marine organisms, and other wastes washed off the continents. If the ocean was 3 billion years old or older, then these deposits on the deep ocean floor should be extremely thick.

To measure these sediments, scientists developed a seismic device for use under water. An explosive charge was set off on the ocean floor. Because seismic waves travel slower in soft sediments and faster in hard rock, scientists could calculate the thickness of different layers.

Another technique involves lowering a seis-

FIG. 6-2. Possible routes for Marsupials to Australia.

Fig. 6-3. An ocean bottom seismograph. (Courtesy of USGS.)

mograph to the ocean floor (Fig. 6-3) to record microearthquakes. Later the device automatically rises back to the surface to be recovered. These geophysical methods have given scientists information about the ocean floor that could not be obtain by direct methods. Some findings came as quite a surprise. Instead of miles of sediment, they found an average thickness of only a couple thousand feet. Could this mean that the oceans were much younger than they had expected or was there some sort of natural vacuum cleaner sweeping the ocean floor clean? To further confuse things, tests using magnetometers towed behind ships revealed that the magnetic patterns locked in the sediments on the ocean floor regularly alternated, pointing in some areas North, and other areas South. Gravitational surveys were also confusing. In the deep trenches off the edges of certain continents, it was found that gravity was much too weak to be responsible for the downward pulling of the sediments in vast geosynclines. Temperature surveys showed heat seeping out of the Earth in the mountainous regions of the middle Atlantic. The more scientists probed the ocean floor the more complex it became.

In the late 1950s, during the height of the Cold War American and Soviet oceanographic vessels crisscrossed the seas in a frantic effort to map the ocean floor so that nuclear ballistic missile submarines could navigate deep underwater. After the

TABLE 6-1. Dimensions of Deep Ocean Trenches

TRENCH	DEPTH (miles)	WIDTH (miles)	LENGTH (miles)
Aleutian	4.8	31	2300
Japan	5.2	62	500
Java	4.7	50	2800
Kuril-Kamchatka	6.5	74	1400
Marianas	6.8	43	1600
Middle America	4.2	25	1700
Peru-Chile	5.0	62	3700
Philppine	6.5	37	870
Puerto Rico	5.2	74	960
South Sandwich	5.2	56	900
Tonga	6.7	34	870

FIG. 6-4. Pillow lava on the ocean floor. (Courtesy of WHOI.)

data had been compiled, the maps that were produced showed something that was entirely unexpected.

The submerged mountains and undersea ridges form a continuous 40,000-mile-long, several-hundred-mile-wide, and up to a 10,000-foot-high chain that circles the earth like the stitching on a baseball. Even though it was under water, this mid-ocean ridge system easily became the dominant feature on the face of the Earth, extending over an area greater than all the major land mountain ranges combined. Not only that, if showed many unusual features including massive peaks, saw-tooth ridges, earthquake fractured cliffs, deep valleys, and lava formations of every conceivable shape (FIG. 6-4).

SEA-FLOOR SPREADING

Along much of its length, the ridge system is carved down the middle by a sharp break or rift that is the center of intense heat flows. Also, the mid-ocean ridges are the site of frequent earthquakes and volcanic eruptions that form new islands in the oceans. It appeared then that the system was a giant crack in the Earth's crust and in many places it was crossed at right angles by other cracks or faults similar to those caused by earthquakes. These faults seemed to be the results of lateral strain, as though the ocean floor was moving.

The activity seemed to be more intense in the Atlantic where the ridge is steeper and more

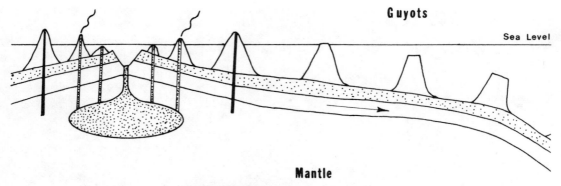

FIG. 6-5. Guyotes on the ocean floor.

jagged than in the Pacific or Indian oceans where branches of oceanic ridges actually dive under continents. The ocean floor was indeed far more active and younger than it had been supposed. Volcanic activity in the ridges gave every indication that the ridge might be adding new material to the ocean floor. In contrast, the trenches off the continents suggested that they were swallowing up old oceanic material, thereby accounting for the missing sediment. The Atlantic ridge is also in a curious position, winding itself midway between continents and paralleling opposing coastlines.

Strange underseas volcanoes called guyots (pronounced "ghee-oh" — FIG. 6-5) formed flat-topped peaks as though the tops of the cones had been sawed off. It appeared that the cones were at one time above sea level and wave action gradually wore them down below the surface of the sea.

What was even more interesting was that the further away the guyots were from the volcanically active areas of the ocean, the older and squatter they became. This seemed to indicate that the guyots wandered across the ocean floor, away from their places of birth. This phenomenon can also be demonstrated with Pacific volcanic island chains such as the Hawaiian Islands (FIG. 6-6). The oldest Hawaiian Islands are to the northwest. Hawaii, the youngest and largest island, is to the southeast and also has the only active volcanoes. It appears that the islands were produced assembly line fashion, with each one moving away in succession from its point of origin — a source of volcanic material lying beneath the crust called a hot spot.

Observation of these and other interesting features along the ocean floor prompted the American geologist Harry Hess to write his classic paper *Evolution of the Ocean and Basins,* published in 1962. Hess proposed a process he called seafloor spreading. Earlier explanations for the cracks in the ocean floor envisioned an expanding Earth due to an increase in the internal heat or a decrease in gravity. The weakening of the gravitational field could cause the Earth to bulge out forming cracks along the crust like those on a boiling egg. Most scientists were dissatisfied with the expansion hypothesis. For one thing, the force of gravity, like the speed of light, remains a constant and has never been shown to change. Also, had the Earth today been significantly larger than it was in the past, there should be obvious effects on the shape of the continents, and they would not fit as well together as they do. The solution Hess came up with relied on an outward movement of a different sort, using the Earth's own convection currents to cause material to rise to the surface.

As the rock material heats up in the asthenosphere, it slowly rises in convective currents. After millions of years, it finally reaches the topmost layer of the mantle called the lithosphere (from the Greek lithos, meaning rock). The rising rock material presses against the underside of the lithosphere and spreads outward, causing fractures to form where it encounters a weak spot. Then, as the current flows out on either side of the crack, it carries the two separated parts of the lithosphere along with it and the fracture widens. Reduced temperature and pressure allows the now soft rock material to rise up through the crack. The material finds easy passage through the 60 miles or so of lithosphere until it reaches the ocean crust. There it melts entirely as it breaks through the ocean floor, at the mid-ocean ridges, where it pours out as molten lava. As the lava cools, it adds another layer to older material on each side of the ridge. The pressure of the upwelling lava forces the ridge further outward on both sides, pushing the ocean floor and the lithosphere it rides on away from the mid-ocean ridge.

Since the Earth is not expanding, any new material added to the ocean floor at one end must be subtracted somewhere else. Hess suggested that the old seafloor and the lithosphere were destroyed in the deep-sea trenches at the edge of continents or along volcanic island chains (FIG. 6-7). The rocks dive back into the Earth, where they are broken up, remelted, and reabsorbed into the mantle to be used again in a continuous cycle.

The theory cleared up a lot of puzzling features of the ocean floor, including the mid-ocean ridges, the relatively young ages of rocks in the ocean crust, and the formation of island chains. But more importantly, at last here was the long-sought mechanism for continental drift.

The continents do not plow through the ocean crust, like an icebreaker plows through frozen seas. Instead, continents ride like icebergs in a moving current of molten rock. As with any new theory, there is always healthy skepticism, and this is one way scientists keep each other honest. Therefore, sea floor spreading was slow to gain acceptance.

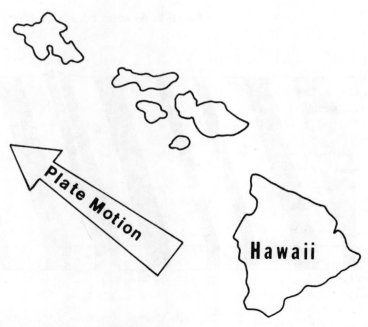

FIG. 6-6. The Hawaiian Islands.

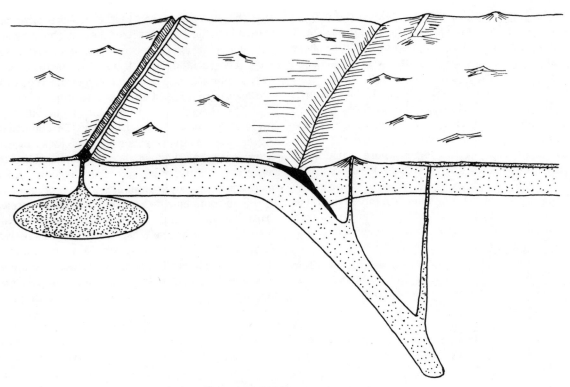

FIG. 6-7. An ocean ridge and subduction zone.

FIG. 6-8. Magnetic reversals at the mid-ocean ridge.

Another offshoot of the Cold War era came in the early 1960s when the United States, the Soviet Union, and other countries signed the Limited Test Ban Treaty, eliminating nuclear tests in the atmosphere and the ocean. In order to police compliance with the treaty, the United States constructed seismic listening posts around the world. Any covert nuclear explosions could easily be picked up, and their position accurately plotted, by the sensitive instruments. This provided a secondary benefit for scientists because these seismic stations could also accurately plot the positions of earthquakes.

After mounds of data had been accumulated, it became apparent that the majority of the earthquakes occurred in the vicinity of the mid-ocean ridges and the deep-sea trenches, especially around the Pacific ocean in an area known as the circum-Pacific belt. Because these areas are considered to be sites of intense earth movements, one would expect shallow tremors in the mid-ocean ridges and deep-focus earthquakes in the deep-sea trenches. Also, according to the theory, if the lithosphere is reentering the Earth at the trenches, it should do so at an angle of 45 degrees.

Not only was the seismic data able to measure a slope of about 45 degrees, but it could also trace the outline of the descending lithospheric plate, known as the Benioff zone after the American seismologist Hugo Benioff, who first discovered it in 1954. Therefore, another piece of uncovered evidence inadvertently proved the existence of sea floor spreading.

MAGNETIC REVERSALS

Recognition of the reversal of the Earth's magnetic field began in the early 1950s. Over the Earth's long history, the magnetic poles, for unknown reasons (possibly large meteor impacts or very high magnitude earthquakes), have flip-flopped many times. The magnetic fields captured in the rocks not only show the past position of the magnetic poles but also their polarity. Over the past 110 million years, the Earth's magnetic field

has reversed at least 80 times. The last time this happened was about 700,000 years ago, and some scientist believe that the earth is overdue for another one. The Earth's magnetic field seems to have been weakening over the past 150 years and could go into another reversal within the next few thousand years.

In 1963, two British geologists, Fred Vine and Drummond Mathews, thought magnetic polarity could be a decisive test for seafloor spreading. As the basalts of the mid-ocean ridges cool, their iron molecules are polarized in the same direction as the Earth's magnetic field. As the ocean floor spreads out on both sides of the ridge, the basalts record the Earth's magnetic field during each successive reversal.

Normal polarities in the rocks are reinforced by the present magnetic field; reversed polarities are weakened by it. This produces parallel bands of magnetic rocks on both sides of the ridge with identical successions of reversing magnetic fields, a sort of geological stereo tape recorder (FIG. 6-8). Magnetometers towed behind ships did indeed show stripes of reversed magnetic fields along the mid-ocean ridges, just as the scientists predicted.

Magnetic reversals also provided a means of dating practically all of the ocean floor. The reversals do not follow any particular cycle. Therefore, any set of patterns are unique in geologic history. The Canadian geophysicist J. Tuzo Willson calculated the age of a number of magnetic stripes in selected parts of the ocean floor. What was significant about this was that it offered a means of determining the rate of sea floor spreading.

For instance, if the age of a particular stripe is known, and the distance to its point of origin is also known, then, by dividing the distance by time, the rate is established. It turns out that near an area known as the East Pacific Rise the rate was about 2 inches per year. In the mid-Atlantic, the rate was a bit slower. This means that the Atlantic must have opened up 150 million to 200 million years ago. This is remarkably concurrent with Wegener's estimates for the breakup of the continents and the age of the ocean floor.

FIG. 6-9. A geologist analyzes core. (Courtesy of U.S. Department of Energy.)

DEEP SEA DRILLING

The only thing that seemed to be missing and held back many conservative geologists from believing in sea floor spreading, despite the overwhelming evidence in its favor, was the lack of rock specimens. On dry land it is nothing for a geologist to go to his favorite outcrop and pick out a rock to take to the lab. In the deep oceans it is another thing entirely to reach down and pluck a rock from the ocean floor. For one thing, the oceans are on average, 2 miles deep and blanketed by layer upon layer of thick sediments. If the geologist wanted to

correctly date these sediments, he would have to recover them in the order in which they were formed; therefore, dredging techniques would be of limited value. Fortunately, a technique known as seafloor coring was developed. A hollow pipe is drilled into the sediments and a long cylindrical sample is brought up to the surface. Although on land, drillers are successful in recovering cores at great depths (FIG. 6-9), early attempts at coring in deep water only penetrated a few feet into the upper sediments of the ocean floor.

In the mid 1960s the National Science Foundation sponsored a deep-sea drilling program called

FIG. 6-10. The Glomar Pacific deep-sea drilling ship. (Courtesy of USGS.)

Project Mohole (a hole in the Moho). Andrija Mohorovicic calculated the contact between the mantle and the Earth's crust, or Moho, by seismic techniques. In the oceans, the crust is the thinnest at only about 3 to 5 miles thick. It was hoped that the Moho would provide new clues about the origin, age, and composition of the Earth's interior. Such information cannot be obtained on the Earth's surface. Unfortunately, the task of drilling through miles of ocean crust in waters as much as 2 miles deep became too expensive and time-consumming. Congress was forced to stop funding the project, thousands of feet short of its goal, after spending over $100 million.

The British research vessel *Glomar Challenger* was built for the Deep Sea Drilling Project (FIG. 6-10). The objective was to drill a large number of shallow holes, in widely scattered parts of the ocean floor, in an attempt to prove seafloor spreading. The ship was designed with a 140-foot drilling derrick amidships and special computerized thrusters located fore and aft to maintain the ships station over the bore hole even in rough seas.

The string of drill pipe dangled in the ocean as much as 4 miles below the ship before it finally touched bottom. The drill bit was able to cut

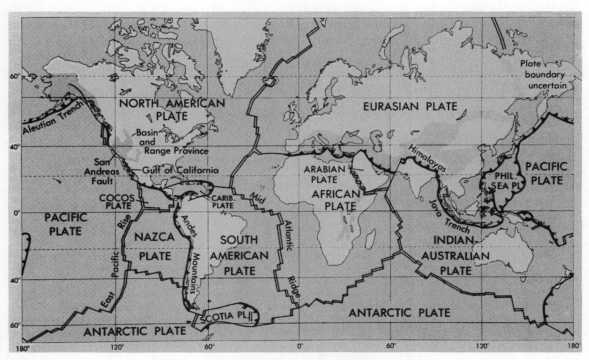

FIG. 6-11. The lithospheric plates. (Courtesy of USGS.)

through the sediment by the weight of the heavy drill collars above it. There was no need for the ship to push downward on the drill sting. The core was retrieved through the drill stem by a removable inner barrel so that the drill bit could remain in the hole. Otherwise, the crew would have to bring the core barrel and bit back up to the surface and then try to reenter the drill hole, a feat requiring a special funnel-like apparatus to guide the drill bit back into the hole and extraordinary skill. This method also allowed much longer sections of core to be collected before the drill bit became too dull and had to be pulled up and replaced.

By the late 1960s and early 1970s, the *Glomar Challenger* gave geologists almost unrefutable evidence for seafloor spreading. As predicted, the sediments were older and thicker the further the ship drilled from the mid-ocean ridges. The rate of spreading calculated from the age of the cores was remarkably close to the rates predicted by the theory. It so happens that Iceland straddles the Mid-Atlantic Ridge, and here the rate of spreading can be measured directly across the exposed rift valley by standard survey methods. It appeared that the North Atlantic opened up between 170 million and 180 million years ago, with Eurasia and North America separating at an average rate of about an inch a year. In some areas, like the East Pacific Rise, the rate was considerably more rapid, up to several inches a year.

PLATE TECTONICS

Despite all the mounting evidence pointing toward continental drift, there were scientists, especially in the Soviet Union, who were still having doubts about the breakup and drifting of the continents. They question whether the currents in the Earth's interior were powerful enough to propel the continents around. Even some believers in drift, thought this energy source might not be sufficient enough and suggested that supplementary mechanisms such as gravity might have helped.

If Earth processes are essentially uniform throughout time, why did this event happen so late in the Earth's history? Regardless of these objec-

tions, the overwhelming majority of Earth scientists accept continental drift as scientific certainty. So convincing was the evidence that, by the late 1960s, it gave rise to an entirely new way of looking at the Earth, called the theory of plate tectonics (tectonics is any process by which the Earth's surface is shaped). The theory was first publicized, in 1967, by the British geophysicists Dan McKenzie and R.L. Parker and it incorporates the processes of seafloor spreading and continental drift into one coherent model. Therefore, all aspects of the Earth's history and structure could be unified by the revolutionary concept of movable plates.

The theory was also developed independently by the American geophysicist Jason Morgan at Princeton University. He regarded the Earth's outer shell as neither rigid nor fixed, but made up of seven major plates, and about a dozen minor plates, each about 60 miles or so thick (FIG. 6-11). The plates are composed of the lithosphere and the overlying continental or oceanic crusts. The plate

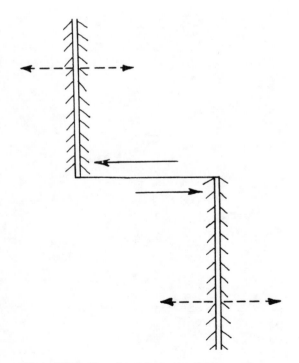

FIG. 6-12. Transform faults on the ocean floor.

boundaries are the mid-ocean ridges and the deep-sea trenches. The plates ride on the asthenosphere and carry the continents along with them like ships frozen in floating icesheets. The breakup of plate could cause the formation of a continent. An example is breakup of Laurasia at the mid-Atlantic ridge to create North America. On the other hand, if two plates should collide, the thrust of one plate under the other would uplift the crust to form mountain ranges or create long chains of volcanic islands.

Much can be learned about crustal plates in motion by observing ice floes in the arctic. Sea currents and lateral stresses might cause a large sheet of ice to crack down the middle. The sheet separates into two parts with one going one way and the other going another, leaving an ever-widening gap which is filled in with new ice. This corresponds to the mid-ocean ridges. Because water expands as it freezes, it exerts a great pressure on the two halves, pushing them further apart. Being confined with limited space in which to move, the two sheets of ice slam into adjacent sheets, breaking and thrusting up the ice into ridges at points of contact. Along the sides, the ice sheets simply slide past adjacent sheets with little or no distortion, corresponding to the lateral faults of crustal plates (FIG. 6-12).

In actual practice, thousands of feet of sediments are deposited along the seaward margin of a continental plate in deep ocean trenches (FIG. 6-13) and the increased weight presses downward on the oceanic crust. As the continental and oceanic plates merge, the heavier oceanic plate is subducted or overridden by the lighter continental plate, forcing it further downward. The sedimentary layers of both plates are squeezed, causing a swelling at the leading edge of the continental crust, which forms mountain belts. The sediments are faulted at or near the surface, where the rocks are brittle, and folded at depth where the rocks are more plastic.

As the oceanic crust is descending, the topmost layers are scraped off and are plastered against the swollen edge of the continental crust. In the deepest part of the continental crust, where temperatures and pressures are very high, rocks are partially melted and metamorphosed. As the descending plate dives further under the continent, it reaches depths where the temperatures are extremely high. Part of it melts forming a silica-rich magma that rises because it is lighter than the surrounding rock. The magma intrudes the overlying metamorphic and sedimentary layers to form large bodies of granite or breaks through the surface and erupts as a volcano.

When two continental plates converge, little or no subduction occurs because of the equal buoyancy of the continents. Instead mountains are formed (FIG. 6-14). This is what happened when India crashed into southern Asia to form the Himalayans. The Urals in the Soviet Union were created under similar circumstances.

Continents are neither created nor destroyed by the process of plate tectonics. Divergence of lithospheric plates creates new crustal material, and convergence destroys crustal material in well-developed subduction zones. This condition is prevalent in the western Pacific where deep subduction zones are responsible for the island arcs (FIG. 6-15). Volcanoes of the island arcs are highly spectacular because the lava is silica rich, contrasting strongly with the basalt of other volcanoes or mid-ocean ridges. The volcanoes are mostly explosive and build up steep-sided cinder cones. Island arcs are also associated with belts of deep-seated earthquakes 200 to 400 miles below the surface.

Not only do rifts open in ocean basins but also under continents. This is happening in eastern Africa, creating a great rift valley which will eventually widen and flood with seawater to form a new subcontinent.

Extinct rift systems, where the spreading activity has stopped, are overrun by continents. For example, the western edge of North America has overrun the northern part of the now extinct Pacific rift system. The North American continental mass has run into the northern extension of the active Pacific rift system, called the East Pacific Rise, creating the San Andreas Fault of California. A similar fault, known as the Great Glen Fault is causing the Scottish highland to the north to slide pass the lowlands to the south.

F<small>IG</small>. 6-13. Major ocean trenches.

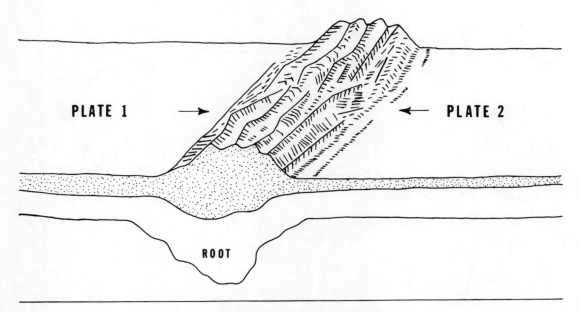

FIG. 6-14. The formation of mountains.

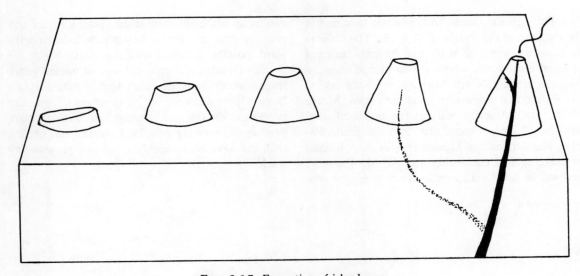

FIG. 6-15. Formation of island arcs.

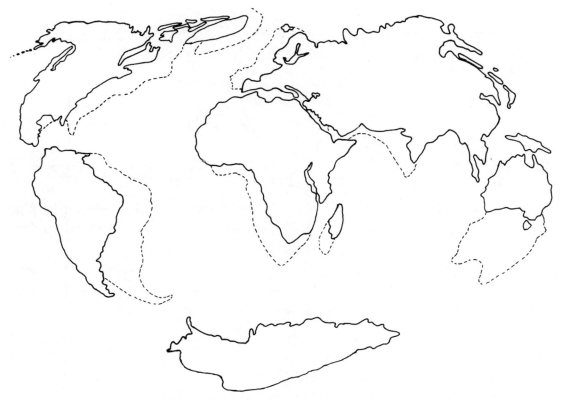

FIG. 6-16. The future position of the continents.

The Atlantic Ocean will continue to widen at the expense of the Pacific (FIG. 6-16). The California coast will break off at the San Andreas fault and proceed northward, where it will plunge into the Aleutian trench. North America will slide across the Pacific and eventually crash into Asia. Meanwhile, South America will cut the umbilical cord with North America and drift into the South Pacific. The African and Eurasian plates will continue pressing against each other and the Mediteranian Sea will be filled with new land mass. A new sub-continent will have torn off of eastern Africa and possibly drift into India. Australia will drift northward, possibly colliding with Southeast Asia.

Eventually, a couple of hundred million years from now, all the continents might reunite into one large supercontinent, or Neopangaea. Then, the process of continental breakup and drift can start over again, forming new land masses and oceans that will have no resemblance to our present-day world.

7

The Earth In Rage

THE oldest known record of man's encounter with volcanoes is from the Great Rift Valley of East Africa (FIG. 7-1). A place known as Laetoli, a short distance southeast of Olduvai Gorge in Tanzania is where Louis and Mary Leakey made so many discoveries of man's primitive past. Here in 1976, well-preserved footprints of two of our ancestors were found embedded in a volcanic ash bed.

After years of eroding the thick overlying layers, the footprints appeared — looking fresh and remarkably modern — with rounded heels and arches, pronounced balls, and forward-pointing toes, all the features necessary for walking erect. The ash bed was dated by radiometric methods at 3.5 million years old, and the footprints became, one of the earliest pieces of evidence that man walked upright at that time. The ash came from the eruption of a nearby volcano called Sadiman. What these early hominids, who were no more than four feet tall, thought of the booming, fire-belching mountain can only be surmised, but later eruptions buried their footprints (and probably them too) with more ash, preserving their departure for posterity.

The East African Rift Valley which has become so much a part of our cradle of civilization extends all the way from the shores of Mozambique to the Red Sea where it splits up to form the Afar Triangle in Ethiopia, a popular hunting ground for ancient human and prehuman remains. It was here that one of the most important finds was discovered in 1974. It was a remarkable collection of bones belonging to a 3.2 million year old female, scientists named, Lucy. The rift is a complex system of extensional faults which could be an indication that the continent is in the initial stages of rupture. Much of the area has been uplifted thousands of feet by an expanding mass of molten magma which lies just beneath the crust. This heat source is responsible for the numerous hot springs and volcanoes along the rift valley. Some of the largest and oldest volcanoes in the world stand nearby, including Mounts Kenya and Kilimanjaro which at 19,590 feet is the highest mountain in Africa.

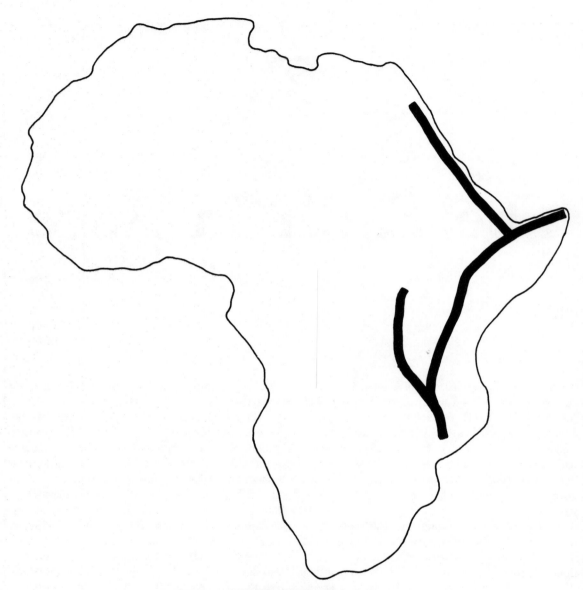

FIG. 7-1. The East African rift system.

Since the dawn of man, thousands of volcanoes have erupted from the depths of the Earth. Just during the past 400 years, over 500 volcanoes have erupted, killing 200,000 people and causing billions of dollars in property damages. Presently, there are approximately 600 active volcanoes in the world and many thousand dormant or extinct ones. Next to earthquakes, volcanoes are the most terrifying forces on Earth. Yet, it should not be forgotten that they also play a constructive role for the benefit of mankind. Not only do they provide rich soils and magnificent scenery, but without

Date	Volcano	Area	Death Toll
TABLE 7-1. Chronology of Major Volcanic Eruptions			
—	Stromboli	Lipari, Italy	
1480 B.C.	Santorin (Thira)	Mediterrananean	
79 A.D.	Vesuvius	Pompeii, Italy	16,000
1104	Hekla	Iceland	
1169	Etna	Sicily	15,000
1616	Mayon	Philippines	
1661	Vesuvius	Naples, Italy	4,000
1669	Etna	Sicily	20,000
1701	Fujiyama	Japan	
1759	Jorullo	Michoacan, Mexico	200
1772	Papandayan	Java, Indonesia	3,000
1776	Mayon	Philippines	2,000
1783	Laki	Iceland	
1790	Kilauea	Hawaii	
1793	Unsen Island	Japan	50,000
1793	Tuxtla	Veracruz, Mexico	
1814	Mayon	Philippines	2,000
1815	Tambora	Sumbawa, Indonesia	12,000
1822	Galung Gung	Java, Indonesia	4,000
1835	Coseguina	Nicaragua	
1845	Hekla	Iceland	
1850	Osorno	Chile	
1853	Niuafou	Samoa	70
1856	Pelee	Pierre, Martinique	
1857	St. Helens	Washington	
1873	Mauna Loa	Hawaii	
1877	Cotopaxi	Ecuador	1,000
1881	Kilauea	Hawaii	
1883	Krakatoa	Java, Indonesia	36,000
1886	Tongario	New Zealand	
1888	Bandai-san	Japan	461
1897	Mayon	Philippines	
1902	La Soufriere	St. Vincent, Martinique	15,000
1902	Pelee	Pierre, Martinique	28,000
1902	Santa Maria	Guatemala	6,000
1903	Colima	Jalisco, Mexico	
1906	Vesuvius	Naples, Italy	
1910	Irazu	Costa Rica	
1911	Taal	Philippines	1,335
1912	Katmai	Alaska	
1912	Virunga	Belgian Congo	
1914	Lassen	California	
1914	Whakari	New Zealand	

table continues on p. 106

1914	Sakurajima	Japan	
1917	San Salvador	El Salvador	
1919	Keluit	Java, Indonesia	5,500
1924	Kilauea	Hawaii	
1926	Mauna Loa	Hawaii	
1927	Anak Krakatoa	Java, Indonesia	
1928	Rokatinda	Dutch East Indies	
1929	Vesuvius	Naples, Italy	
1929	Calbuco	Chile	
1931	Merapi	Java, Indonesia	
1932	Volcan del Fuego	Guatemala	
1932	Las Yeguas	Argentina	
1935	Kilauea	Hawaii	
1935	Mauna Loa	Hawaii	
1935	Coseguina	Nicaragua	
1938	Nyamlagira	Belgian Congo	
1943	El Paricutin	Michoacan, Mexico	
1944	Vesuvius	Naples, Italy	
1952	Binin Island	Japan	
1957	Capelinhos	Azores	
1963	Surtsey	Iceland	
1963	Agung	Bali, Indonesia	
1969	Kilauea	Hawaii	
1973	Helgafell	Iceland	
1977	Nyiragongo	Zaire	70
1980	St. Helens	Washington	62
1983	El Chichon	Chipas, Mexico	187
1985	Nevado del Ruiz	Armero, Columbia	22,000
1986	Augustine	Alaska	

them there could be no life on Earth, for they supply the waters of the ocean, carbon dioxide for photosynthesis, and other important elements in the atmosphere.

THIRA ISLAND

One of the earliest recorded episodes of what might well have been the most violent volcanic eruption in man's ancient history occurred on the volcanic island of Thira, also called Santorin, seventy five miles north of Crete. The Greek scholar Plato probably ascribed his fictitious story about the lost continent of Atlantis to the disaster. Thira was an outpost of the Minoan civilization which flourished on Crete from 3000 B.C. until about 1480 B.C. whereupon it collapsed so suddenly and violently it has long baffled archaeologists. The Egyptians must have heard the large booming sound, and they were almost certainly showered by a mysterious ash that blew in on the North wind. Shortly afterwards, Minoan traders suddenly stopped arriving on their shores. The Egyptians probably came to the conclusion that the homeland of the Minoan's blewn up and sank below the sea.

When the first tremors occurred, the Minoans

on Thira probably had the good sense to evacuate their doomed island and moved to Crete, for only a few human remains have been found among the ruins. When the volcano erupted in a final colossal explosion, the cone of the volcano collapsed into the emptied magma chamber beneath the island, forming a deep water-filled crater. The collapse of Thira created an immense sea wave or tsunami, hundreds of feet high that probably battered the shores and harbors of Crete, totally destroying the economy of that seafaring nation. Also, the thick ash fall probably destroyed the crops and rendered the soil unproductive for years. The weight of the thick ash might account for the mysterious blow from the sky which destroyed Minoan palaces. Although the initial toll on human life probably was only modest, the Minoan culture rapidly declined and never recovered.

VESUVIUS

On a sweltering afternoon on August 24, 79 A.D., the citizens of Pompeii were going about their business, never mindful that nearby Mount Vesuvius (FIG. 7-2) was about to viciously come to life. No one suspected that the old extinct volcano posed any serious threat, even after several years of ground shuddering and even though wisps of steam could be seen rising from its crater. Then all of a sudden, without warning, the seaward side of Vesuvius was blown off. For a long time, pressures had been gradually building in a chamber of molten rock, deep within the mountain's roots. The pressure was released explosively, bursting through the floor of the ancient crater and hurling huge quantities of ash and pumice into the air. The Roman writer, Pliney the Younger best describes the disaster from eighteen miles away. He wrote that a strange cloud shot up and outward from the mountain. The ground shook with violent earthquakes and the waters of the Bay of Naples rose and fell and dashed upon the beaches. The mountain top soon disappeared behind black, smokey steam which was pouring constantly from the crater with red flames and bright flashes of lightning darting through it. There were increasing

FIG. 7-2. The 1944 eruption of Mount Vesuvius. (Courtesy of USGS).

roars and explosions deep inside the mountain. For eight days the black cloud spread over towns around the mountain, day was turned into night, and showers of hot pumice and globs of molten lava fell to earth.

Many residents of Pompeii had no chance at all as searing hot ash mixed with steam and other gasses, rained down upon them. People were caught in mid stride as they were buried almost immediately. As many as 16,000 lost their lives, mostly by suffocation. Pompeii was promply buried under twenty feet of ash, while nearby Herculaneum was submerged in a sea of boiling mud. Strangely, there was no lava flow associated with this eruption as there was with succeeding ones. In 472 A.D., another great deluge of volcanic ash was added to the covering of the two doomed cities. Pompeii was rediscovered around 1740 and was once again brought to the light of day by archaeologists. Various treasures were recovered and casts of many inhabitants were made, showing in explicit detail, expressions of stark terror on their faces.

Mount Vesuvius which is about seven miles southeast of Naples, Italy is perhaps the best known volcano in the world and now the only active volcano on the European mainland. Vesuvius lies within the rim of an earlier prehistoric volcano, called Mount Somma, and rises to a height of about 4000 feet above sea level. Vesuvius has erupted frequently since that ignoble day back in 49 A.D. A particularly violent eruption in 1631 destroyed several nearby villages and took 18,000 lives. In this century, in 1906 and later in 1929, Vesuvius blew its top, devastating whole areas around it. A rude awakening of the volcano occurred during World War II on March 18, 1944. Vesuvius again put on a show of might, its most explosive eruption of this century, making the destructive forces of man's armies look puny by comparison. This time the eruption threatened to interfere with the Allied invasion of Italy and the military advance was temporarily halted until several thousand inhabitants of Naples were evacuated to safety. Bombers of the 12th Army Air Force were caught on the ground near the base of the mountain and lava flows caused extensive damage to the air base.

FIG. 7-3. Mount Etna, Italy. (Courtesy of Univ. of Colorado, NOAA/EDIS.)

MOUNT ETNA

Mount Etna (FIG. 7-3) lies on the eastern shore of Sicily and is the largest and highest of the European Volcanoes, rising 10,902 feet above sea level. The base of the volcano is 87 miles in circumference and almost completely surrounded with lava flows. Etna is so tall that eruptions rarely have sufficient energy to make it to the top, so numerous parasitic cones erupt all around the flanks of the mountain, becoming a cluster of volcanoes instead of a single volcanic cone. There are about 200 of these subsidiary cones, some of them over 3000 feet high. Doubtless, Etna is as old as man himself and records of its eruptions by the early Greeks go back several centuries B.C.. Thousands of lives and many towns have been destroyed by the numerous outbursts of Etna during its long history. In the eruptions of 1169, about 15,000 were buried in the ruins of Catania, and 500 years later, in 1669 20,000 people perished. Perhaps, Etna's most spectacular eruption was in 1853 and in this century, Etna wiped out the town of Mascati

and almost entirely destroyed the village of Nunziata in 1928. Despite its frequent eruptions, Sicilians tenaciously cling to their mountain, refusing to give up their vineyards and farms, for the volcanic soil is said to be among the richest in the world.

STROMBOLI

Stromboli (FIG. 7-4) is located on one of the Lipari islands 40 miles north of Sicily and ranks as one of the most active volcanoes in the world. Throughout its long history, it has never wholly ceased erupting but only varied its intensity from time to time. For centuries this remarkable volcano has been relied upon by sailors who called it "The Lighthouse of the Mediterranean" because its regular flashes could be seen for a hundred miles out to sea. World War II Allied bombers used the volcano's beacon as a navigational checkpoint to and from their raids on Europe. The principle crater is about two-thirds the way up the mountain which is 3040 feet tall. There are also several smaller craters on one side. Stromboli is as regular

FIG. 7-4. The eruption of Stromboli in March 1951. (Courtesy of Howell Williams, NOAA/EDIS.)

as clock work with the more violent eruptions spaced some fifteen minutes apart, interspersed with more moderate activity. The crater floor seems to be always choking on semi-solid lava. The pressure beneath eventually becomes strong enough to violently blow the floor upwards, clearing the obstruction for a short while, and the cycle starts over again.

TAMBORA

The year 1816 was known as the "year without summer." Crops in New England and Western Europe fell short and famine threatened many parts of the northern hemisphere. This climatic havoc was attributed to the eruption of Mount Tambora on the island of Sumbawa in Indonesia (see FIG. 7-5). The eruptions began on April 5, 1815 with a series of deep shocks which sounded like cannon fire and could be heard some 450 miles away. Dutch troops were even sent out to investigate what was thought to be pirates attacking nearby military posts. The most explosive erup-

tions occurred on the 11th and 12th of April and did not entirely cease until July. The sound of the explosions were heard in Sumatra one thousand miles away to the west. Only a few out of a total population of 12,000 survived on the island, and 45,000 or more additional lives were lost on adjacent islands. Volcanic ash was so heavy that there was darkness at noon. The ash was carried as far as Java, 300 miles away and in sufficient quantities to darken the sky. According to some meteorologists, this eruption sent more dust into the upper atmosphere and obscured sunlight more than any other volcano in the past 400 years. It could well have been the most explosive eruption in the last 10,000 years.

KRAKATOA

The most destructive eruption in modern history took place on an island in the Sundra Strait between Java and Sumatra, called Krakatoa (FIG. 7-6). In May 1883, a dormant volcano began a series of violent eruptions. It belched out vast clouds of ash that obscured the sun, and the explosions were heard seventy miles away. After dying down somewhat toward the end of May, large scale eruptions began again in mid June. This time the eruptions were even more violent and earth tremors were felt in many parts of Java and Sumatra. The main crater was blown away and in its place were as many as ten other cones belching out steam and pumice dust so high that ash fell on villages 300 miles away. The climax came on the morning of August 27 with an explosion equal to three thousand Hiroshima size atomic bombs. The island of Krakatoa disappeared with a bang that was heard as far as Australia, Sri Lanka (Ceylon) off the tip of India, and Madagascar off southeast Africa, 3000 miles away. The pressure wave from the explosion was recorded on barographs all around the world. It circled the globe two or three times, taking as long as four days to die down. It was the loudest noise known to man.

After the eruption, most of the damage and loss of lives followed in the wake of sea waves, called tsunamis, some over a hundred feet high.

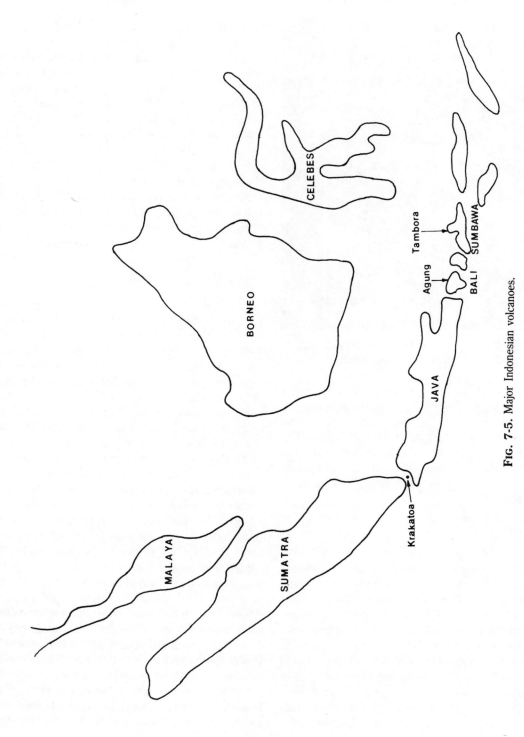

FIG. 7-5. Major Indonesian volcanoes.

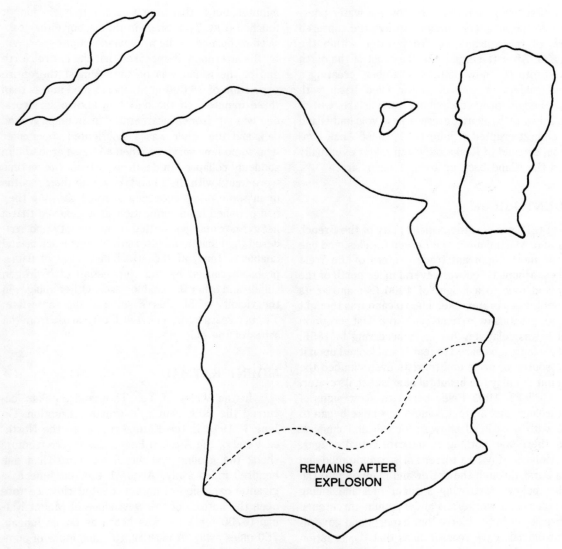

REMAINS AFTER
EXPLOSION

FIG. 7-6. The Island of Krakatoa.

The tsunamis were registered on tidal gages as far away as the English Channel. For a hundred miles around Krakatoa the tsunamis ripped over low lying areas wiping out mainland towns and villages. The giant waves flatten everything in their paths and even carried a Dutch gunboat well over a mile inland. It is estimated that 36,000 people throughout the area died by drowning. Half the island of Krakatoa disappeared, much of it into the upper atmosphere. The dust rose fifty miles high, circled the earth, and produced magnificent red sunsets for years afterwards. The dust also cut down the amount of sunlight reaching the lower atmosphere causing a drop in worldwide temperatures. What probably made Krakatoa so spectacular was that the explosion was partially powered by the expansion of steam generated either by sea water pouring into the magma chamber through the ruptured walls of the volcano, or from water within the magma. After the explosion, the crust of the earth caved into the now emptied chamber, creating a large caldera, a sort of water filled basin with jagged edges protruding above the surface. Out of the ashes of Krakatoa arose a new volcanic island which first erupted in June 1927, called Anak Krakatoa, or child of Krakatoa which might eventually build the island back up to its former size.

MOUNT PELEE

St. Pierre was the principal city of the French Island of Martinique in the Lesser Antilles, and one of the most important trade centers of the West Indies. Mount Pelee was several miles north of the city and rose to a height of 4000 feet and at its summit was a crater lake. The volcano was thought to be practically extinct with the last eruption which was relatively harmless occurring in 1856. People long ago ceased to fear it and looked upon it as a source of pride and tourists even climbed the summit to enjoy the beautiful blue lake in its crater. On April 23, 1902 Pelee began to show signs of disturbance and a great column of smoke began to rise with occasional showers of ash and cinders. Yet, there was nothing to indicate actual danger. On Monday May 5, a torrent of steaming mud and lava burst through the crater and plunged into the valley below, destroying a sugar mill and killing several dozen workers. Pandemonium threatened to break out in St. Pierre, but experts and government officials gave reassurances that the eruption was normal and no threat to the city.

On Thursday morning, May 8, red flames were seen leaping from the mountain high into the sky, and there was a constant muffled roar as enormous clouds of black smoke belched from the volcano. Then there was a tremendous explosion, and the seaward side of the volcano was ripped out, and a solid sheet of flame rolled down the mountain and headed for the city. Clouds of hot ashes and suffocating fumes swept through the city and out to sea. The blast of fire from the volcano lasted only a few

minutes, but in that time it set fire to everything it touched (FIG. 7-7). Ships in the harbor either capsized or burned as the firey wind swept over them. By the afternoon, it appeared that the entire North end of the island was on fire. Almost the entire population of 28,000 in St. Pierre died in less than three minutes. Of the only two known survivors, one was a prisoner incarcerated in an underground cell, and the other was a disoriented shoemaker who some how survived when all those around him suddenly collapsed in death. Nearly all the victims were found with their hands covering their mouths or in some other agonizing attitude showing they had perished from suffocation. It is believed that a heavy, noxious gas settled upon the city and rendered the inhabitants insensible or unconscious and unable to fend off the attaching waves of flame, probably caused by the combustion of hydrogen sulfide and other flammable gases. Other villages in the vicinity of St. Pierre suffered the same fate. Twenty years later, a new St.Pierre arose from the ashes of the old.

MOUNT KATMAI

In the Valley of Ten Thousand Smokes, occurred the 20th century's greatest eruption. On June 1, 1912 in the Katmai region on the Northeast end of the Alaskan Peninsula, severe tremors shook the ground and were felt more than one hundred miles away. About 1 P.M. on June 6, a gigantic explosion of unprecedented violence tore open the bottom of the west slope of Mount Katmai (6700 feet) and was heard as far as Juneau, 750 miles away. A mass of 10 cubic miles of pumice, ash, and gas invaded the valley, burning entire forests in its path and filling the valley at some places to a height of 600 feet. For two days, powerful explosions ejected millions of tons of volcanic material from a single fissure five miles west of Katmai (FIG. 7-8A, B). In the town of Kodiak about 100 miles away, the sky was so clogged with pumice and ash, the sun was totally blocked out, and visibility was down to a couple of yards. Volcanic material piled up in the streets and on roof tops, and houses crumbled under the weight. Landslides

FIG. 7-7. The May 8, 1902 Mount Pelee eruption. (Courtesy of USGS.)

roared down the mountains and into town. For four days the townspeople endured the onslaught of the volcanic eruption before a feeble light of day finally broke through a dust clogged sky.

The top 1200 feet of Mount Katmai exploded and collapsed into a giant caldera one and a half miles wide and 2000 feet deep which later filled with water and formed a crater lake. The heavier particles from the eruptions spread out in a radius of 600 miles while the finer dust was blown up into the stratosphere where it circulated for months above the northern hemisphere. A series of explosions excavated a depression at the west base of the volcano whereupon viscous lava rose pancake-shaped, 800 feet in diameter and 195 feet high. The entire valley became a hardened yellowish-orange mass, 3 miles wide by 12 miles long. Thousands of white fumaroles (volcanic steam vents) which gave the valley its name gushed out of the ground and shot hot water vapor as much as a thousand feet into the air.

Alaska is known for its numerous active volcanoes. Thousands of years ago, Mount Augustine (4025 feet) built an obscure island out of lava and ash in the Cook Inlet 175 miles southwest of Anchorage. On Thursday March 27, 1986, Augustine, one of Alaska's more active volcanoes, awoke after ten years of slumber. The initial eruption shot ash nine miles into the atmosphere, and the volcano continued a steady pumping of ash and gasses throughout that Easter weekend. The ash cloud spread as far as 600 miles to the north, and blinding ash in the town of Kenai kept motorists off the roads. Health alerts were sent out to Anchorage and other communities in south-central Alaska, and residents were warned to stay home and avoid exercise. Planes were grounded to avoid clogging their engines, and some electrical power had to be

Fig. 7-8A. Novarupta believed to be the main site of the Katmai region eruption. (Courtesy of USGS.)

FIG. 7-8B. Mount Katmai, Alaska, showing crater lake. (Courtesy of Howell Williams, NOAA/EDIS.)

cut for a short while to avoid ash damage to generator turbines. Ash was thick enough at the coastal town of Homer, 70 miles east of the volcano, for the street lights to come on. Tsunami warnings were given in case there was a violent eruption, similar to the one in 1883, when debris on the flanks of the volcano crashed into the inlet and sent a 30 foot wave into Port Graham, 60 miles to the east, destroying boats and flooding homes.

HAWAIIAN ISLANDS

The Hawaiian islands are a chain of volcanic islands similar to several other Pacific island chains. Only the main island of Hawaii has active volcanoes and these are relatively harmless, despite their spectacular and violent outbursts. Volcanic eruptions on Hawaii are treated as though

they were a Forth of July fireworks display. In nearly two hundred years, the only known loss of life from the eruptions was when a division of the Hawaiian army was killed after an eruption of Kilauea in 1790. The only other explosive eruptions of Kilauea, since that time, occurred in 1924, killing one person and later in 1969. Legends of sacrificial maidens being offered up to appease the firey gods abound in Hawaiian folklore. Generally, Hawaii's volcanic eruptions are so mild that the United States created the Hawaii Volcanoes National Park on August 1, 1916. The park consists of Mounts Kilauea and Mauna Loa (FIG. 7-9), the only active volcanoes, and extinct Haleakala on the nearby island of Maui. In 1911, the Hawaiian Volcano Observatory (FIG. 7-10) was established to study volcanic activity in the Hawaiian Islands where a considerable amount of knowledge about volcanoes has been acquired.

FIG. 7-9. Mauna Loa, Hawaii. (Courtesy of U.S. Air Force and USGS.)

FIG. 7-10. The USGS Hawaiian Volcano Observatory. (Courtesy of USGS.)

The four great mountains forming the island of Hawaii are probably the most unusual group of volcanoes on earth. Mauna Kea (White Mountain) is in reality the tallest mountain in the world, for it rises some 32,000 feet from the ocean floor. Geologists believe that, when the sprouting stream of lava which originated 20 to 30 miles down in the bowels of the earth raised Mauna Kea to its present height of 13,825 feet above sea level, it could force itself no higher and was compelled to seek outlets elsewhere. These side shows formed Hualalai (8269 feet) and Kilauea (4090 feet). Kiluea is a vast pit of molten lava that intermittently rises and falls as though someone pulled out and then replaced the drain plug. Mauna Kea then transformed its energies again and erected Mauna Loa which at 13,680 feet is the giant of them all. Although Mauna Loa is quite active with great fountains of white-hot lava shooting several hundred feet high, forming a characteristic "curtain of fire", no lava flow has issued from its crater within historic times. Instead, lava seeps out in submarine flows which continue to build up Hawaii from the ocean floor and bursts from the sides of the volcano at elevations between 7000 and 13,000 feet. Near the end of 1933, one such parasitic flow headed towards the seaport of Hilo and threatened to engulf the town until it was halted in its tracks by the Army Air Corps which dropped bombs on the lava.

PARICUTIN

One of the strangest eruptions in recent times took place in a farmers cornfield near the town of Paricutin, 200 miles west of Mexico city. For days, the farmer noticed the ground beneath his feet was getting warmer, and everywhere, little wisps of smoke (steam) arose from cracks in the soil. Every day the smoke rose higher and higher, until finally on February 20, 1943, the farmer heard a loud rumble, the earth began to tremble, and more smoke came out of the ground. A great earthquake tore open the earth, and smoke along with sand and rocks shot up into the air. When darkness came, the whole countryside lit up with glowing rocks and cinders that every few seconds leapt like flames from the ruptured earth. The roaring increased its intensity and great masses of red hot rock were hurled high into the air whereupon they fell back and began piling up around the opening to form a cone.

This was a birth of a volcano which began at once to build a mountain in a valley where only a cornfield had been before in a region known for its numerous extinct volcanoes. Within a radius of seventy-five miles from the new vent, stand several hundred ancient volcanic cones of various ages and various sizes from 200 to 800 feet high. The volcano was seen and heard from far away and the earthquake tremors were recorded on seismographs as far away as New York. The growth of the cone was spectacular. After the first day it was 120 feet tall. In one week, it was 550 feet high. Within ten weeks, it was 1100 feet high and spread out over hundreds of acres. Initially, no lava issued from the cone, so this was what is known as a cinder cone. Instead, two days after the first explosion, lava flowed from a fissure in a field about a thousand feet north of the cone. Within two months, this flow grew 6000 feet long, 3000 feet wide, and over 100 feet high and rushed over the country side destroying everything in its path.

Named for the village which was its first victim, Paricutin (FIG. 7-11) brought sightseers and scientists from all around the world to witness the birth of a volcano. The volcano put on quite a show,

making thirty to forty deafening explosions a minute. Geologist got a first hand look at the development of a volcano and set up instruments to measure the intensity of the eruptions. On June 10, 1943, the volcano quieted down, and a new lava flow began pouring out one side of the cone. The lava covered several hundred feet an hour and headed for the now abandoned village of Paricutin two miles away which was practically obliterated with ash, volcanic debris, and lava. Surprisingly, no one was killed by the eruption, but whole forests, several farms, and an entire village were destroyed.

MOUNT ST. HELENS

On a quiet Sunday morning in southwest Washington on May 18, 1980, sightseers and scientists alike came to see the first volcano to come alive in the continental United States in over 60 years. For seven weeks, the mountain had been venting steam and ash in preparation for what volcanologists thought would be a mild eruption. Mount St. Helens was an old dormant volcano with an almost perfectly symmetrical cone and is among 15 other major volcanoes in the Cascade Range. It has erupted at least 20 times in the past 4500 years, and the last eruption was in 1857. On the north side, the top of the 9,677 foot peak bulged out as much as 400 feet and created avalanches on the mountain's upper flanks. The heat from the crater melted the snow and formed numerous mud flows which scarred the slopes. There were a multitude of earth tremors registering between 3 and 5 on the Richter scale. Triggered by a larger earthquake, ice blocks from glaciers on the south side fell into the crater. Seconds later, an immense landslide on the north side, one of the largest in historic times, plunged into Spirit Lake in the valley below. From the weakened north flank came a lateral blast, and with hurricane force, a superheated gas cloud, 900 degrees or more, raced ahead of the landslide down to the valley floor and bound over the north valley wall, devastating everything in its path for 18 miles. This was a classic Mount Pelee type eruption with the explosion

FIG. 7-11. Paricutin Volcano, Mexico.

cloud fanning out from the northeast to the northwest.

Mount St. Helens (FIG. 7-12) literally blew its top. The upper one-third of the peak was blown away, and from the crater, a dark "cauliflower cloud" of ash and steam billowed high into the air, reaching 60,000 feet within minutes of the initial eruption and lasting throughout the day. This cloud headed in a north and east direction and for 30 miles, dropped rock fragments and pumice in its path and carried ash well beyond. As the summit eruption grew, portions of the south crater wall were removed and a dense ash cloud rolled down the south flank of the volcano. This was a much smaller cloud than that on the north side and did not go far beyond the base of the volcano. The rim was reduced to an elevation of 8390 feet with the

north flank opening to the crater only 4400 feet in elevation. The crater was enlarged into a U-shaped basin 2 miles long from north to south, 1 mile wide, and nearly a mile in depth. Throughout the day, lava flows, reaching speeds in excess of 70 miles per hour, periodically poured out of the crater and down the the north flank into the valley below. The lava, along with hot ash and debris, melted the remaining snow and ice blocks on the flanks of the mountain. This melt water was added to water from torrential rains precipitating from the eruption cloud, the purged water table, and water displaced from Spirit Lake. The waters were mixed with the ash and debris creating large mud flows which moved down the valley of the North Fork of the Toutle River and various other drainages.

The destruction was beyond imagination with

FIG. 7-12. The 1980 Mount St. Helens eruption, Washington. (Courtesy Jim Hughs and Roland V. Emetaz, U.S. Forest Service, USGS, and U.S. Dept. of Agri.)

more than 200 square miles devastated by what was equivalent to a 400-megaton hydrogen bomb explosion. Trees stripped of their bark and branches, lay toppled like toothpicks from the force of the gaseous eruption (FIG. 7-13). Vehicles were overturned as though they were toys scattered by an angry child. The shock wave created by the explosion was felt as far away as Vancouver, British Columbia. Ash was carried northeastward by strong prevailing winds and fell as far as Montana 600 miles away. The valley of the North Fork of the Toutle River was transformed into a bleak, gray, hummocky landscape of craggy mounds of rock, blocks of melting glacial ice, narrow winding gullies, and steaming fumarole pits. A mud-laden Spirit Lake was choked with battered logs and dotted with islands of rock debris. Floods swept through the valleys of the Toutle River, and mud laden waters jammed with logs destroyed several bridges and clogged the channels of the Cowlitz and Columbia Rivers (see FIG. 7-14). At least 62 people lost their lives and 200 were left homeless. Total damage was estimated at $2.75 billion. Enough timber to build 80,000 houses was flattened and damages to eastern Washington crops were estimated at $200 million.

EL CHICHON

Near midnight on March 28, 1982, a volcano which had been dormant during historic times, suddenly came to life in a series of explosive eruptions. This was El Chichon (FIG. 7-15), one of the dirtiest volcanoes in recent history. Located in the southeastern state of Chiapas, Mexico, the volcano killed 187 people and left 60,000 homeless. The last major eruption, occurring a few days later on April 4, sent a dense cloud of dust and gas into the stratosphere and was observed to travel in a narrow band completely around the world in three weeks. This cloud was the largest and longest-lasting so far observed by satellites in their twenty-five year history. The highest dust concentration was at an altitude of 16 miles, and the cloud did not dissipate for at least one month after the eruption. On the ground, a light-gray ash cloud spreading

predominantly northeast of the volcano blocked out the sun until it was near total darkness with visibility less than fifteen feet. Ten miles away, 20 inches of ash was measured and diminished to an average of 8 inches 50 miles down wind from the volcano. The worst case was in Palenque, 75 miles east of the volcano, where thicknesses of over 16 inches were measured.

El Chichon produced notable effects on the climate, and the dust cloud and volcanic gases cooled the northern hemisphere by as much as any other volcanic eruption in the past 150 years, since the eruption of Mount Tambora. In Autumn, the cloud spread its way northward over the United States and was well on its way to enveloping the entire northern hemisphere. The cloud absorbed sunlight in the stratosphere where it caused a 3 degree centigrade warming, the warmest its been since records were kept, beginning in 1958. The stratospheric warming caused a substantial cooling near the surface, as much as .5 degrees centigrade. This translates into unpredictable extremes in regional weather patterns such as changes in the amount of storminess, precipitation, heat, and cold. The volcano might also have effected a coincidental appearance of El Niño, a heatwave in the waters of the Pacific ocean.

NEVADO DEL RUIZ

Just after 11:00, in the evening of November 13, 1985, when most citizens of Armero, Columbia were fast asleep, a heavy downpour fell on the city — not rain, but volcanic ash. Within an hour, a 130 foot wall of mud and ash careened down the narrow canyon of the Lagunilla River. On the edge of town the mudflow spread out and rapidly flowed through the city streets with ten foot high waves. During the next quarter of an hour, the mudflow, having the consistancy of mixed concrete, carried off everything in its path including trees, cars, houses, and people. Nevado del Ruiz turned out to be the deadliest volcano in recent history, claiming the lives of 23,000 people and leaving 60,000 others homeless.

When the Arenas crater erupted inside the

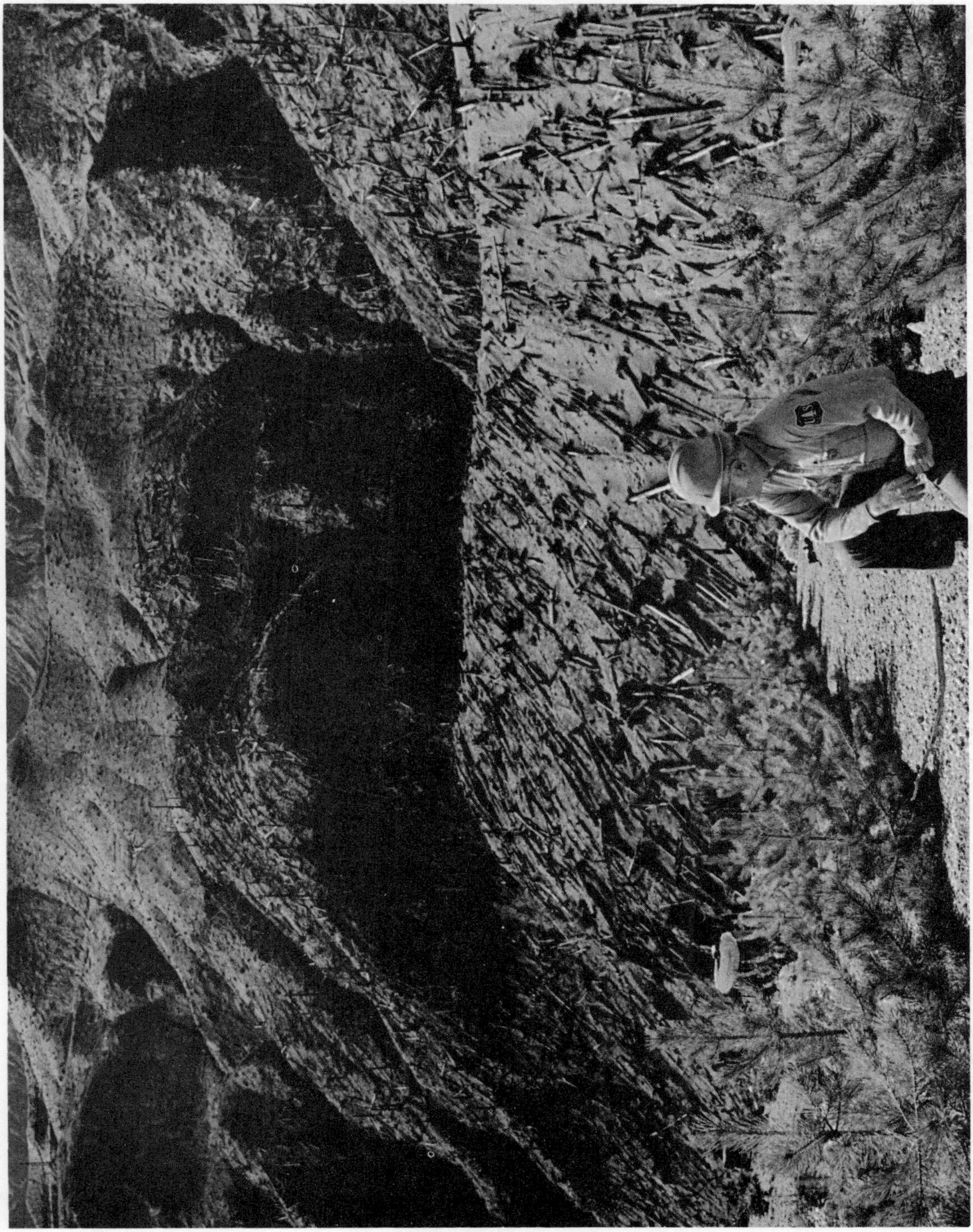

Fig. 7-13. Timber destruction from the 1980 Mount St. Helens eruption.

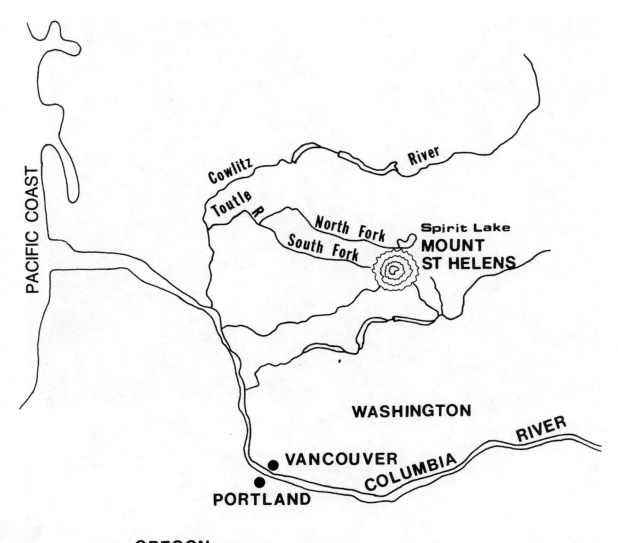

FIG. 7-14. Location of Mount St. Helens.

18,000-foot peak, it melted the mountain's icecap and sent floods and mud flows cascading 30 miles per hour down its sides into the nearby Lagunilla and Chinchina river valleys (FIG. 7-16). The deluge buried almost all of Armero (population 25,000) 30 miles from the volcano and badly damaged 13 smaller towns where some 3000 additional people lost their lives. The mountain belongs to a chain of active volcanoes that runs through the western part of the country. The volcano has erupted at least a half-dozen times in the past 3000 years, and in 1845 a similar eruption killed 1000 people. The two large explosions of the recent eruption blasted out the northeast side of the volcano probably simi-

FIG. 7-15. El Chichon Volcano, Mexico. (Courtesy of USGS.)

lar to the way Mount St. Helens erupted, but with one very notable exception—this volcano was located near a heavily populated area.

LAKE NIOS

Another chain of volcanic peaks and valleys covered with lush tropical vegetation runs along northwest Cameroon in central Africa. The fertile volcanic soil makes the region ideal for agriculture which is conducted by local tribes whose straw huts dot the hillsides in small clusters. About 200 miles northwest of the Capital city of Yaounde, lies a crater lake named Nios. Around 9:00 P.M. on August 21, 1986, the residents of three villages located in a river valley downstream from the lake were eating their evening meal or fast asleep, when suddenly they heard a large explosion. The frightened villagers quickly ran outside only to be met by a wall of toxic fumes. The hot, humid gases clung to their clothing which the people frantically tried to tear off. Almost all the villagers were immediately asphyxiated either in their homes or a short distance away. Nothing was destroyed, but over 1700 people died along with thousands of cattle and other animals as though by chemical warfare. A total of about 20,000 people were affected in one way or another over a ten square mile area.

The disaster might have been triggered by a small earth tremor or landslide which cracked open the deep lake bottom, releasing volcanic gases under great pressure. This created a huge bubble which burst explosively through the surface of the

FIG. 7-16. Mudflow from the November 13, 1985 eruption of Nevado del Ruiz, Columbia. (Courtesy of USGS.)

lake. The clear blue water was churned to a murky reddish-brown from mixing with the bottom sediments and the temperature was nearly ten degrees C above normal. The heavy gas cloud consisted mostly of carbon dioxide along with poisonous gases such as sulfur dioxide, hydrogen sulfide, carbon monoxide, and cyanide. This deadly "cocktail" swepted down the hill side and spread out in a low-hanging blanket for over three miles down wind from the lake. Victims enveloped by the carbon dioxide had no access to oxygen and therefore could not breath. The presence of poisonous gases might have made death swift, although probably extremely agonizing. Survivors were treated for burns, scarred lungs, and paralyzed limbs. Almost exactly two years earlier in the same mountain range, a similar eruption at Lake Manoum killed a reported 37 people. This indicates that the disaster at Lake Nios was no freak of nature and all crater lakes worldwide are suspect.

8

The Ring of Fire

VOLCANOES generally come in clusters, seldom erupting in non-volcanic regions but nearly always at the junction of plate boundaries. The theory of plate tectonics has given scientists a new tool that aids in understanding why volcanoes erupt where they do. They normally exist in areas where the Earth's crust is under great stress, such as rift valleys and subduction zones. In those areas where continental plates collide with each other, mountains are formed but no volcanoes. In other places where plates merely slide past each other, lateral faults are created but still no volcanoes. Only under special conditions are the fires below stoked sufficiently to cause the eruption of a volcano. Therefore, unless you live in a volcano prone area, chances are very slim that a volcano will erupt in your backyard or cornfield.

LOCATION OF VOLCANOES

Mount Vesuvius is associated with a string of famous volcanic peaks near the toe of the Italian peninsula. Mounts Etna and Stromboli have been active almost continuously throughout recorded history. A near straight line can be drawn between these active volcanoes. This indicates that the source of heat that stokes the furnaces of these mountains is the result of two crustal plates in collision. Heat generated along the subducting plate melts some of the overlying rock. The magma finds its way to the surface and pours out as lava. If the passage is blocked, the magma builds up explosive forces that can destroy whole islands and towns.

Most of the 600 active volcanoes of the world are in the Pacific Ocean, and nearly half are in the western Pacific area. There is an almost continuous ring of fire along the edges of the Pacific. Starting with the western tip of the Aleutian Islands off Alaska, the ring continues along the Aleutian archipelago and includes peaks such as Mounts Augustine, Katmai, and Bogoslov. The ring then turns south across the Cascade Range of British Columbia, Washington, Oregon, and Northern California and includes the volcanic peaks of Mounts

Baker, Rainier, St. Helens, Hood, Shasta (FIG. 8-1), and Lassen Peak. The ring also runs down Baja California, southwest Mexico where Paricutin and El Chichon live, and western Central America with their numerous active cones, including Nevado del Ruiz of Columbia. In addition, the ring follows the course of the volcanic range of the Andes Mountains along the western edge of South America. It then turns toward Antarctica and the islands of New Zealand, New Guinea where Vulcan makes his home, Indonesia, the Philippines, and Japan were Mt. Fujiama rises majestically, and ends on the Kamchatka Peninsula in eastern USSR.

A large proportion of volcanoes occur in island arcs, a series of volcanic islands mostly in the Pacific, that describe a graceful curve. The longest island arc is the Aleutian Islands, extending more than 3000 miles from Alaska to Asia. The Kurile Islands just to the south form another long arc. The islands of Japan, the Philippines, Indonesia, New Hebrides, Tonga, and the arc from Timor to Sumatra, all form island arcs. The island arcs have similar curves and each is associated with deep ocean trenches.

One explanation for the arcs is that the Pacific plate is spinning very slowly, completing a turn in 3 billion years. As the plate moves Westward away from the volcanic source, volcanic islands pop up in an arc due to the circular motion of the plate. This would also set up stress fractures on the rim of the plate, where it comes in contact with other plates, and might account for why two-thirds of the worlds active volcanoes and most earthquakes exist on the edges of the pacific plate.

FIG. 8-1. Mount Shasta, California. (Courtesy of C.D. Miller, USGS.)

In the Atlantic Ocean, volcanic activity is far less extensive and generally occurs in two localities, the mid-ocean ridges and the West Indies. Parts of the Mid-Atlantic Ridge that extend above the water, such as Iceland, the Azores (FIG. 8-2), the Canary and Cape Verde islands, Ascension Island, and Tristan da Cunha, are volcanic in origin. Rift volcanoes account for only about 15 percent of the world's known active volcanoes. Most rift volcanoes are in Iceland and East Africa. It is estimated that there are about 20 eruptions of deep submarine rift volcanoes every year.

Shallow water volcanoes like Surtsey (FIG. 8-3) in Iceland are explosive because of the rapid boiling of seawater in contact with the magma chamber. But once the volcanoes rise above sea level, they produce relatively quiet lavas. Rift volcanoes on continents such as East Africa produce a greater variety of volcanic rocks than their oceanic counterparts.

VOLCANIC CONES

Volcanoes come in a variety of shapes and sizes. Cinder cones result from explosive eruptions

FIG. 8-2. The July 1958 eruption on Fayal Island, Azores. (Courtesy of Howell Williams, NOAA/EDIS.)

FIG. 8-3. Lava flows from Surtsey Island Volcano into the sea. (Courtesy of Howell Williams, NOAA/EDIS.)

and are relatively short, usually less than 1000 feet high, with steep slopes. These are built up by accumulating layer upon layer of pumice, ash, and other volcanic debris. Deep within the earth, viscous magma contains dissolved water, carbon dioxide, and other gases. When the magma reaches the surface, the reduced pressure forces the bubbles out explosively, causing the volcano to spew its contents into the air (similar to the way carbon dioxide bubbles are released violently when a bottle of beer is shaken). The larger fragments fall back toward the portal of the volcano while lighter debris is carried on the wind. Later, as things settle down, lava might seek an outlet near the base, on the side, or even in the crater. Paricutin is a good example of a cinder cone with lava erupting from a fissure near its flanks.

If a volcano erupts only basaltic lava from a central vent, it forms a shield volcano, without building a mountain or cone. Highly fluid molten rock is violently squirted out in firey fountains of lava from pools in the crater or it just oozes out of the central vent. As the lava builds up in the center it flows to the outside in all directions, providing a dome-shape appearance when it cools and hardens. The slope on the flanks of the volcano rises only a few degrees and no more than 10 degrees near the summit. The lava spreads out to cover large areas, as much as one thousand square miles. Mauna Loa is a magnificent example of a shield volcano, with a great sloping dome rising 13,675 feet above sea level. It and its four sister volcanoes have built and are still building the island of Hawaii.

If a volcano erupts both cinder and lava, it becomes a composite or stratovolcano. The hardened plug in the throat of the volcano is blasted into small fragments by the buildup of pressure from trapped gas below. Along with molten rock, these fragments are sent aloft and fall back on the volcano as cinder and ash. The cinder layers are reinforced by layers of lava from less explosive eruptions, forming cones with a steep summit and gently sloping flanks.

The most famous and tallest volcanoes of the world, such as Vesuvius, Fujiyama, and Mount St. Helens are of the composite type and are usually associated with subducting plates. The almost perfectly symmetrical cones of composite volcanoes are everyone's idea of what a volcano should look like. Unfortunately, their beauty gives way to the most devastating type of volcanic activity. Unexpected violent eruptions occur from what was once thought to be dormant cones.

VOLCANIC CRATERS

At the summit of most volcanoes is a steep-walled depression called a crater. The crater is connected to the magma chamber through a conduit or vent (FIG. 8-4). When fluid magma moves up the pipe, it is stored in the crater until it fills up and overflows. During periods of inactivity, back flow can drain the crater completely. Highly viscous lava often forms a plug in the crater that can slowly rise to form a huge spire or dome, or the lava can be blown outward, enlarging the crater.

If the crater is unusually large, one or more miles wide, it is called a caldera (Spanish for caul-dron). Most calderas form when the summit of a volcano collapses into a partially emptied magma chamber. Calderas are also formed when a volcano decapitates itself and blows off its upper peak leaving a broad crater behind. If dormant calderas fill with fresh water they form crater lakes. Crater Lake in Oregon (FIG. 8-5) formed when the upper 5000 feet of the 12,000 foot composite cone of Mount Mazama collapsed and filled with rainwater and melting snow. The lake is 6 miles across and 2000 feet deep, the sixth deepest lake in the world. At one end is a volcanic peak called Wizard Island.

VOLCANIC GASES

The products of volcanic eruptions include gases, liquids, and solids. The main factors controlling the physical nature of volcanic products are the viscosity of the magma, its water and gas content, the rate of emission, and the environment of the vent. If the vent happens to be under water or under a glacier, the same type of magma can produce entirely different rock deposits due to the difference in cooling rates.

Many subduction-zone or island-arc volcanoes have higher concentrations of gas in the upper parts of their magma chambers before the eruption. This is why Indonesian volcanic eruptions such as Tambora and Krakatoa have been so explosive. The eruption begins with the emission of pyroclastics. Pyroclastics means fire fragments (FIG. 8-6). This is followed by thick, viscous lava flows.

Volcanic gases include steam, carbon dioxide, sulfur dioxide, and hydrochloric acid that are dissolved in the magma and released as the magma rises to the surface and the pressure decreases. The texture of pyroclastics and lava is largely controlled by the number and size of the gas-bubble holes formed in the erupting material. Pumice, the lightest of volcanic materials, is full of holes and can even float on water. During the eruption of Krakatoa in 1883, floating pumice several feet thick posed a hazard to shipping in the area.

On the other end of the spectrum is dense basalt that is formed at high temperatures with

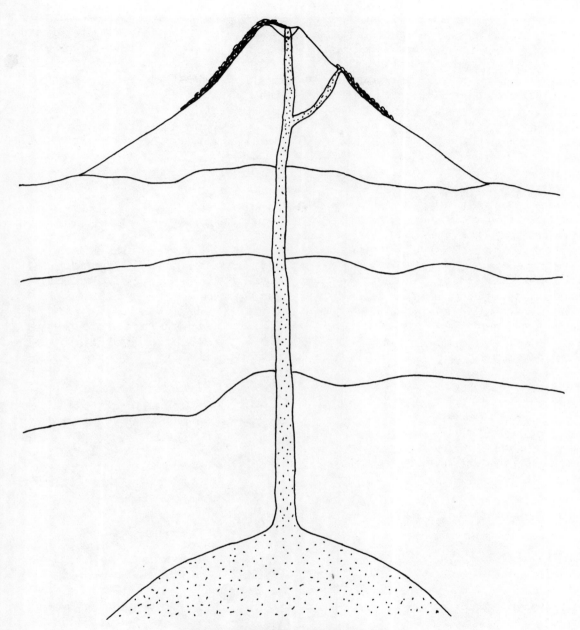

FIG. 8-4. A typical erupting volcano.

FIG. 8-5. Crater Lake Oregon. (Courtesy of USGS.)

C-1. Inner workings of a volcano.
(Adapted from NOAA pub. 1985-579-010/25212)

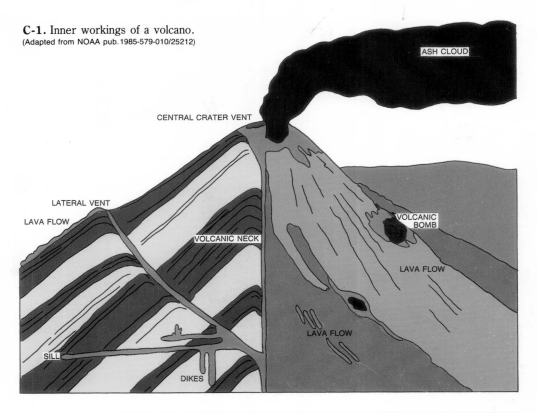

ASH CLOUD

CENTRAL CRATER VENT

LATERAL VENT

LAVA FLOW

VOLCANIC NECK

VOLCANIC BOMB

LAVA FLOW

LAVA FLOW

SILL

DIKES

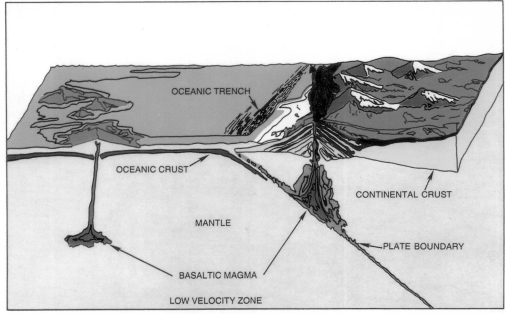

OCEANIC TRENCH

OCEANIC CRUST

CONTINENTAL CRUST

MANTLE

PLATE BOUNDARY

BASALTIC MAGMA

LOW VELOCITY ZONE

C-2. Diagram of a volcano in oceanic and continental environments. (Adapted from USGS pub. 1985-461-428/10009)

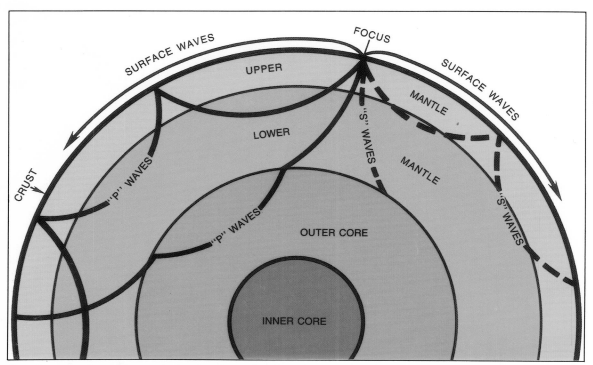

C-3. Cross section of the earth showing the paths of earthquake waves. (Adapted from USGS pub. 1985-461-428/10010)

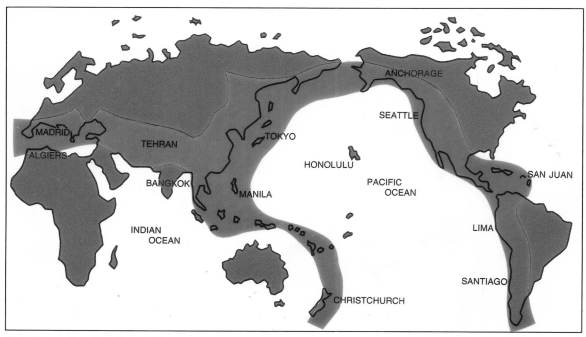

C-4. Zone of earthquake activity. (Adapted from USGS pub. 1985-461-428/10012)

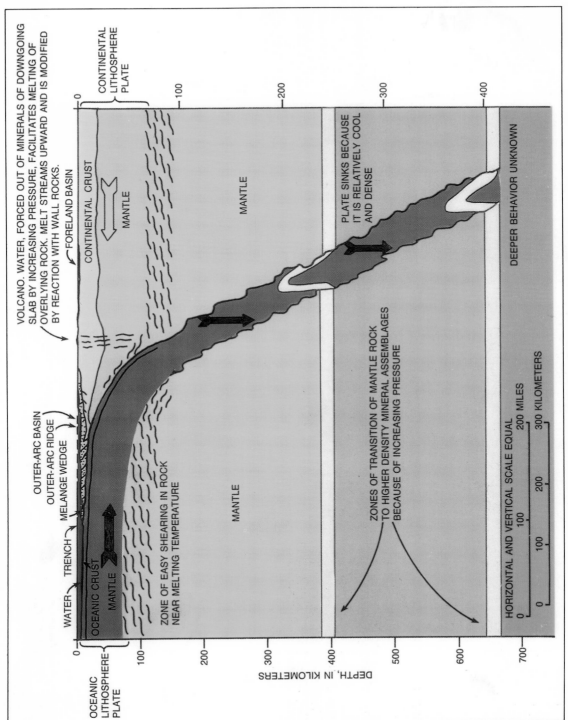

C-5. Cross section of a subducting plate. (Adapted from USGS pub. 1980-311-348/60)

(NGDC)

C-6.(above) Subsidence of a building from the July 29, 1967 Caracas, Venezuela earthquake.
(Courtesy of NOAA/EDIS)

C-7. (left) Devil's Tower, Wyoming showing the root of a volcano.
(Courtesy of Univ. of Colorado, NOAA/EDIS)

COLLAPSED CALDERA

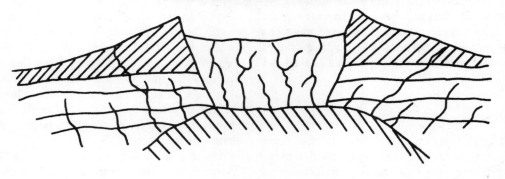

FIG. 8-6. Pyroclastic flow from the 1980 Mount St. Helens eruption. (Courtesy of Lionel Wilson, USGS.)

practically no holes. It is the commonest rock formed from solidifying magma extruded on the surface of the Earth, Moon, and perhaps other bodies in the Solar System. Most volcanic rocks are somewhere in between these two extremes and include andesites and rhyolites (TABLES 8-1 through 8-4).

TEPHRA

All solid particles ejected into the air from volcanic eruptions are collectively called tephra, from the Greek word meaning ash, and includes an assortment of fragments from large blocks to dust-size material. Tephra results when molten rock containing dissolved gases rises through a conduit and suddenly separates into liquid and bubbles as it nears the surface. With decreasing pressure, the bubbles grow.

If this event occurs near the orifice, a mass of froth might spill out and flow down the sides of the volcano. If the reaction occurs deep down in the throat, the bubbles expand explosively, burst the surrounding liquid which fractures the magma into fragments. Like pellets from a shotgun, the fragments are driven upward by the force of their own expansion and hurled far above the volcano. The fragments cool and solidify during their flight through the air. Fine fragments are caught by the wind blowing across the eruption cloud and carried as far as thousands of miles, with various bits and pieces dropped on the ground along the way. Blobs of still fluid magma, called volcanic bombs, might splatter the ground nearby. If they cool in flight, they form a variety of shapes, depending on how fast they are spinning, and sometimes whistle like incoming cannon shells (FIG. 8-7). If the bombs are the size of a nut, they are called lapilli, Latin for little stones, and form strange gravellike deposits along the countryside.

Nearly all volcanoes produce some tephra. Even relatively quiet eruptions occasionally throw up fountains of very fluid lava, whose spray solidifies into a form of tephra. This tephra is usually small in quantity and confined to the neighborhood of the vent. If water from a lake, ocean, or water table finds its way into the magma chamber, it instantaneously flashes into steam, and violent explosions rise through the conduit accompanied by little or no new magma.

Most of the tephra produced in this manner comes from the walls of the conduit or from shattered parts of the crater. Tephra, supported by hot gases, called a nuee ardente, flows streamlike near the ground and might follow existing river valleys for tens of miles — traveling upwards of 100 miles per hour. The eruption of Mount Pelee in 1902 was a classic example of this type of eruption.

TABLE 8-1. Types of Volcanic Products

FORM	TYPE	CHARACTERISTIC
Gas	Fume	Gaseous cloud without ash content
Liquid	Lava	
	Aa	Rough, blocky surface
	Pahoehoe	Smooth, ropy surface
Solid	Airfall fragments	
	Dust	<1/16 mm
	Ash	1/16 – 2 mm
	Cinder	2 – 64 mm (0.05 – 1.6 in)
	Blocks	>64 mm solid
	Bombs	>64 mm plastic
	Pyroclastic flows	Hot fluidized flows
	Mudflows	Flows fluidized by rain, melting ice and snow, or displaced crater lakes

FIG. 8-7. Volcanic bombs at base of cinder cone in Cascade Mountains, California, 1891. (Courtesy of J.S. Diller, USGS.)

When the tephra cools and solidifies, it forms deposits called ash-flow tuffs that can cover an area of a thousand square miles or more.

Ejecta from volcanoes have a wide range of chemical, mineral, and physical properties. Nearly all volcanic products are silicate rocks, composed mainly of oxygen, silicon, and aluminum, with lesser amounts of iron, calcium, magnesium, sodium, potassium, and other elements. Basalts are relatively low in silica and high in calcium, magnesium, and iron. Magmas that are more siliceous have more sodium and potassium and less magnesium and iron.

Magmas of different composition are indicative of their source materials and the depths of their environments. Degrees of partial melting of mantle rocks, partial crystallization which enriches the melt with silica, and assimilation of a variety of crustal rocks in the mantle effect the composition of the magma. When the erupting magma rises to the surface, it incorporates a variety of rock types along its way and the magma changes its composition. This can have a dramatic effect on the type of eruption.

LAVA

Lava is molten rock or magma that manages to reach the throat of the volcano or a fissure without exploding into fragments and flows onto the surface. The magma that produces lava is much less viscous than that which produces tephra, allowing volatiles and gases to escape with comparative ease and giving rise to much quieter and milder eruptions. Mostly, lava is composed of basalt that is only about 50 percent silica, dark in color, and quite fluid.

Outpourings of lava come in two general classes, which are Hawaiian names, and typical of Hawaiian eruptions: pahoehoe (pronounced, Pah-

TABLE 8-2. Classification of Volcanic Rocks			
PROPERTY	BASALT	ANDESITE	RHYOLITE
Silica content	Lowest about 50%, a basic rock	Intermediate about 60%	Highest more than 65%, an acid rock
Dark mineral content	Highest	Intermediate	Lowest
Typical minerals	Feldspar Pyroxene Olivine Oxides	Feldspar Amphibole Pyroxine Mica	Feldspar Quartz Mica Amphibole
Density	Highest	Intermediate	Lowest
Melting Point	Highest	Intermediate	Lowest
Molten rock viscosity at the surface	Lowest	Intermediate	Highest
Tendency to form lavas	Highest	Intermediate	Lowest
Tendency to form pyroclastics	Lowest	Intermediate	Highest

HOE-ay-hoe-ay) means satinlike, and aa (pronounced, AH-ah) which is the sound of pain when walking over them bare foot.

Pahoehoe or ropy lavas (FIG. 8-8) are highly fluid basalt flows produced when the surface of the flow congeals and forms a thin plastic skin. The melt beneath continues to flow, molding and remolding the skin into billowing or ropy-looking surfaces. When the lavas eventually solidify, the skin retains the appearance of the flow pressures put upon it from below.

Aa or blocky lava (FIG. 8-9) forms when vis-

TABLE 8-3. Common Igneous Rocks			
	FELSIC	INTERMEDIATE	MAFIC	ULTRAMAFIC
---	---	---	---	---
Intrusive	Granite	Diorite	Gabbro	Peridotite
Extrusive	Rhyolite	Andesite	Basalt	None
Mineral composition	Quartz Potassium feldspar	Hornblend Sodium feldspar Calcium feldspar	Calcium feldspar Pyroxenes	Olivine Pyroxenes
Minor mineral constituents	Sodium feldspar Muscovite Biotite Hornblend	Biotite Pyroxenes	Olivine Hornblend	Calcium feldspar

Characteristic	Subduction	Rift Zone	Hot Spot
Location	Deep ocean trenches	Mid-ocean ridges	Interior of plates
Percent active volcanoes	80 percent	15 percent	5 percent
Topography	Mountains island arcs	Submarine ridges	Mountains geysers
Examples	Andies Mts. Japan Is.	Azores Is. Iceland	Hawaiian Is. Yellowstone
Heat source	Plate friction	Convection currents	Upwelling from core
Magma temperature	Low	High	Low
Magma viscosity	High	Low	Low
Volitile content	High	Low	Low
Silica content	High	Low	Low
Type of eruption	Explosive	Effusive	Both
Volcanic products	Pyroclasts	Lava	Both
Rock type	Andesite Rhyolite	Basalt	Basalt
Type of cone	Composit	Cinder fissure	Cinder shield

TABLE 8-4. General comparison of types of volcanism

cous, subfluid lavas press forward, carrying a thick and brittle crust with them. As the lava flows, it puts stresses on the overriding crust, breaking it into rough, jagged blocks that are pushed ahead of or dragged along with the flow in a disorganized mass.

Highly fluid lava moves rapidly anytime, but it travels especially fast down steep volcano slopes. The flow rate is also determined by the viscosity and how long it takes the lava to harden. Most lavas flow at a walking pace to about 10 miles per hour. Some lava flows have been clocked at only a snail's pace while others are as fast as 50 miles per hour. Some very thick lavas creep ahead slowly for months or even years before they become hard enough to stop completely.

After a stream of lava has become crusted over and has hardened on the surface, and if the underlying magma continues to flow away, a long cavern or tunnel called a lava tube is formed. Tubes can reach 10 yards across and extend for hundreds of yards. The walls and roof of the lava cave are occasionally adorned with stalactites while the floor is covered with stalagmites of deposits of lava. In some cases, especially on the ocean floor, the lava solidifies into pillow-shaped masses called pillow lava (FIG. 8-10).

As lava cools it shrinks, causing cracking or jointing. The cracks can shoot vertically through the entire lava flow, breaking it into six-sided pillars or columns such as those found at Devils Postpile National Monument, California (FIG. 8-11).

Lava lakes such as those on Mount Kilauea are basalt flows that have been trapped in large pools and do not solidify to any great extent. The magma that feeds the lakes rises from 30 miles below the surface and is stored in a reservoir about 2.5 miles below the summit. In the formation of a

HOT SPOTS

Scattered around the world are more than 100 small regions of isolated volcanic activity known as hot spots. Unlike most of the world's active volcanoes, they are not always found at plate boundaries and many lie deep in the interior of a plate. Most hot spots move even slower than the oceanic or continental plates above them. In some cases, the movement of the plates past the hot spot has left a trail of volcanoes to mark their passage. When a continental plate hovers over a hot spot, the molten rocks welling up from deep below create a broad dome in the crust on average about 125 miles across. As the dome grows, it develops deep fissures that make their way to the surface.

Hot spot volcanoes are distinguished by their very isolation — such as in the middle of a rigid lithospheric plate far from centers of volcanic and earthquake activity — and might be the only distinctive feature in an otherwise monotonous landscape. Almost all hot spot volcanism occurs in regions of broad crustal uplift or swelling. Lavas of hot-spot volcanoes are different from volcanoes of rift systems and subduction zones and are basalts containing larger amounts of alkali minerals such as sodium and potassium. Hot spots might be the result of plumes of hot material rising up from deep within the mantle. The distinctive composition of hot-spot lavas seems to indicate a source outside the general circulation pattern of the mantle. Plumes might also arise from stagnant regions in the center of convection cells or from below the region that is stirred by convection currents.

The most prominent and most easily recognizable hot spot is the one which created the Hawaiian Islands. Apparently all the islands in the Hawaiian chain were formed by a single source of lava, over which the Pacific plate has passed, proceeding on a northwesterly course. The volcanic islands popped out on the ocean floor, conveyor belt fashion, with the oldest being the one furthest to the northwest away from the hot spot. There are also similar chains of volcanic islands in the Pacific that trend in the same direction as the Hawaiian Islands. (FIG. 8-12).

This effect might indicate that the Pacific

FIG. 8-8. Pahoehoe lava from eruption of Kilauea Volcano, Hawaii. (Courtesy of D.A. Swanson, USGS.)

lava lake, lava from the reservoir erupts to the surface and flows into a depression. The depth of the lakes is substantial — as much as 400 feet. Therefore, it takes a long time for them to cool and solidify. This might take from one year for shallow lakes, to as long as 25 years for the deepest ones. Eventually, the natural dikes that channel the lava into the lake collapse, and so the lake is cut off from its sources and begins to solidify. Some lava lakes disappear completely down the bottom of the crater as though someone pulled the drain plug.

FIG. 8-9. Aa lava in Hawaiian Volcanoes National Park. (Courtesy of USGS.)

plate is slowly rotating around a single pole. It could also indicate that the African plate is stationary, while the Pacific plate is moving off in the direction defined by the volcanic chains.

The trail of volcanoes left by the hot spots changes abruptly to the north where it follows the Emperor Seamounts. The Seamounts are isolated underwater volcanoes strung out in a chain across the interior of the Pacific plate. This deflection occurred just at the time when the Pacific plate collided with the North American plate. Therefore, hot spots could be a reliable means for determining the direction of plate motion, provided they remain reasonably stationary.

More than half of the hot spots are on continents with the greatest concentration, about 25 in all, in Africa. Hot spots might have been responsible for the unusual topography of the Africa conti-

nent, which is characterized by numerous basins, swells, and uplifted highlands. The effect might also support the hypothesis that the African plate has come to rest over a population of hot spots.

Another piece of evidence indicating that Africa is stationary is that hot-spot lavas of several different ages are superimposed on one another. If the continent were moving, they should be spread laterally in a chronological sequence. There also appears to be a direct relationship with the number of hot spots with the rate of drift of a continent.

The Antarctic and Eurasian plates also have numerous hot spots. Therefore, it can be expected that these regions are only moving slowly. In contrast, on rapidly moving continental plates, such as North and South America, hot-spot volcanism is rare.

Yellowstone National Park is more than 1000

FIG. 8-10. Pillow lava on Ingot Island, Alaska, 1924. (Courtesy of F.H. Moffit, USGS.)

FIG. 8-11. Devils Postpile National Monument, California. (Courtesy of F.E. Mattes, USGS.)

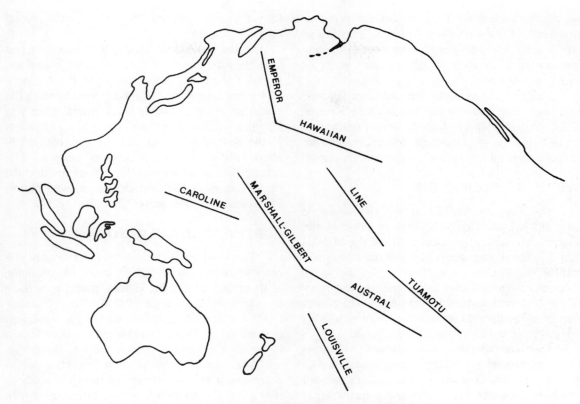

FIG. 8-12. Linearity of volcanic islands on the Pacific plate.

miles from the nearest plate boundary. Nevertheless, it is one of several mid-plate centers of hot spot activity. Beneath the park is a hot spot that is responsible for the continuous thermal activity giving rise to a multitude of geysers such as Old Faithful. The geysers are produced when rain water seeps into the ground, is heated near the magma chamber, and rises explosively through fissures in the torn crust. The region is frequently shaken by earthquakes. The largest in recent history occurred in 1959 and triggered a massive landslide at Hebgen Lake, Montana (more on this in Chapter 14).

The hot spot did not always exist under Yellowstone, and its early travels can be traced in volcanic rocks of the Snake River Plain for 400 miles in southern Idaho. Over the past 15 million years, the North American plate slid southwestward across the hot spot, placing it under its temporary home at Yellowstone. During the past 2 million years, there have been at least three episodes of intense volcanic activity in the region. Eventually, as the plate continues westward, the hot spot will move its way eastward across Wyoming and Montana.

The output of pyroclastics and lava for a single volcanic eruption ranges from a few cubic yards to as much as 5 cubic miles. Together, the volcanoes of the world's subduction zones produce about 1 billion cubic yards of new, mostly pyroclastic, volcanic material per year. Rift volcanoes generate about 2.5 billion cubic yards per year of mainly submarine flows of basalt. Volcanoes over hot spots produce about 0.5 billion cubic yards per year as mostly basalt flows in the oceans and pyroclastics and lava flows on the continents. This brings the Earth's average yearly total output of new volcanic rock to about 4 billion cubic yards or nearly a cubic mile.

Many years can go by without large volcanic eruptions from sources like Krakatoa or Katmai. Even giant eruptions of historic times are dwarfed by the volumes of prehistoric volcanic rocks that probably poured out in single enormous eruptions.

THE EAST PACIFIC RISE

The East Pacific Rise is a 6-thousand-mile long rift system along the eastern edge of the Pacific plate and is the counterpart of the Mid-Atlantic Ridge. Using deep-diving submersibles, scientists were able to explore this underwater mountain range and made an astonishing discovery in the cold, dark waters. Flourishing on the almost barren ocean floor $2\frac{1}{2}$ miles down were rich living communities unlike any others on Earth.

These unexpected oasis of bizarre life forms clustered around hot water vents associated with the rifting crust. Cool seawater percolates through cracks in the ocean floor and is heated near magma chambers that lie just below the rifting crust. The heated water, rich in dissolved minerals, is expelled upward to the surface through vents like undersea geysers where some of the minerals precipitate out of the water to build up exotic-looking chimneys. Some of the chimneys spew out water blackened by sulfide minerals and have been called "black smokers." Others ooze out water that is milky white and are called "white smokers." Because of their warm and mineral laden waters, the vents sustain colonies of huge clams, giant crabs, and 10-foot-long tubeworms (FIG. 8-13).

About 30 million years ago, the North American continent began approaching the East Pacific Rise. The first part of the continent to override the axis of seafloor spreading was the coast of Southern California and Northwest Mexico. As the rift system and the subduction zone converged, the intervening oceanic plate was totally consumed. The deep sediments in the trench were caught in

the big squeeze and heaved up to form the coastal ranges of California.

At the same time, Baja California was ripped from the mainland. In northwest United States and British Columbia, the consuming of the northern part of the East Pacific Rise took place beneath the continent. As the 50-mile thick crustal plate was forced down into the mantle, the heat melted parts of the descending plate and the adjacent lithospheric plate, forming pockets of magma. The magma melted its way to the surface and formed the volcanoes of the Cascade Range, with Mount St. Helens the most active peak (FIG. 8-14).

CONTINENTAL VOLCANOES

The Western United States has scores of volcanoes that are likely to erupt in the future. Some of them, like Mount St. Helens, might be waking from long slumbers. Even 50,000 years of quietude might not be long enough to silence the rumblings of some volcanoes, and volcanoes have been known to awake after over a million years of slumber.

One way to forecast future eruptions is to determine a volcano's behavior from the study of its rocks. The volcano can then be grouped with others in a descending order of hazard. More than 35 volcanoes in the United States are likely to erupt sometime in the future. The first group includes volcanoes that have erupted on average every 200 years, that have erupted in the past 300 years, or both. This group includes Mount St. Helens, the Mono-Inyo Craters, Lassen Peak, Mounts Shasta, Rainier, Baker, and Hood.

The second group includes volcanoes that erupt less frequently than every 1000 years and last erupted more than 1000 years ago. These include Three Sisters, Newberry Volcano, Medicine Lake Volcano, Crater Lake Volcano, Glacier Peak, Mounts Adams, Jefferson, and McLoughlin.

The third group includes those volcanoes that last erupted more than 10,000 years ago but still overlie large magma chambers. These include the Yellowstone caldera, Long Valley caldera, Clear Lake Volcanoes, Coso Volcanoes, San Francisco Peak, and Socorro, New Mexico.

FIG. 8-13. Black smokers and tube worms on the East Pacific Rise. (Courtesy Robert D. Ballard and Kathleen Crane, WHOI.)

Scientists have compiled a map of geologically recent eruptions that shows 75 centers of activity arrayed in broad bands (FIG. 8-15). These extend from the Cascade Range in Northern California, Oregon, and Washington eastward through Idaho to Yellowstone and southeastward along the entire California and Nevada border.

Another band extends from Southeast Utah through Arizona and New Mexico. Because the pattern of activity 5 million years ago closely resembles the pattern since 10,000 years ago, it could be concluded that all 75 centers might have the potential for future eruptions, and new centers

of activity might form within these bands at any time.

Historical records show that before the 1980 Mount St. Helens eruption, only two other eruptions have disturbed the Cascade Range of the United States in 90 years. There was a minor ash eruption of Mount Hood in Oregon in 1906, and the more spectacular eruptions of Lassen Peak in California between 1914 and 1917 (FIG. 8-16). Between 1832 and 1880, four volcanoes, Mounts Baker, Rainier, St. Helens, and Hood, erupted ash or lava with periods between eruptions of 10 to 30 years for each volcano and perhaps as many as

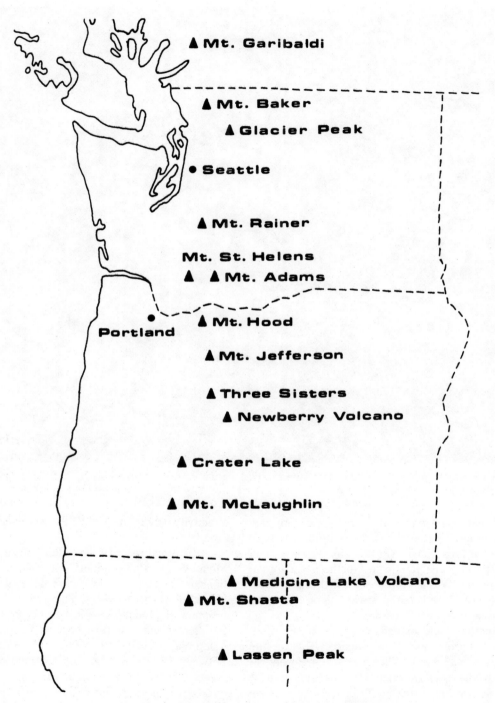

FIG. 8-14. Active volcanoes of the Cascade Range.

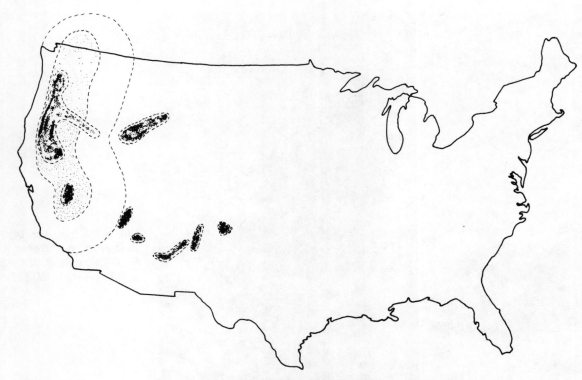

FIG. 8-15. Volcanic hazard areas.

three volcanoes erupting in the same year. In 1851, an eruption near Lassen Peak came out of nowhere, like the Paricutin volcano in Mexico, and spewed lava over four square miles of forest land. None of these recent eruptions came near the size of the larger eruptions of Mount St. Helens since its reawakening in 1980.

PREDICTING ERUPTIONS

Predicting when a volcano will erupt is not by any means an exact science. Scientists can get some warning from seismographs that measure the intensity of earthquake activity near the volcano. In many volcanic regions, such preliminary quakes are accompanied by deep rumblings and by avalanches from the walls of the craters. The tilting of the ground around the volcano might be the most reliable clue to impending activity. The under-

ground movement of magma causes rapidly changing tilts on the surface that can be measured by tiltmeters (FIG. 8-17) placed strategically around the volcano. The volcano might bulge along one of its flanks or begin to heave up the crater floor. The heat generated within the volcano might melt the ice and snow on its summit.

As the magma rises in volcanic vents it distorts the Earth's magnetic field, which can be measured by airborne magnetometers. Along with the magnetic changes, there are changes in electrical currents in the Earth that can be measured by sensitive resistivity meters. Other indications of impending eruption include a sudden rise in the temperature of nearby hot springs, gas vents, and near surface rocks.

Given sufficient warning, it is sometimes possible to minimize the damage caused by a volcano's eruption. Channels can be dug and levees built to

FIG. 8-16. The June 14, 1914 eruption of Lassen Peak, California. (Courtesy of B.F. Loomis, USGS.)

divert the flow of lava away from inhabited areas. The lava stream can be doused with water to cause it to slow down and solidify. The Air Force has even tried, with some success, bombing the lava flows from Mauna Loa in Hawaii. Dams were built in Java to divert volcanic mudflows away from cities and agricultural lands. Artificial hillocks were built in some villages to serve as islands of refuge from volcanic mudflows. People who have made active volcanoes their neighbors learned to live with their unruly behavior and have treated them as though they were just a normal part of their lives.

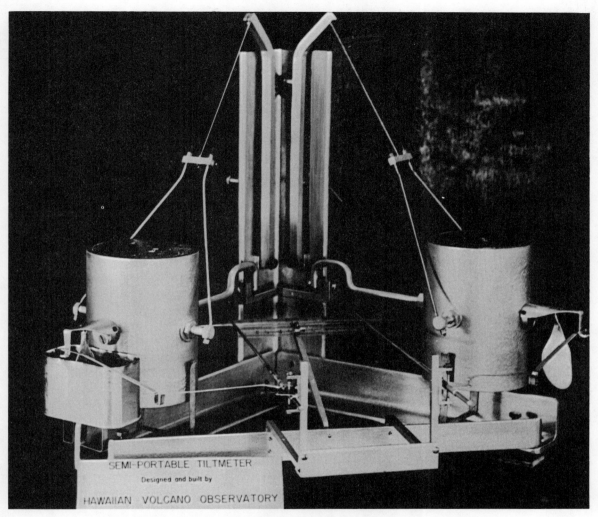

Fig. 8-17. A semiportable tiltmeter. (Courtesy of R.H. Finch, USGS.)

9

Volcanoes
In Outer Space

WHEN Galileo first turned his crude telescope on the Moon in 1609, he shattered the accepted belief that the Moon, as seen with the naked eye, appeared to be a small planet with continents and oceans, called maria. What Galileo discerned through his telescope was a Moon with a pockmarked surface of craters and flat plain (FIG. 9-1). Twice as much of the Moon's surface on the visible side is covered with continents, or highlands, than with maria.

When the Soviet *Luna 3* photographed the far side in 1959, it was found to be 90 percent highland. In July of 1969, 360 years after Galileo made his lunar discovery, Neil Armstrong became the first man to set foot on the Moon. The site was the Sea of Tranquillity and the mission was *Apollo 11*. The Moon's surface was dusty and much darker than it looks from Earth. The astronauts gathered up Moon rocks to take home with them so that scientists might learn something of the Moon's origin.

LUNAR VOLCANOES

From a study of the rocks, it appears that the Moon formed roughly about the same time as the Earth, some 4.6 billion years ago. The Moon has a crust 30 to 60 miles thick, a brittle intermediate layer about 700 miles thick, and a relatively dense —possibly partly molten core—with a radius of 300 miles. Early in its life the Moon's surface was melted by a furious bombardment of meteorites. Then the Moon began to slowly cool.

About 4 billion years ago, the Moon was bombarded a second time. Numerous huge impact craters, ranging up to 240 miles across, destroyed most of the earliest rocks on the Moon's surface. During the next few hundred million years, huge flows of basaltic lava welled up through the weakened crater floors and flooded over great stretches of the surface, filling and submerging many of the larger meteor craters. The Moon's seas were composed of molten rock which hardened into maria.

FIG. 9-1. The Earth's moon. (Courtesy of Kitt Peak National Observatory.)

There are numerous narrow, sinuous depressions called rills in the lava flows. Many of the rills emanate from craters that might have been volcanic in origin. In some areas, wrinkles break the lava surface and might have been due to faulting that could be responsible for the high order of earthquake activity on the Moon. There are also areas of chaotic mountain building, probably of volcanic origin, throughout the Moon's surface. Some ridges are several hundred feet high and extend for hundreds of miles. When the last of the lava hardened about 3 billion years ago, except for some fresh meteor impacts, the Moon looked very much then as it does today.

Moon rocks brought back from the Apollo missions (TABLE 9-1) vary in age between 3.2 and 4.5 billion years old. The oldest rocks are primitive and have not been remelted since their original solidification from molten magma. These rocks formed the original lunar crust and are called Genesis Rock. They are composed of anorthosite, a coarse-grained, pure feldspar granite that was formed deep within the Moon's interior. The youngest rocks are all of volcanic origin and were melted and reconstructed, probably by giant meteor impacts. After the basalt flows ended, new Moon rock formation appears to have ceased, and no known rocks are younger than 3.2 billion years old.

The Moon rocks resemble Earth rocks but with some notable differences. All the rocks are igneous, meaning they came from magma, and together they are called the regolith. They include coarse-grained gabbro basalt, meteoric impact breccia, pyroxine peridotite, glass beads, and dust-size soil material composed mainly of anorthosite. The regolith is generally about 10 feet thick but is believed to be thicker in the highlands. The lunar basalt has much more iron, titanium, and less alkali. Gas holes are common, and glass is embedded in cavities of the rock. The rocks collected on the surface have a density between 3.1 and 3.5, while

TABLE 9-1. Summary of Major Space Probes

PROBE	YEAR	MISSION
Mariner 2	1962	Fly-by of Venus; first probe to any planet
Mariner 4, 6, 7	1965	Fly-by missions of Mars
	1969	
	1969	
Apollo 8	1968	Astronauts circle the moon and return to earth
Apollo 9	1969	First astronaut landed on the moon
Mariner 9	1971	Orbiter of Mars
Apollo 17	1972	Last of six Apollo missions to carry people to the moon
Mariner 10	1974	Orbited the sun, allowing it to pass Mercury several times; fly-by mission to Venus
Pioneer 10, 11	1973	First close-up views of Jupiter
	1974	
Venera 8, 9, 10	1972	Soviet landers on Venus (operative about one year each due to harsh surface conditions)
	1975	
	1975	
Viking 1, 2	1976	*Orbiters and landers of Mars*
Voyager 1, 2	1979	Fly-by of Jupiter
	1980	Fly-by of Jupiter
Voyager 2	1986	Fly-by of Uranus
	1989	Expected fly-by of Neptune

the entire moon is only 3.34. This might indicate that some parts of the Moon are denser than others. It could also mean that the Moon is undifferentiated and homogeneous.

On Earth, volcanoes are responsible for our atmosphere and oceans. The Moon has one-sixth the gravity of Earth, and it seems reasonable to conclude that all gases and water vapor from volcanic eruptions on the Moon escaped into space. So far, no trace of water has ever been found on our nearest neighbor. All metal oxides on the surface appear to be in their lowest states of oxidation, indicating no atmosphere similar to ours ever existed. Because of the dark color of the Moon's surface rocks, like the basalts, the Moon is a poor reflector of light from the Sun, and only about 7 percent of the light is reflected to Earth. Otherwise, if the rocks were lighter in color, people could read their newspapers at night by the light of a full Moon.

MERCURY

Looking very much like the Moon and not much larger, Mercury (Fig. 9-2), the innermost planet, is also pockmarked with numerous meteorite craters. The similarity is so striking that photographs of Mercury sent back from *Mariner 10* in March 1974, could easily have been mistaken for the back side of the Moon. It differs from the Moon in not having jumbled mountainous regions and wide lava planes and, instead, displays long, low,

TABLE 9-2. Summary of Solar System Data

Body	Orbit in Millions of Miles	Radius Miles	Mass	Density	Axis Tilt	Rotation	Year	Temp. (°C)	Atmospheric Composition
Mercury	36	1,500	0.1	5.1	10	58.6 days	88 days	425	Carbon dioxide
Venus	67	3,760	0.8	5.3	6	242.9 days	225 days	425	Carbon dioxide minor water
Earth	93	3,960	1.0	5.5	23.5	24 hours	365 days	15	78% nitrogen 21% oxygen
Mars	141	2,110	0.1	3.9	25.2	24.5 hours	687 days	−42	Carbon dioxide minor water
Jupiter	483	44,350	318	1.3	3.1	9.9 hours	11.9 years	2000	60% hydrogen 36% helium 3% neon 1% methane and ammonia
Saturn	886	37,500	95	0.7	26.7	10.2 hours	29.5 years	2000	Same as Jupiter
Uranus	1,783	14,500	14	1.6	98	10.8 hours	84 years		Similar to Jupiter, no ammonia
Neptune	2,793	14,450	18	2.3	29	15.7 hours	165 years		Same as Uranus
Pluto	3,666	1,800 750	0.1	1.5		6.4 days	248 years		

winding cliffs or scarps that resemble fault lines hundreds of miles long. Its density of 5.45 is very close to that of the Earth. The crust is Moonlike and its composition is much like the interior of the Earth. Mercury evolved similar to the way the Moon evolved — having been bombarded with meteors between 3.9 and 4.2 billion years ago — and, like the Moon, little has happened since.

Mercury is the swiftest planet, with a year that only 88 days long. Its rotational period is 59 days; therefore, Mercury rotates 1.5 times for every revolution around the Sun. This makes for long, hot days with temperatures soaring to 315 degrees centigrade, hot enough to melt lead, and long cold nights with temperatures falling to −140 degrees centigrade. This gives Mercury the greatest temperature extremes of any planet. There is very little atmosphere, consisting mostly of helium. There is an appreciable magnetic field that indicates the presence of an iron core similar in composition to the Earth's and extends for approximately 1100 miles (about 75 percent of Mercury's radius). This would account for why Mercury is so much denser than the Moon. Above the core floats a silicate mantle 375 miles thick. There does not appear to be any upwelling of magma to the surface and the craters are all believed to be from meteor impacts.

VENUS

The second planet from the Sun, named for the goddess of love, is often called the sister planet of the Earth because of its similar size and mass. Venus (FIG. 9-3) is second only to the Moon in brilliance in the night sky. It is covered by a dense layer of clouds that makes for a good reflector of sunlight but also makes observations of the surface of Venus and very difficult.

In December 1978, the *Pioneer Venus* orbiter was able to penetrate the clouds with several probes to learn something about the Venus landscape. The surface temperature reaches 900 degrees centigrade. Therefore, liquid water bodies are not possible and only minor traces of water exist in the atmosphere. Radar mapping has revealed large elevated plateaulike tracts that rise 3 to 6 miles above the surrounding terrain, elongated ridges, and circular depressions that might have resulted from meteor impacts. A great trench 8 miles deep, 175 miles wide, and 900 miles long might well be the Solar System's grandest canyon. The surface could have been shaped by deep-seated tectonic forces and volcanic activity, producing a pattern that is far from Earth-like.

Venus orbits the Sun in a nearly perfect circle once every 225 days. Its rotation is retrograde, meaning that it is the only planet in the Solar System that spins in the opposite direction of the other planets. A clockwise turn is completed every 243 days. Carbon dioxide makes up about 93 percent of the atmosphere and causes a runaway greenhouse effect that is responsible for the high surface temperatures.

The heavy gas produces air pressures on the surface as much as 90 atmospheres. The pressure would be equivalent to the pressure at 3000 feet beneath Earth's oceans. The primary source of the carbon dioxide was outgassing during volcanic eruptions. Hot acid rains composed mainly of concentrated sulfuric acid fall to the surface. Along with the extremely hot temperatures and high pressures acid contributes to a very short life span for Venus probes. The surface appears to be much smoother than the Moon or Mercury, and rocks observed by the Soviet *Venera* spacecraft were angular in some places while at other locations they were flat and rounded and might have been due to wind erosion. The rocks have a density identical with that of terrestrial granites. The soil has a composition similar to basalts found on the Earth and Moon.

The internal structure of Venus is thought to be much like the Earth. Venus possesses a liquid, metallic core surrounded by a mantle and a rocky crust. The core has about one-quarter of the planet's mass and half its radius. There is almost a complete absence of a magnetic field. This could be due to the slow rotation of the planet that would prevent the generation of electrical currents for the dynamo effect. The density of the mantle ranges from 5.6 near the top to 9.5 near the core.

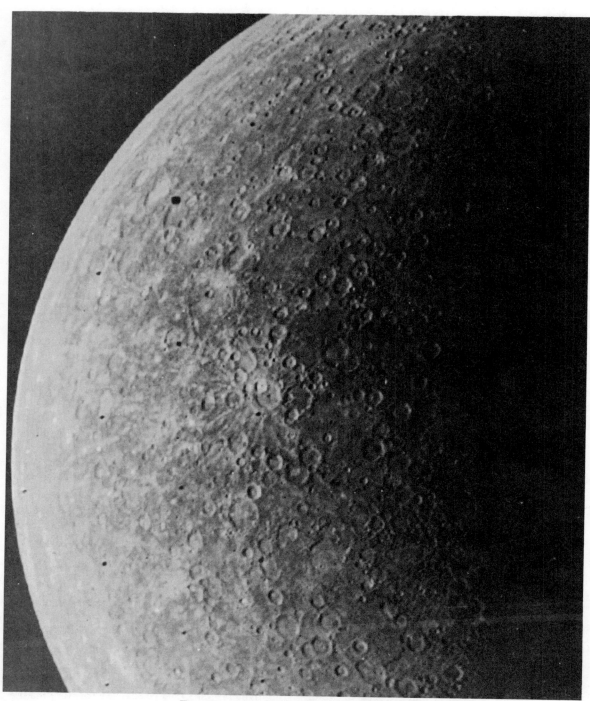

FIG. 9-2. Mercury. (Courtesy of NASA.)

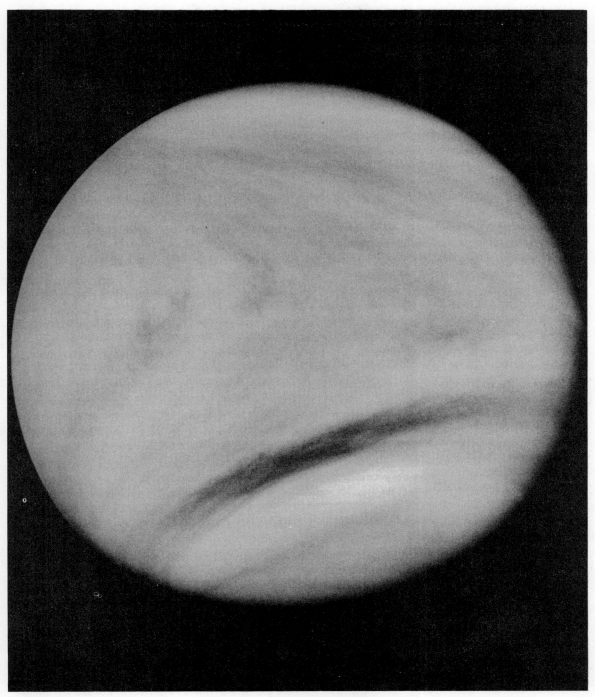

FIG. 9-3. Venus. (Courtesy of NASA.)

The density of the crust averages 2.9. The presence of radioactive uranium, thorium, and potassium in the crust are in amounts comparable with those on Earth. It might be safe to say that the amount of heat generated inside Venus is comparable with that of Earth. As on Earth, the best escape route for excess internal heat is volcanoes.

Radar maps from *Pioneer Venus,* high-resolution radar images from Soviet spacecraft, and radio telescopes on Earth have recently revealed volcanolike structures on the surface of Venus. The abundance of sulfur dioxide in the upper atmosphere suggests that Venus has undergone massive volcanic eruptions within the past decade. A region known as Beta Regio appears to have numerous huge volcanoes. Some volcanoes are as tall as three miles, and a single shield volcano has a diameter of over 400 miles, much larger than any on Earth.

One theory implies that upwelling of magma below the region caused horizontal movement in the crust, just as it does on Earth and created a major linear rift system, flanked by volcanic structures. Also, isolated peaks have been detected near the equator and might be individual volcanoes. Soviet spacecraft have observed great circular features as much as several hundred miles in diameter and relatively low in elevation. These are attributed to huge volcanic domes that have collapsed to leave large calderas with folds of crust around their periphery.

MARS

The red planet has envoked greater interest and has been studied in greater detail than any other planet. Like the Moon and Mercury, the surface on Mars is cratered, but there are a number of terrain features caused by wind, water, ice, and tectonic activity—including volcanism. Mars, about half the size of Earth, approximates both Earth's length of day and the tilt of its axis. It rotates on its axis once in 24 hours and 37 minutes, inclined at an angle of 24 degrees. This gives Mars seasons much like Earth, except they are longer and colder because it is farther from the Sun.

Mars has polar ice caps, similar to those on Earth, composed of ice and frozen carbon dioxide. In the winter, polar ice can grow halfway to the equator, and in the spring it begins to diminish rapidly, until only a small island of ice is left at the pole during the summer.

The Martian atmosphere is only 1 percent as dense as that on Earth and is 95 percent carbon dioxide, with minor amounts of other gases and water vapor. Even though the atmosphere is thin, violent seasonal dust storms, with 170 mile an hour winds that last for weeks, are responsible for the planet's red glow. Sand dunes similar to those in the deserts on Earth are created by blowing dust and sand. There are large canyons such as Valles Marineris, which is as much as 4 miles deep, over 100 miles wide, and 3000 miles long. Such canyons are thought to have formed by slippage of the crust along great faults, like the rift valleys of Africa, and have branching tributaries that look much like dry river beds. It could be that heat from volcanic activity or meteoroid impact melted subsurface ice, and rapid release of water and flowing mud carved out these huge channels.

Images radioed back from *Mariner 9,* the first artificial satellite to orbit a planet, revealed in 1971 and 72 a Martian northern hemisphere with numerous volcanoes. The largest volcano, called Olympus Mons (FIG. 9-4), covers an area the size of the state of Ohio and is 75,000 feet high, over twice as tall as Mauna Loa, the tallest volcano on Earth.

These volcanoes most closely resemble shield volcanoes similar to those that built Hawaii. Their extreme size is thought to be the result of the absence of plate movements. Rather than a chain of relatively small volcanoes forming, one very large cone developed. Impact craters are notably less abundant in the regions where volcanoes are most numerous. This indicates that at least some of the volcanic topography formed more recently in Mars' history but is still ancient by Earth standards.

The Southern hemisphere has a surface that is more highly cratered and is comparable in age to the Lunar highlands—between 3.5 and 4.0 billion years old. The discovery of several highly cratered

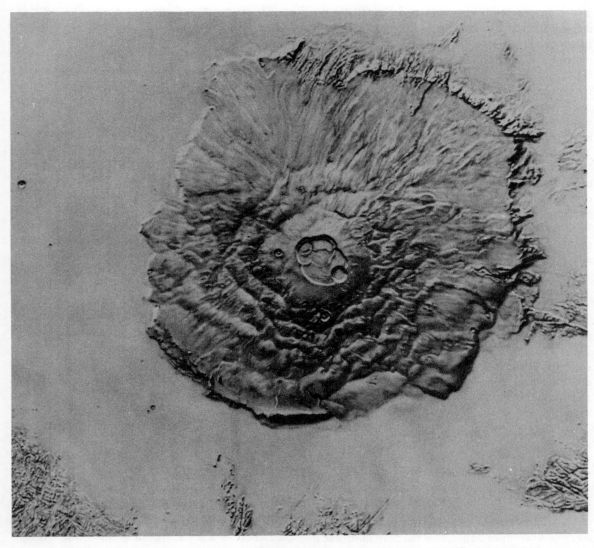

FIG. 9-4. Olympus Mons, the largest shield volcano on Mars. (Courtesy of M.H. Carr, USGS.)

and weathered volcanoes indicates that volcanic activity began early and has a long history. Even the fresh-appearing volcanoes and lava planes of the northern hemisphere might be older than 1 billion years. The fact that there is no seismic activity, as indicated by the *Viking* lander's seismographs, points toward a now tectonically dead planet.

There appears to be no horizontal crustal movement of individual plates on mars, and the crust is probably much cooler and more rigid than that on Earth. That is why there are no folded mountain ranges. Because Mars has only 10 percent of the Earth's mass, it could not have generated and stored nearly as much heat.

Because Mars does not possess any appreciable magnetic field, it is surmised that it has no appreciable metallic core or lacks a fluid core due to low internal heat. Therefore, it generates no dynamo effect. There is no evidence of plate tectonics. Therefore, heat could not be generated by friction between plates. For Mars to exhibit large-scale volcanism under these conditions, heat pockets would have to exist below the surface. The heat might have been supplied by radiogenic sources.

Evidence for polar wandering on Mars indicates that the entire crust might have moved as one plate due to instabilities in the interior caused by the planet's rotation. This movement could have been caused by convection currents in the mantle that would also force molten rock to the surface and produce volcanoes.

JUPITER

The outer planets, except for Pluto, are referred to as the giant or gaseous planets because gases make up the bulk of their mass. This alone indicates that these bodies are totally unlike the inner, dense, Earth-like planets. The gaseous planets, although spectacular, are not as geologically active as their moons, which are solid bodies. The *Voyager I* and *II* spacecrafts passed near Jupiter in January and June 1979, respectively, and close views of the larger inner satellites were obtained (FIG. 9-5).

Jupiter is the largest planet and has a mass 2.5 times greater than the combined masses of all other orbiting bodies in our Solar System. If Jupiter were several times larger, it could have lit up like a miniture Sun, and our Solar System would become like many other binary star systems in the universe.

Despite its huge size, Jupiter rotates faster than any other planet, completing one rotation in less than 10 hours. This rapid rotation causes the equator to bulge and the poles to flatten. The planet is covered with alternating bands of multicolored clouds that are aligned parallel to the equator. The most striking feature on the planet's surface is a great red spot, whose color varies intensely. The red spot also varies in size but has been measured by the *Voyager* probes at some 14,000 miles wide and about 7000 miles deep. The cause of the red spot, and other smaller but similar spots, sometimes has been attributed to volcanic activity on the planet's surface. More likely they are large hurricanelike storm systems.

Jupiter's atmosphere is mostly hydrogen and helium and there are smaller amounts of methane, ammonia, sulfur, and water. The wind systems generate the light and dark colored bands that are similar to high and low pressure zones on Earth. Because of the immense pressure of the atmosphere on the planet's surface, Jupiter is thought to be covered by a gigantic ocean of liquid hydrogen that might extend halfway into the interior. Jupiter is also thought to contain as much rocky and metallic material as is found on the inner terrestrial planets. This could make up the planet's core. Due to the thickness and density of the overlying layers of liquids and gasses, direct observation of the solid part of the planet might be impossible.

Jupiter's satellite system consists of 15 moons, resembling a miniture solar system. The four largest moons, first discovered by Galileo, travel in nearly circular orbits with periods of from 2 to 17 days. The largest of these Galilean moons, Callisto and Ganymede are about the size of Mercury. The two smaller Moons, Europa and Io, are about the size of the Earth's Moon. The surface of Callisto, the outermost of the Galilean satellites, is densely cratered like the back side of the Earth's Moon, except these meteoric impacts were made on a crust of a dirty, frozen ocean of ice.

Ganymede is the largest of the Jovian moons, and its surface resembles the near side of our Moon. There are densely cratered regions and smooth areas where young lava flows covered the scars of older craters. Numerous grooves suggest that some type of tectonic activity has taken place in the not-too-distant past.

Europa has a smooth, icy surface that is devoid of major impact craters and crisscrossed by numerous linear features a hundred miles wide and

FIG. 9-5. Io with Jupiter in background. (Courtesy of NASA.)

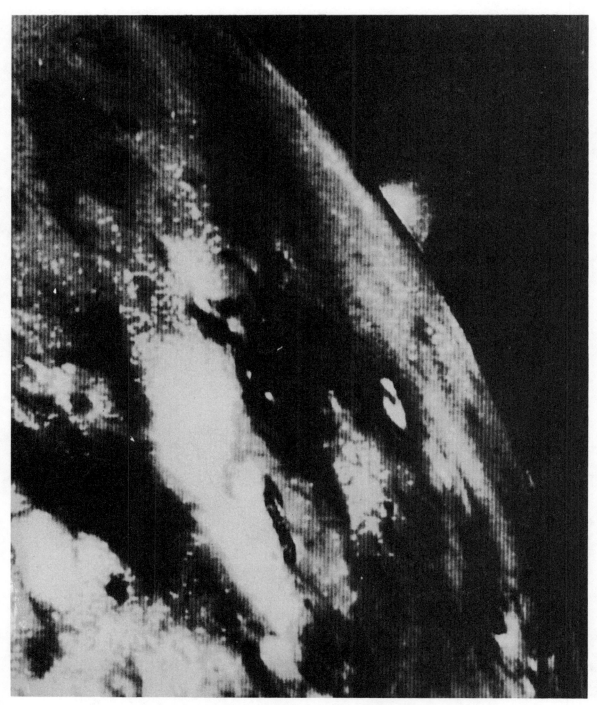

FIG. 9-6. Volcanic eruption on Io. (Courtesy of USGS.)

thousands of miles long. These might be fractures in the icy crust filled with material pushed up from below. The moon probably formed after the later bombardment period, 4 billion years ago, when meteoroids were much more abundant.

There is only one body in the Solar System, other than Earth, where actual volcanic eruptions have been observed. Io is the innermost of the Galilean moons. The surface of Io is dotted with hundreds of volcanic features and is very colorful as a result of its sulfurous rocks. The almost total lack of impact craters indicates that the surface of Io has recently, within the last million years, been paved over with lava.

Eight active volcanoes have been identified on Io. On Earth, there might not be eight major eruptions in a whole century. Umbrella-shaped volcanic plumes have been seen rising from the surface to heights of 150 miles and more (FIG. 9-6). If the Earth suddenly became as volcanically active as Io, several Mount St. Helens-size volcanoes would be popping up in the most unlikely places every few years.

Io's volcanoes are not only more numerous, but they are also more energetic than those on Earth. Material ejected from Io's volcanic vents reaches velocities of over 2000 miles per hour (or as fast as a high-powered bullet). This is about 10 times greater than the most explosive volcanoes on Earth. There are what appear to be numerous molten rock or sulfur lakes existing on a surface that is typically −150 degrees centigrade.

The source of all this thermal energy is believed to be the result of a gravitational tug-of-war between Jupiter and the other moons with Io caught in the middle. Io is gravitationally locked onto Jupiter so that its same side always faces its mother planet. The other moons, particularly Europa, cause Io's orbit to be highly irregular. The constant push and pull perturbs the moon's motions, causing it to nod back and forth with respect to Jupiter. This nodding action could produce internal friction that heats the interior and keeps it in a molten state. However, Io is emitting so much heat that even this tidal process cannot account for all the energy. Other processes might be involved as well.

SATURN

Being very similar in composition and only slightly smaller than Jupiter, Saturn is only half as dense as Jupiter. Saturn is nearly twice as far from the Sun, at 886 million miles, and takes 29.5 years to make one revolution. The most spectacular feature of Saturn is its rings (FIG. 9-7). First discovered by Galileo, the rings appear to be three distinct bands of ice particles about 10 miles thick. There are also some 95 concentric ringlets that are like grooves on a phonograph record.

The rings begin about 7,500 miles from the surface of the planet and extend to about 40,000 miles. The middle ring, which is also the brightest, is separated from the other two by a gap on both sides called the Cassini gap. Saturn's 15 moons must orbit outside the rings. If a Moon should approach the edge of the outer ring, it would be destroyed by the gravitational tidal force of Saturn, which would pull the moon apart. For this reason, the rings — which might be leftover material from which Saturn was formed — could not coalesce into new moons.

The moons of Saturn are among the most interesting in the Solar System, and Titan is the granddaddy of all moons. It is larger than Mercury, and it is the only moon known to possess an atmosphere. It was once thought that the Titan atmosphere was composed of methane gas as dense as Earth's atmosphere. Titan would have then resembled the early Earth just when life began and might have been the best place in the Solar System to look for life.

The surface temperature is estimated at −150 degrees centigrade, hardly warm enough to support life. Yet, if Titan had an internal heat source, then volcanism could provide the warmth needed to sustain life. Recent data from *Voyager I* indicates, however, that instead of methane, the Titan atmosphere is believed to be composed of mostly all nitrogen. If that is the case, there is not the least chance for life.

FIG. 9-7. Saturn. (Courtesy of NASA.)

Another strange moon is Iapetus, which has no counterpart anywhere else in the Solar System. Iapetus is black and white with one hemisphere as dark as basalt while the other is as white as snow. This causes the moon to be visible only on the west side of Saturn. When its orbit takes the moon east, it disappears from view because its leading hemisphere is incapable of reflecting enough sunlight to be seen at such a great distance.

URANUS

At twice the distance as Saturn, Uranus is nearly 1.8 billion miles from the Sun. First mistaken for a faint star, the discovery that Uranus is indeed a planet was made by the English astronomer William Herschel on march 13, 1781. Uranus is a bland, pale green ball. Like Saturn, it has rings that resemble nine brownish circles around the planet. The unique feature about Uranus is that its axis of rotation lies only 8 degrees from the plane of its orbit. Uranus appears to be rolling along in its orbit instead of spinning as the other planets do. Thus, the Sun is overhead at one pole during one-half of a revolution and the other pole during the other half.

The fly-by of *Voyager II* in January 1986 (Fig. 9-8) showed images of a slight brownish yellow haze over the south pole and greenish blue cloud bands rotating with the planet at the middle and low latitudes. These are the only features on an otherwise barren landscape composed mostly of frozen ammonia and methane. Therefore, Uranus more closely resembles a huge comet in structure.

Voyager's discovery of a new moon closer in to Uranus and eight other tiny moons, less than 30 miles across, puts the total number of satellites at 14. Of the five major moons, Ariel is the brightest and has a diameter of about 750 miles. The surface is heavily cratered and cut by fault scarps and grabens. This indicates that the moon has undergone tectonic activity, and possibly volcanism, during its past.

Bright ray craters sprall across the sunlit side of the 1000 mile-diameter Titania. This moon shows signs of mild internal activity indicated by large trenches. Images of Oberon reveal cratering, a 4-mile-high mountain, and a large crater with a dark floor that could have been caused by extrusion of volcanic fluids.

Miranda, the smallest of the major moons, is barely 300 miles wide. The dark terrain appears to be layered and rimmed by a high range of mountains. Deep trenchs run parallel with scarps and terraces. An unusual dark, chevron-shaped feature covers a good part of Miranda and is identified as closely spaced parallel mountain ridges.

NEPTUNE

In August 1989, *Voyager II* will fly by Neptune. The existence of Neptune was predicted before it was even sighted. Something was having gravitational effect on Uranus, speeding it up and then slowing it down as it passed; therefore, it had to be another planet. If any two planets could be considered twins, it is Uranus and Neptune. Although they are 1 billion miles apart, the two planets are almost identical in size, mass, and color. Their composition and structure are thought to be similar, too. Because it is farther out, Neptune experiences colder temperatures. Neptune has two known moons. Triten is about 3000 miles across and is unique among large satellites in that its orbit is retrograde. The other moon, Nereid, is extremely faint and small. Scientists will learn more about Neptune and its moons when *Voyager II* makes its rendezvous.

PLUTO

Our most distant planet is truely an oddity. Pluto has an eccentric path that brings it within the orbit of Neptune. There is no danger of collision because Pluto is also the only planet whose orbit is not in the same plane as the others. Instead, the orbit is tilted at 17 degrees. Because of this unusual behavior, Pluto is thought to have once been a satellite (or two satellites) of Neptune that was somehow knocked out of orbit. Actually, Pluto and Charon make a double planet system. Pluto, the larger member, is about 1,800 miles in diameter,

FIG. 9-8. Uranus. (Courtesy of NASA.)

which is smaller than our Moon. Charon is about one-third that size. Pluto might be best described as a large, dirty iceball made up of a mixture of frozen gasses and rock.

Although a tenth planet outside the orbit of Pluto has been predicted, it so far remains only a prediction.

10

Shake, Rattle, and Roll

Fʀᴏᴍ the time man began to walk upright, he often lost his balance because of the unstable ground beneath his feet. Along the East African Rift Valley, where man first made his home, tremors caused by the spreading rift system threatened to tear the continent apart. There were large, violent shakes and the Earth reeled as though hit by a giant wave. The ground ripped open and a great rent in the Earth traveled rapidly as far as the eye could see. Huge boulders showered down from ridge tops and landslides tore open large gashes in mountain sides. With wild terror in his eyes, primitive man must have ran along side frightened animals trying to escape the danger, only to find safety for only a while. Then the Earth reminded him once again what a precarious place this is to live.

EARLY EARTHQUAKE BELIEFS

Common to many ancient religions around the world is the idea that the Earth was carried on the backs of oxen, tortoises, fish, frogs, or serpents. Earthquakes were thought to strike when the load shifted as the animal moved. To the early religions, earthquakes represented all sorts of foreboding evil and destruction, resulting from man's punishment by the gods. The Semitic tribes wandering through the deserts of the Middle East believed that the shaking of the Earth was a sure sign of God's displeasure, and they had better mend their ways. The Greeks were often shaken off their feet from time to time. When an earthquake struck, they fell to their knees in supplication to angry Poseidon, god of sea and earthquakes. A Rumanian legend has it that the Earth is supported by three pillars named Faith, Hope, and Charity. When one of these symbols of morality wavered through the misdeeds of the people, the Earth shook. Throughout the centuries and even into the present, some religious teachings proclaimed that earthquakes occur in those areas where people needed chastening.

More rational men strove for a logical or scientific explanation for the violent and destructive movements. The Greek philosopher Thales (640?–546 B.C.) held the view that the world floated on water and this would account for the new springs that often spurt forth during and after an earthquake. The Greek philosopher Anaxagoras (500?–428 B.C.) proposed that earthquakes resulted when sections of the Earth cracked and caved in. After observing earthquakes and volcanic eruptions along the shores, he concluded that earthquakes might be the aftermath of fires that rage inside volcanoes, forcing their fragile crust to tremble, crack, and finally collapse. The succession of aftershocks accompanying most earthquakes were brought on by huge rocks that were loosened from the inside walls of the mountains and bounced around inside the Earth before they finally came to rest deep in the Earth. Democritus, who lived about the same time, imagined that earthquakes were related to rainwater or seepage from lakes and seas. He was close to the truth. Under certain conditions, earthquakes do occur in a such a manner.

One of the longest-standing accepted theories on earthquakes came from the fourth century B.C. Greek philosopher Aristotle. He mused upon the fact that often a stifling and listless atmosphere preceded most earthquakes. He thought there were times when all the winds in a given area somehow were forced into the Earth's interior. There, they mixed with other trapped masses of air and gas, and raged through the Earth's internal cavities seeking a way out. These tremendous winds rushing about, hurling themselves against the restraining rocks, were responsible for setting off earthquakes. The Roman poet Ovid (43 B.C.–A.D. 17) thought that when the Sun wandered too close, the Earth trembled as it tried to shield itself from the scorching heat.

Earthquakes are shrouded by all sorts of superstition and belief in the supernatural. Earthquakes were thought to throw out venomous fumes, causing vile diseases. Pills were even sold claiming to protect against the perils of earthquakes. Unbelievers and sinners were burned at the stake for sacrilege and causing earthquakes. There have been many tales about giant cracks opening in the earth and swallowing up whole civilizations.

The residents of Boston complained that the lightning rods Benjamin Franklin installed around town caused the electrical substance to be drawn from the air, which might lead to earthquakes. Indeed, on November 18, 1755 an earthquake shook Boston and much of New England. One of the most strongly held beliefs was that earthquakes are tied directly with the weather and when the air is stifling, earthquakes are bound to happen. Even today, some believe in "earthquake weather" and that high winds and hot temperatures are responsible for the trembling of the Earth.

ANCIENT EARTHQUAKES

The ancient Chinese were the first to keep records and collect data on earthquakes. During the Yin Dynasty (1532–1028 B.C.), historians wrote about political affairs and natural phenomenon. What might well be the oldest earthquake on record occurred in 1831 B.C. After an earthquake in 1177 B.C., the Chinese began to keep regular records.

In the Fen and Wei River valleys of northern China, accurate records of earthquake activity occurring in that region have been kept since 466 B.C. The first large earthquake, recorded in A.D. 7, destroyed the entire city of Hsien. Among the greatest natural disasters, the Shenshu earthquake in A.D. 1556, had the highest earthquake death toll in history. Some 830,000 people lost their lives and the devastated area was more than 500 miles long.

The Mediterranean area is well known throughout the annals for its destructive earthquakes. Since the latter part of the second millennium B.C., tablets found in Iraq, Syria, and other towns on the Mediterranean coast told of local rulers being unable to pay taxes after earthquakes destroyed their cities. Roman tax records indicated that numerous towns received financial aid from the government to help repair earthquake damage. After the volcanic destruction of Santorin around 1480 B.C., the Minoan civilization on Crete continued to be weakened by numerous earthquakes for two centuries, until it finally declined altogether.

One of the most disastrous earthquakes on

record occurred on July 21, A.D. 365. It affected an area of about a million square miles in the eastern Mediterranean, encompassing Italy, Greece, Palestine, and North Africa. The earthquake leveled coastal towns and a gigantic seismic sea wave destroyed the Egyptian port of Alexandria, drowning 5000 people.

The ancient city of Curium in southern Cyprus was totally leveled by the earthquake, and for centuries a part of classic Roman civilization was buried in the rubble. Archaeologists excavating in the area have uncovered well-preserved artifacts and bones of humans and animals. Analysis of walls and objects that hit the ground indicated that the earthquake was of extreme intensity, causing near total destruction with the epicenter about 30 miles to the Southwest. People and animals were immediately trapped in buildings as the walls shattered. The situation was analogous to Pompeii; people had little or no time to get away when the earthquake hit.

The ancient city of Antioch, which is now Antakya, Turkey was built partly on soft ground and has suffered from earthquakes since it was founded. In A.D. 115, the city was almost totally destroyed. Because of its strategic military position in southern Turkey, near the border with Syria, it was rebuilt on the same site. In A.D. 458, Antioch was almost totally destroyed again by another earthquake and rebuilt on the same spot even though it was pointed out that reconstruction here was likely to be unwise. As predicted, the part of the city that was rebuilt on the worst ground near the river was totally destroyed a generation later when another earthquake hit with the loss of 30,000 lives. Again, the city was rebuilt on the same site and became an important religious center. The city was destroyed a final time by the Persians in A.D. 540.

PORT ROYAL, JAMAICA

Port Royal on the Island of Jamaica was the center of English commercial activity in the New World. It was one of America's busiest ports and had well-stocked warehouses and stores with prosperous merchants. It was the hangout for some of the roughest, most drunken sailors ever found in one place. It was also home port for many pirates of the Spanish Main who sailed to Port Royal to loot Spanish treasure ships and sack New World towns.

Just before noon on June 7, 1692, the town began to shake in three separate shocks. The ground rose and fell in waves, cracking open and closing again, swallowing people, and crushing them to death. There was a great roar, and the whole north end of town slowly slid and fell into the sea. All along the water front, buildings toppled over and slowly sank beneath the waves. Ships in the harbor were capsized by the turbulence of the sea. Two thousand people disappeared and two-thirds of the city was destroyed. In its place, the new port of Kingston was built. In 1907, the city was destroyed by fire after an earthquake.

LISBON, PORTUGAL

Lisbon was a crowded port city on the north bank of the Tagus River and had a population of 235,000. On November 1, 1755, deep below the ocean, not many miles southwest of the city, a tremendous force was unleashed. In Lisbon, people felt a series of quick, sharp vibrations. After a minute, the vibrations came slower and much stronger. A thunderous roar deafened their ears, and clouds of dust appeared over the city as buildings began crumbling and falling to the ground.

In another minute, the motion of the ground changed to a violent up-and-down whiplashing that finished off most of the remaining buildings. Fires broke out among the rubble and, fanned by a high wind, they developed into a vast inferno that lasted for days.

A second earthquake struck 20 minutes after the first. People sought safety on the river front. In the renewed shaking, the stone quay gave way and sank into the river, taking people with it. A 20-foot sea wave generated by the earthquake, forced its way up the river and destroyed bridges and overturned ships.

The shock was felt throughout Portugal, Spain, and other parts of the world as far away as the United States. Many areas along the coast of

Portugal came to rest at new levels. The effects of the earthquake were seen in other parts of Europe. Unusual wave motions were observed on lakes in Sweden and Scotland, and in Amsterdam, boats on the canals were torn loose from their moorings. Well waters rose and springs stopped flowing or threw up muddy water. The sea wave reached the coast of Britain by mid-afternoon, and the West Indies by early evening. The earthquake might have been responsible for triggering sympathetic earthquakes in North Africa, hundreds of miles away, causing heavy damage. The Lisbon earthquake totally leveled the city and killed 60,000 of its inhabitants.

NEW MADRID, MISSOURI

On December 16, 1811, the greatest earthquake to strike the continental United States in recorded history took place in New Madrid in southeastern Missouri on the banks of the Mississippi River. The ground rose and fell, as though it were long waves upon the sea, and the sky was darkened by rising dust. Nearly all the buildings in New Madrid, which had a population of less than a thousand people, were destroyed. Trees tilted until their branches interlocked and then sprang back again, snaping their trunks (FIG. 10-1). The soil opened up in deep cracks, and the ground slid down from bluffs and low hills. On the Mississippi River, great waves were created, overturning many boats and washing others high upon the shore. Thousands of broken trees fell into the river and sandbars, and whole islands disappeared.

Luckily the area was sparsely populated. Missouri had just recently been admitted into the Union. A study of the historic records gave this earthquake the highest rating of any earthquake, a 12 on the modified Mercalli scale (shown on TABLE 11-1). There were actually three separate shocks of maximum intensity.

When the aftershocks died down from the first, a second shock struck on January 23, 1812. Then there were two weeks of quiet. On February 7, the last furious jolt was felt. This changed the course of the Mississippi River and two large lakes,

FIG. 10-1. The 1811-12 New Madrid, Missouri earthquake. (Courtesy of M.L. Fuller, USGS.)

FIG. 10-2. Reelfoot Lake, Tennessee. (Courtesy of M.L. Fuller, USGS.)

St. Francis and Reelfoot (FIG. 10-2), were created in the basins of down dropped crust.

The shocks were felt in many parts of the country. The vibrations alarmed the inhabitants of Chicago and Detroit as they experienced slight tremors. The shocks woke people in Washington, D.C. and rang church bells in Boston, more than a thousand miles away. Pendulum clocks were stopped throughout the eastern part of the country. Near New Madrid, minor aftershocks were felt for as long as two years.

ASSAM, INDIA

On June 12, 1897, the Assam region of the Himalayas in northeastern India witnessed an earthquake of equal or greater magnitude than that of New Madrid. India had been known for its major earthquakes. A very strong earthquake hit Calcuta on October 11, 1737, killing 300,000 people. Unfortunately, little is known about this earthquake; apparently, the Indians did not keep accurate records.

Every major earthquake had been preceded by a long period of quiescence. In Assam, just as in New Madrid, changes of ground level occurred over large areas (FIG. 10-3). The 4000-foot Assam Hills, south of the Brahmaputra River, were uplifted some 20 feet. Loose rocks and boulders were tossed into the air, leaving cavities in the ground where they originally rested. Fence posts came upward out of their holes. The ground was torn up, throwing huge clods in every direction, and in some cases, the clods were overturned so that roots were visible. The area of total destruction covered up to 9000 square miles. The area where the vibrations were felt was twice that of the Lisbon or New Madrid earthquakes.

A repeat performance occurred on August 15, 1950, resulting in one of the most violent earth-

quakes since the use of modern seismic instruments. Registering 8.7 on the Richter scale, its energy has been estimated at 100,000 Hiroshima-size atomic bombs. Ten thousand square miles of land were churned into desolation. As luck would have it, the area was sparsely inhabited by primitive mountain tribesmen and the death count was probably low.

Scientists, 25 miles from the epicenter, reported that the earthquake felt as though a powerful ram was hitting against the earth below them. There was a deep rumbling noise from the Earth like a kettledrum and mixed with it was a terrifying clatter as though hundreds of steel rods were being rapidly raked over sheets of corrugated iron.

The noise was unbelievably agonizing, and perhaps never before had human ears been subjected to such an onslaught of sound. Soon, the hammer blows weakened and the main shock was over. Then, from high in the sky, came a quick succession of short, sharp explosions that were clear and loud like exploding anti-aircraft shells. These booms were characteristic of tremors produce by the collapse of underground structures. Since that time, the area has been suspiciously quiet and scientists say that it is overdue for another major earthquake.

SAN FRANCISCO, CALIFORNIA

California was known for its large earthquakes, but luckily they occurred in relatively scarcely populated regions. A major earthquake struck Fort Tejon, near Los Angeles in 1857. The hamlet of Lone Pine in the Owens Valley, east of the Sierra Mountains, was destroyed on March 26, 1872. This was one of the largest earthquakes in California's history, and it opened up a deep fissure along a 100-mile line in the Owens Valley (FIG. 10-4). At least 30 people died when their fragile adobe huts collapsed on them. More than 1000 after shocks ran through the area during the next three days.

California was not the only state in the Union to be struck by major earthquakes near the turn of the century. On August 31, 1886, Charleston,

FIG. 10-4. A fissure from the 1872 Owens Valley, California earthquake. (Courtesy of NOAA/EDIS.)

South Carolina was hit by a violent shock that tore down buildings (FIG. 10-5) and killed 110 people. The earthquake was felt as far away as Boston, Milwaukee, and New Orleans. On September 10, 1899, Yakutat Bay, Alaska was shook by two violent earthquakes one of which was 8.6 magnitude. The shore line was lifted as much as 50 feet and the gigantic Yakutat glacier reversed its direction and spilled huge ice slabs into the sea.

San Francisco, in 1906, called the "Pride of the West," was a prosperous port and a large modern city of half a million people. In the early morning of April 18, San Francisco appeared to shudder for about a minute and then quieted for about 10 seconds. Then 12 minutes past five o'clock when most people were still asleep, an earthquake of shattering intensity, 7.9 magnitude, struck the city (FIG. 10-6), and the shaking lasted for about three minutes. The streets, largely deserted at this hour, weaved and twisted as though they were waves upon the sea, and people were thrown to the ground unable to get up again until it was over.

All across the city, the rumble of the Earth, the deafening roars of falling masonry and tumbling

FIG. 10-5. The August 31, 1886 Charleston, South Carolina earthquake. (Courtesy of J.K. Hillers, USGS.)

FIG. 10-6. The April 18, 1906 San Francisco, California earthquake. (Courtesy USGS and NOAA/EDIS.)

walls drowned out all other noise. Houses reeled and tumbled over and, in moments, Market Street was piled high with debris. Roadways buckled and heaved while leaving street car tracks suspended in the air. The streets filled with people in their bed cloths, abandoning their homes and hotels in droves with many clinging onto their valuables. Gas mains fractured and were ignited by overturned stoves and electrical sparks from overhead wires. Wooden beams and rafters fell across open flames scattered throughout the city and created the seeds of a raging inferno.

The damage was greatest in the low-lying business section. Almost all the buildings in the downtown area of the city were destroyed or structurally weakened. Because of the early hour, office buildings were mostly empty. Had the earthquake occurred during working hours, the death toll could have been very high. The wooden shanties of Chinatown almost all collapsed with the first tremor

The ground subsided several inches under some buildings and caused them to collapse. Those buildings that did manage to survive the earthquake were utterly destroyed by the subsequent fire. The earthquake ruptured the water mains and firemen along with the townspeople stood by helplessly, watching their city burn to the ground. By the second morning, the city was nearly completely engulfed by flames and the fire raged out of control for three days and two nights. Between 700 and 800 people lost their lives and 300,000 were left homeless. Four square miles, 75 percent of the city, was totally destroyed. Property damages were estimated at $400 million (a lot of money in those days).

Damage was also severe in other areas. The town of Santa Rosa, 50 miles to the north, was almost entirely wrecked. There were secondary effects throughout the county. Avalanches and landslides occurred in many places. An entire hillside slid down a shallow valley for a distance of half a mile. South of Cape Fortunas, a hill slid bodily into the sea and created a new cape. The road between Point Reyes Station and Inverness was broken apart and offset horizontally 21 feet where it crossed the San Andreas Fault.

Trees were uprooted, fissures and springs appeared in many districts, and ceiling lamps swung to and fro as far as 370 miles from San Francisco. Water in irrigation canals, pools, and ponds became violently agitated at a distance up to 240 miles. Ships at sea experienced a distinct and intense shock up to 150 miles from the coast.

KWANTO PLAIN, JAPAN

The citizens of Tokyo and Yokohama were looking forward to a fine Saturday morning, September 1, 1923. Then about a minute before noon, three shocks of incredible intensity, 8.3 magnitude, struck the Kwanto Plain in central Honshu, the principal island of Japan. The area of total destruction was 90 miles by 50 miles; this encompassed the two great cities. At first, the movement was slow. Then in the space of a few seconds it built to a tremendous crescendo. On the Kwanto Plain, huge fissures appeared in the ground and great landslides permanently altered the landscape.

The triple shocks brought every building of consequence in Yokohama tumbling to the ground. The wreckage was total. Tokyo fared not much better and the downtown area was almost obliterated (FIG. 10-7). In both cities, the earthquake interrupted the noon meal preparations, and hot charcoal spilled out of overturned braisers. In an instant, matchbox houses were in flames. The flames were fanned by the wind, and the fires merged to become a mighty inferno. Within minutes, the fires were totally out of control. With water supplies cut off, firefighting was utterly hopeless.

As if Tokyo did not have enough problems, at four in the afternoon, a cyclone hurtled toward the city at 125 miles an hour. Small boats were lifted into the air and water was sucked up in a huge muddy column. When the cyclone hit the blazing city, it snatched up burning timbers, furniture, clothing, and bodies and threw them skyward. Then it hurled them down again, spread the fire, and a deadly firestorm enveloped the city.

FIG. 10-7. The September 1, 1923 destruction of Tokyo, Japan. (Courtesy of O.K. Brehmer, NOAA/EDIS.)

Forty-thousand people with all their possessions were engulfed in one roaring mass of flames and were roasted alive. Nearly three-quarters of the capital city was wiped out. The fire burned for two days until there was nothing left to burn. Over 300,000 buildings were turned into a charred mess. Similar whirlwinds in Yokohama swept the flames through every part of the city and 60,000 buildings burned to the ground (FIG. 10-8). The earthquake destroyed about 3 billion dollars worth of property and left over 1 million homeless. The earthquake took the lives of over 140,000 Japa-

FIG. 10-8. The destruction of Yokahama, Japan. (Courtesy of O.K. Brehmer, NOAA/EDIS.)

FIG. 10-9. The March 27, 1964 Alaskan earthquake. (Courtesy of NOAA/EDIS and USGS.)

nese, about the same number as the World War II fire raids over Tokyo or the atomic bombings of Hiroshima and Nagasaki.

ANCHORAGE, ALASKA

The Good Friday Alaskan earthquake of March 27, 1964, which devastated Anchorage and other seaports (FIG. 10-9), was the largest ever recorded on the North American continent. Formerly 8.5 magnitude, but upgraded to 9.2, the earthquake struck without warning at 5:36 in the afternoon. For three to four minutes, the ground rolled and lurched. The pavement in downtown Anchorage came apart and buildings wobbled. Along a section of Forth street, one whole block gave way. A row of cafes and pawnshops, along with the street and cars, dropped down to the basement level. The earthquake set off landslides and 30 blocks of Anchorage were destroyed when the city's slippery clay substratum slid toward the sea.

Huge fissures opened in the outlying areas, and the greatest crustal deformation ever known took place. The area of destruction was estimated at 50,000 square miles, and the earthquake was felt over an area of half a million square miles (FIG. 10-10). The epicenter was beneath Prince William Sound some 65 miles southeast of Anchorage.

The ocean crust ruptured along an area, 500 miles long, parallel to the Aleutian trench. The seafloor in this area was thrust up an average of 10 feet, and in places, the vertical offset was as much as 30 feet. This generated large undersea waves, a giant tsunami, that struck the shores of the Kenai Peninsula and Kodiak Island.

In the port of Valdez, cargo was being unloaded from a ship when the earthquake struck. The shock caused the vessel to bob up and down, 20 to 30 feet, like a cork. Apparently the ship was not heavily damaged because it immediately set out to sea.

The port of Seward experienced a remarkable landslide as tons of shoreline slid into the bay. Oil tanks caught fire one by one in a chain reaction, and the skies were clouded with black smoke.

At Resurrection Bay, the water was disturbed by incredible turbulence as it rebounded from one side of the narrow inlet to the other. Thirty minutes after the initial shock, a 30-foot high tsunami picked up burning oil as it approached what was once the water front of Seward. In all, three waves hit the town and swept anything movable out to sea.

Kodiak suffered similar tsunami damage, but remarkably Anchorage, which had the greatest earthquake damage, was not hit by the tsunamis. The earthquake took 131 lives, destroyed a half billion dollars in property, and all but crippled Alaska's economy.

LATIN AMERICA

The mountainous spine that runs along the west coasts of Central and South America produces some of the shakiest ground in the world. In this century, at least two dozen earthquakes of 7.5 magnitude or more have taken place in Central and South America. In the last decade, Central America has seen two catastrophic earthquakes. One of 6.2 magnitude in Managua, Nicaragua (FIG. 10-11) destroyed 36 city blocks and killed 10,000 in 1972. The other of 7.5 magnitude hit Guatemala City, Guatemala in 1976 (FIG. 10-12), killing 23,000, injuring 77,000, leaving 1 million homeless, and causing $2 billion in property damages.

Because of its great length, running halfway along the Andes Mountain range, Chile seems to have received more than its fair share of earthquakes. In 1730 and again in 1751, Chile was shaken by enormous earthquakes. Spectacular ground movements were recorded at Riocamba during the earthquake of 1797. A major earthquake struck Valdivia and Concepcion in 1835. Concepcion was destroyed for a sixth time and Valdivia, Puerto Montt, and other ports were wrecked by an earthquake of 9.5 magnitude on May 22, 1960. Giant seismic sea waves raced across the coast, landslides wasted the countryside, and two dormant volcanoes came to life, all in an area of 90,000 square miles. Fifty thousand homes were destroyed and 5700 people lost their lives

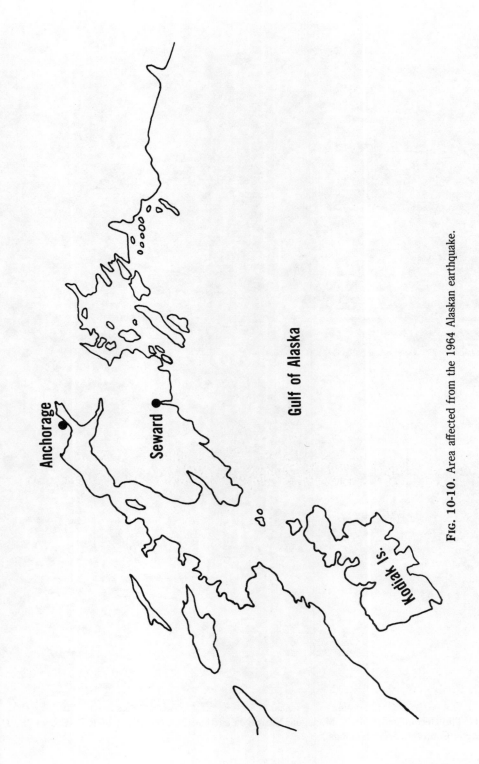

FIG. 10-10. Area affected from the 1964 Alaskan earthquake.

Fig. 10-11. The December 23, 1972 Managua, Nicaragua earthquakes. (Courtesy of R.D. Brown Jr., USGS, and EERI, Managua Conference Proceedings.)

FIG. 10-12. The 1976 Guatemala earthquake. (Courtesy USGS.)

Across the Pacific, Hawaii (FIG. 10-13), the Philippines, and Japan were hit with tsunamis 15 to 35 feet high, causing considerable death and destruction.

TANGSHAN, CHINA

In 1976, 15 major earthquakes struck around the world. Because of high population density, China has had both the largest and second largest earthquake tolls in recorded history. In a 12-year-period spanning 1920 and 1932, three major earthquakes struck population centers, killing a total of 450,000 people.

The city of Tangshan lies in northeast China, about 110 miles east of Peking (Beijing). Chinese seismologists prided themselves on their successful earthquake predictions, especially in a country that is highly prone to earthquakes. But the catastrophy at Tangshan (FIG. 10-14) somehow slipped through their seismological net. There were no indicators of impending disaster prior to the fact. If there had been indications, perhaps over half the population of 1.2 million people might have been saved.

Some of the most spectacular earthquake lights ever reported were seen at the time of the great Tangshan earthquake. Viewed from Peking, the lights lit up the sky like daylight in the vicinity of the earthquake. The lights were mainly red and white, and they were bright enough to awaken people. The lights were reported as far away as 200 miles from the epicenter.

One explanation for this eerie phenomenon (FIG. 10-15) is that a sudden release of built-up strain in rocks before a large earthquake, could generate stress on the quartz grains to produce the luminescences by what is known as the piezoelectric effect — the same effect that makes a phonograph needle convert vibrations on a record into electrical impulses. Another suggestion is that violent low-level air oscillations might transport a space charge that could set up temporary electrical imbalances in the atmosphere. A lot of what people claim as earthquake lights is nothing more than lightning in a heavy dust cloud. Scientists would like to learn more about pre-quake glows in order to help predict earthquakes.

FIG. 10-13. Tsunami damage of Hilo, Hawaii. (Courtesy of NOAA/EDIS.)

FIG. 10-14. The 1976 Tangshan, China earthquake. (Photos courtesy H.C. Shaw, J.M. Gere of Stanford U., and USGS.)

FIG. 10-15. Earthquake lights in Matsushiro, Japan. (Courtesy of T. Kuribayashi, USGS.)

MEXICO CITY, MEXICO

Our nearest neighbor to the south has been frequently hit by earthquakes, and earth tremors are so common that they are mostly ignored. This is especially true in Mexico City, which has been continuously subsiding for decades. At 7:18 on Thursday morning, September 19, 1985, what was called the gravest disaster in Mexico's history struck the Western Hemisphere's greatest metropolis of 18 million people (FIG. 10-16).

An earthquake whose epicenter was 220 miles west of the Capital and measuring 8.1 on the Richter scale was the most devastating ever to strike North America. So violent was the earthquake, that buildings trembled in Texas and water sloshed in Colorado swimming pools. Buildings in downtown Mexico City vibrated wildly with their walls and girders groaning from the extreme stress. Metal lamposts swayed and bent like rubber in the shuddering streets. Telephone and electrical wires snapped, windows shattered, and huge chunks of concrete broke off buildings and smashed to the pavement below.

The motion of the ground had a rippling effect. People rushed from their homes in panic, and the sky was darkened from the dust and smoke.

After three minutes, it was all over, and the ground felt oddly still. At least 250 buildings were leveled and the death count from the initial quake was estimated at 3000.

Thirty-six hours later, on Friday evening, another earthquake with a 7.6 magnitude struck Mexico City. Dozens of buildings, damaged earlier, collapsed completely, and workers had to stop in mid-search for victims trapped from the first devastation. More than 9000 people died in the catastrophe, over 30,000 were injured, and 95,000 were left homeless. Some 400 buildings crumbled in the two quakes, 700 others were severely damaged, and thousands of other structures suffered some damage. More than 200 schools were leveled or heavily damaged.

Surprisingly, most of the industrial plants remained intact, and subways, railroads, highways, and ports were soon back in operation. Reconstruction costs were estimated at $4 billion, a lot of money for a country that is reeling in debt. Mexico City, whose population grows by more than half a million yearly, appears to have been lucky this time. Had the earthquakes been one point higher on the Richter scale, making them 30 times more powerful, it might well have been the greatest tragedy in human history.

FIG. 10-16. The September 19, 1985 Mexico City earthquake. (Courtesy M. Celebi, USGS.)

FIG. 10-17. Collapsed buildings from the Mexico City earthquake. (Courtesy M. Celebi, USGS.)

11

Faults of the Earth

ARTHQUAKES are by far the most destructive, short-term natural forces on our planet. A glance at TABLE 11-1 will give an idea of the death toll arising from some of the major earthquakes in the past. In the last 500 years, about 3 million people have died in earthquakes and property damage has been astronomical. Whereas, volcanic eruptions are fairly localized, damage arising from earthquakes is widespread, covering areas thousands of square miles. Hundreds of thousands of earthquakes occur each year but, fortunately, only a few are destructive (TABLE 11-2). Earthquakes not only destroy whole cities, but their disruptive effects on the sociology and economy of a country can be devastating, leading to starvation, disease, and other secondary effects. As the world's population continues to grow, especially in the Third World countries which are barely holding their own as it is, a catastrophy arising from an earthquake could be monumental.

STRIKE-SLIP FAULTS

The mechanism for earthquake formation was poorly understood until after the 1906 San Francisco earthquake. The American geologist Harry Reid found that for hundreds of miles along the San Andreas fault (FIG. 11-1), fences and roads crossing the fault had been displaced by as much as 21 feet.

The San Andreas Fault is a 650-mile-long, 20-mile-deep fracture that runs northward from the Mexican border through Southern California. This large fault zone represents the separation of the North American plate from the Pacific plate.

During the San Francisco earthquake, the Pacific plate slid as much as 21 feet northward past the North American plate. During the 50 years prior to the earthquake, land surveys indicated displacements as much as 10 feet along the fault. Tectonic forces ever so slowly deformed the

	TABLE 11-1. Chronology of Major Earthquakes		
DATE	AREA	MAGNITUDE	DEATH TOLL
373 B.C.	Helice, Greece		
365 A.D.	Eastern Mediteranium		+5,000
478	Antioch, Turkey		30,000
856	Corinth, Greece		45,000
1042	Tabriz, Iran		40,000
1158	London, England		
1556	Shenshu, China		830,000
1596	Uryu-Jima, Japan		4,000
1692	Port Royal, Jamaica		+2,000
1737	Calcutta, India		300,000
1750	London, England		
1755	Lisbon, Portugal		60,000
1755	Boston, Massachusetts		
1757	Concepcion, Chile		5,000
1772	Java, Indonesia		2,000
1783	Calabria, Italy		
1803	Tokyo, Japan		200,000
1811	New Madrid, Missouri		<1,000
1812	Caracas, Venesuela		10,000
1822	Valparaiso, Chile		10,000
1835	Concepcion, Chile		5,000
1857	Tokyo, Japan		107,000
1857	Naples, Italy		
1857	Southern California		
1865	Lima, Peru		
1866	Peru and Ecuador		25,000
1872	Owens Valley, California		+30
1877	Ecuador		19,500
1883	Dutch Indies		36,000
1886	Charleston, South Carolina		
1891	Mino-Owari, Japan		7,000
1899	Yakutat, Alaska	8.6	
1902	Martinique, West Indies		40,000
1902	Guatemala		12,000
1906	San Francisco, California	7.9	+700
1906	Taiwan		1,300
1906	Valpariso, Chile		1,500
1907	Kingston, Jamaica		1,400
1908	Messina, Sicily	7.5	73,000
1915	Italy		29,000
1920	Kansu, China	8.6	180,000
1923	Tokyo and Yokohama, Japan	8.3	143,000
1927	China		200,000
1927	Tango Peninsula, Japan		3,000
1931	North Sea, England	8.0	
1932	China		70,000
1933	Long Beach, California	6.3	100
1935	Quefta, Pakastan		40,000

1939	Concepcion, Chile		50,000
1939	Erzincan, Turkey		23,000
1946	Aleutian Islands	7.4	
1946	Honshu, Japan tsunami		2,000
1949	Tadzhikstan, USSR		12,000
1949	Ecuador		6,000
1949	Seattle, Washington		
1952	Kern County, California	7.7	
1953	Greece		+3,000
1960	Agadir, Morocco	5.7	12,000
1960	Chile	9.5	+6,000
1962	Iran		12,200
1963	Skopje, Yugoslavia	6.0	1,200
1964	Anchorage, Alaska	9.2	131
1964	Niigata, Japan	7.5	
1966	Turkey		2,500
1966	Hsing-t'ai, China		
1967	Caracas, Venezuela	6.5	
1968	Iran		12,000
1970	Peru		67,000
1971	San Fernando, California	6.6	64
1972	Iran		5,400
1972	Managua, Nicaragua	6.2	12,000
1975	Liaoning, China	7.3	(Evacuated)
1975	Bucharest, Rumania		1,500
1976	Guatemala	7.5	22,000
1976	Tangshan, China	7.6	650,000
1976	Turkey	7.3	4,000
1977	Bucharest, Rumania	7.2	4,000
1978	Salonika, Greece	6.5	
1978	Miyogi, Japan	7.5	
1978	Eastern Iran		25,000
1980	Southern Italy		45,000
1981	Southeastern Iran		8,000
1982	Northern Yemen		3,000
1983	Coalinga, California	6.5	
1984	Morgan, California	6.1	
1985	Mexico City, Mexico	7.8	10,000
1986	San Francisco, California	5.3	

crustal rocks on both sides of the fault, which caused the displacements. All this time, the rocks were bending and storing up elastic energy in much the same way a wooden stick stores elastic energy when it is bent.

Eventually, the forces holding the rocks together are overcome and slippage occurs at the weakest point. That point of initial rupture is called the hypocenter or focus and it might be near the surface or deep below it. This displacement will exert strain further along the fault — where additional slippage occurs — until most of the built-up strain is released and, like a stick bent to its maximum, it snaps. The slippage allows the deformed

TABLE 11-2. Summary of Earthquake Parameters

RICHTER MAGNITUDE	SURFACE WAVE HEIGHT (feet)	LENGTH OF FAULT AFFECTED (miles)	DIAMETER AREA QUAKE IS FELT (miles)	NUMBER OF QUAKES PER YEAR	ENERGY OF QUAKE IN WATT-SEC
9	Largest earthquakes ever recorded — between 8 and 9.5				
8	300	500	750	1.5	4×10^{16}
7	30	25	500	15	8×10^{14}
6	3	5	280	150	4×10^{13}
5	0.3	1.9	190	1,500	8×10^{11}
4	0.03	0.8	100	15,000	4×10^{10}
3	0.003	0.3	20	150,000	8×10^{8}

rock to rebound to its original shape, like a stretched rubber band snaps back, when released.

As the rock elastically returns to its original shape, it releases heat generated by friction and produces vibrations called seismic waves. The seismic waves radiate from the hypocenter in all directions. The rocks do not always rebound immediately, but might take days or even years, and the seismic energy produced is then quite small. This slow process is called a seismic slip. Why the seismic energy is released violently in some cases and not in others is not well understood, but it probably has something to do with how freely the plates slide past each other.

DIP-SLIP FAULTS

Not all movements along faults is horizontal. Vertical displacements, where one side is positioned higher relative to the other, are also very common. Faults are classified by the relationship of the rocks on one side of the fault plane with the rocks of the other side (FIG. 11-2).

If the crust is pulled apart, one side slides downward past the other along a plane that is often slanted. This is known as a normal fault (FIG. 11-3), an historical misnomer, because this was once thought to be the way normal faults occur.

Actually, most faults are produced from compressional forces and this arises in what is called a reversed fault where one side is pushed above the other along a vertical or slanted plane. The 1964 Alaskan earthquake produced as much as 50 feet of vertical displacement at one location, forming a high scarp along the fault zone. If the reverse fault plane is nearly flat, and the movement is mainly horizontal for great distances, then it is called a thrust fault (FIG. 11-4).

If a large block of crust, bound by normal faults, is downfaulted it produces a long, trenchlike structure called a graben. If a large block of crust, bounded by reverse faults, is upfaulted it produces a long, ridgelike structure called a horst. Grabens and horsts are found in association (FIG. 11-5) and form long parallel mountain ranges and deep valleys like the Great East African Rift, Germany's Rhine Valley, and the Dead Sea Valley in Israel. If a fault is a combination of both vertical and horizontal movements, it becomes a complex fault system known as an oblique fault.

Vertical and horizontal offsets on the surface indicate that the crust is constantly readjusting itself. These movements are frequently associated with large fractures in the Earth. The greatest earthquakes are produced by sudden slippage along major faults, sometimes with offsets of tens of yards taking place in a few seconds. Most faults are associated with plate boundaries, and most earthquakes are generated in zones where huge plates are shearing past or abutting against each other.

Where the plates interact with each other, rocks at their edges are strained and deformed.

FIG. 11-1. The San Andreas fault. (Photos courtesy G.K. Gilbert, R.E. Wallace, USGS.)

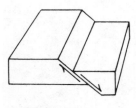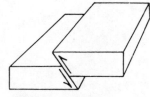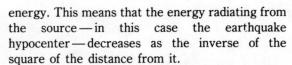

Normal   **Reverse**   **Strike Slip**

Fig. 11-2. Types of earthquake faults.

This interaction can take place near the surface where major earthquakes are produced or several hundred miles below where one plate is subducted under another. Some faulting takes place so deep that it leaves no surface expression. Earthquakes are frequently associated with volcanic eruptions, but their magnitudes compared to faulting are by far much weaker.

SEISMIC WAVES

Seismic waves have a wide range of frequencies and amplitudes, and these can provide basic information about the earthquake source. When a fault slips, the rupture process generally lasts between a fraction of a second for a minor earthquake and as long as five minutes for a major one. The waves generated by the fault's slippage can have periods ranging from years to less than a tenth of a second. The seismic waves with the longest periods correspond to the slow permanent deformation of the ground around the fault, or a seismic slip. The waves with the shortest periods actually fall within the low-audible range and are responsible for the rumbling noises people hear during an earthquake. The waves with periods of about an hour have a frequency that coincides with the resonant frequency of the Earth and causes the entire planet to ring like a bell. This ringing can last for weeks.

The amplitudes of seismic waves can range from a tiny fraction of an inch to tens of yards. The amount of deformation of the ground decreases with the distance from the earthquake and obeys the inverse-square law that applies to all wave energy. This means that the energy radiating from the source—in this case the earthquake hypocenter—decreases as the inverse of the square of the distance from it.

For instance, in the great Chilean earthquake of 1960, with a magnitude of 9.5, the total displacement in some places immediately adjacent to the fault ranged up to 70 feet. At Los Angeles, a quarter of the way around the world, the maximum displacement of the ground was less than a tenth of an inch. These displacements following an earthquake, are measured by seismometer or seismograph stations all around the world.

SEISMOGRAPHS

The earliest seismometer was invented by Chang Heng in China around A.D. 132. The instrument was a highly decorated copper jar, three feet across. It was ringed on top with eight dragon heads, each holding a ball in its mouth. Below each dragon was a frog with an upraised open mouth. Inside the jar hung a pendulum, like a bell clapper, so arranged that, if the ground shook, the pendulum would swing and knock out a ball that fell into the frog's mouth below. This would indicate the direction of the center of the earthquake. However, unless an earthquake was close enough to be felt, the instrument was not sensitive enough to be of much use for locating distant earthquakes.

In 1703, the Frenchman de Hautefeuille took the idea one step further and used a bowl of mercury with eight lips around its sides and little cups below the lips. The shaking of the ground would slop some of the mercury into one of the cups and

FIG. 11-3. Normal faults (upper). Step fault basaltic flow (lower). (Photos courtesy of A. Keith and W.E. Hall, USGS.)

FIG. 11-4. Thrust faults, Atachma Province, Chile. (Courtesy of K. Segerstrom, USGS.)

reveal the direction of the earthquake. Another similar device was a circular trough of wood with notches cut in the edge and filled with mercury. The earthquake would dislodge the mercury and the notch that flooded would indicate the direction of the tremor.

Unfortunately, these instruments, like their Chinese predecessor, were not very sensitive. Several other devices were invented for detecting earthquakes, most of which used bowls of varying sizes filled with water, colored liquid, or mercury. When an earthquake occurred, the vibrations would set up tiny ripples in the liquid. Some used a tiny boat with a long mast. As the boat floated on the liquid, ripples would be indicated by the swinging of the mast. Huge, pointed pendulums were suspended over bowls of sand so that their swing would make marks in the sand, showing the direction of the earthquake waves.

By the late nineteenth century, there were any number of clever devices, using clock mechanisms, flashing lights, or ringing bells, designed to

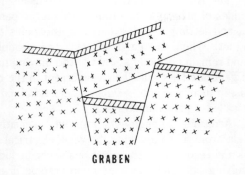

GRABEN

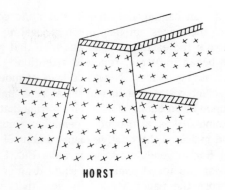

HORST

FIG. 11-5. Grabben and Horst faults. (Courtesy of H.E. Malde, USGS.)

tell when an earthquake struck. But none could measure the waves nor help much in locating the direction of the earthquake. It was then that pendulums began to attract renewed attention.

According to Isaac Newton's laws of motion, an object at rest tends to remain at rest, unless acted upon by an outside force. This means that, as the ground shakes, a suspended pendulum remains still and indicates the relative displacement of the ground. Earlier pendulum seismographs (FIG. 11-6) were unsatisfactory because the slight drag of the pen across the paper spoiled its sensitivity and accuracy.

In the mid 1880s, the English seismologist John Milne, who has been called the father of seismology, made a vast improvement by using a beam of light cast on photographic paper, thus dramatically reducing the friction. He also used moving record paper with clock signals inscribed alongside the wave marks to keep time. Nevertheless, Milne's instrument still did not have sufficient magnification and the timing was also inaccurate.

The Russian scientist Boris Galitzin hit upon the idea of placing a coil of fine wire on the pendulum and letting it swing between the poles of a magnet. When the earth moved, the pendulum would remain perfectly still while the moving magnet generated a small electrical current in the coil. This, in turn, powered a sensitive electrical indicator called a galvanometer.

Additional refinements improved sensitivity by electronically amplifying the weak electrical signals and recording them in various ways, including revolving pen and paper or photographic drums, and tape recorders. Instead of having the pendulum suspended down from a pivot, it was made to be supported in a horizontal position like a swinging gate. This dampened down its natural swinging and made the pendulum even more steady. In order to completely describe the nature of earthquake waves, the seismometers must be aligned in three axes: one vertical and two horizontal. A well-equipped seismograph station can track an earthquake taking place in almost any part of the world.

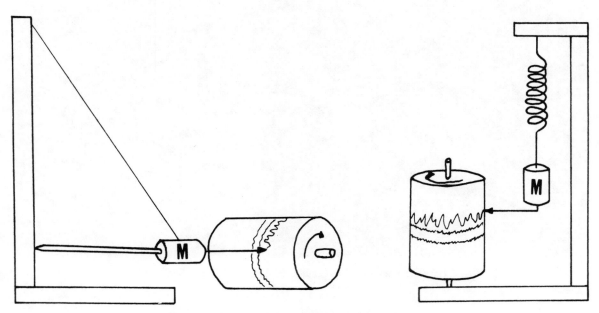

FIG. 11-6. Principal of modern seismometers.

TRAVEL-TIME GRAPHS

The record produced by the seismograph is called a seismogram, and it contains a great deal of information concerning the nature of seismic waves. However, deciphering that information is neither simple nor straightforward. The waves recorded on the seismogram are distorted after passing through the earth. The earth acts like a filter that distorts the seismic waves that are highly complex because the internal structure of the earth is complex, consisting of layers of inhomogeneous rock.

Because the earthquake source is usually deep underground, its seismic radiation cannot be "heard" first hand. A theoretical model is made that duplicates the effects that causes the distortion. This produces a travel-time graph (FIG. 11-7) that is used to specify the location of the hypocenter and the magnitude of the earthquake. Ap-

propriate travel-time graphs are produced for each seismograph station by accurately pinpointing an earthquake in relation to the station. The first travel-time graphs were further refined when seismograms from nuclear test explosions became available. With such tests, the time, location, and size of the detonation were accurately known.

The point on the ground directly above the hypocenter is called the epicenter. The epicenter of an earthquake is located by triangulation using three or more distant seismic stations. There are two general types of seismic waves that travel through the earth: (P) pressure or primary waves, and (S) shear or secondary waves. The S waves can only travel through the solid portions of the earth while the P waves can travel through the deep interior, including the lower mantle and the liquid core.

Because the S waves must take a round-about way from the earthquake center to a distant seis-

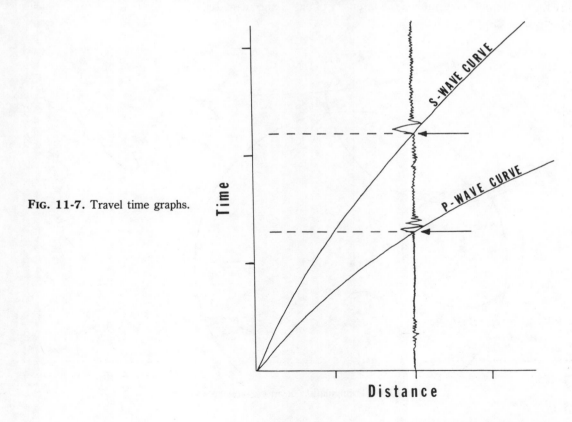

FIG. 11-7. Travel time graphs.

mograph station, they lag behind the P waves significantly. There is a complex relationship involved but, generally speaking, the greater the lag the greater the distance to the hypocenter. For instance, if the earthquake was 2000 miles away, the S wave could lag behind the P wave by as much as 4.5 minutes. By observing the difference in arrival times between the two types of waves, it is possible to calculate the distance of the earthquake from the station by using travel-time graphs.

When observations from three or more station are combined, the location of the earthquake can be determined. This is done by drawing circles on a map around each reporting station, the radius being equal to the distance to the earthquake's hypocenter. Where the circles intercept each other, at a single point, is the epicenter (FIG. 11-8).

THE MERCALLI SCALE

Early attempts to establish the intensity of an earthquake relied heavily on descriptions of the event. The problems with this method is that accounts varied widely, making an accurate assessment of the earthquake's intensity very difficult. In 1902, The Italian seismologist Giuseppe Mercalli devised a fairly reliable scale based on the amount of damage sustained by various types of structures.

A modified version of this tool was used by the U.S. Coast and Geodetic Survey and was called the Modified Mercalli Scale (TABLE 11-3). This scale is divided into 12 categories of intensity that range from the barely perceptible to total destruction. However, the destruction wrought by earthquakes is not an adequate means for comparison. Many factors — including distance from the epicenter, nature of the surface rocks, and building design — provide variations in the amount of damage. Consequently, methods were developed to determine the total amount of energy released during an earthquake; such a measurement is referred to as the magnitude.

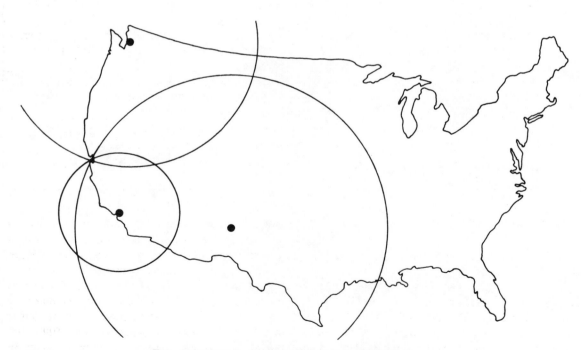

FIG. 11-8. Triangulation of an earthquake's epicenter.

TABLE 11-3. Modified Mercalli Scale of Earthquake Intensity

I	Not felt except by a very few, under especially favorable circumstances.
II	Felt only by a few persons at rest, especially on upper floors of buildings. Delicately suspended objects might swing.
III	Felt quite noticeably indoors, especially on upper floors of buildings, but many people do not recognize it as an earthquake. Standing automobiles might rock slightly. Vibration is like a passing semi-truck. Duration is estimated.
IV	Felt indoors by many, outdoors by few. At night, some awaken. Dishes, windows, doors rattle and walls creak. Sensation is like a heavy truck striking building. Standing automobiles rock noticeably.
V	Felt by nearly everyone, many awaken. Some dishes, windows, etc. broken. A few instances of cracked plaster. Unstable objects overturned. Disturbances of trees, poles, and other objects sometimes noticed. Pendulum clocks might stop.
VI	Felt by all. Many frighten and run outdoors. Some heavy furniture moved; a few instances of fallen or damaged chimneys. Damage slight.
VII	Everybody runs outdoors. Damage negligible in buildings of good design and construction; slight to moderate in well-built ordinary structures; considerable in poorly built or badly designed structures; some chimneys broken. Noticed by persons driving automobiles.
VIII	Damage slight in specially designed structures; considerable in ordinary substantial buildings, with partial collapse; great in poorly built structures. Panel walls thrown out of frame structures. Fall of chimneys, factory stacks, columns, monuments, and walls. Heavy furniture overturned. Sand and mud ejected in small amounts. Changes in well water. Disturbs persons driving automobiles
IX	Damage considerable in specially designed structures; well-designed frame structures thrown out of plumb; great in substantial buildings, with partial collapse. Buildings shifted off foundations. Ground clearly cracked. Underground pipes broken.
X	Some well-built, wooden structures destroyed; most masonry and frame structures destroyed with foundations; ground badly cracked. Rails bent. Landslides considerable from river banks and steep slopes. Shifted sand and mud. Water splashed over banks.
XI	Few Masonry structures remain standing. Bridges destroyed. Broad fissures in ground. Underground pipelines out of service. Earth slumps and slips in soft ground.
XII	Damage total. Waves seen on ground surfaces. Lines of sight and level distorted. Objects thrown upward into the air.

THE RICHTER SCALE

The most widely recognized measure of the strength of an earthquake is the scale of magnitudes developed by the American seismologists Charles Richter and Beno Gutenberg in the 1940s. The Richter scale (TABLE 11-4) is based on the notion that ideally the magnitude should be an absolute measurement of the total energy released by an earthquake and should not be affected by the location of the seismograph station nor the type of seismograph employed. This method for determining the magnitude of an earthquake is actually not all that difficult. The seismologist first measures the maximum amplitude of the ground motion with his seismograph. He then divides the reading by the degree of amplification used in his particular instrument to get a true value for the ground motion at the seismograph station. Then he makes an adjustment for the weakening of the seismic waves

TABLE 11-4. Earthquake magnitude and expected incidence		
RICHTER SCALE	EARTHQUAKE EFFECTS	AVERAGE PER YEAR
<2.0	Microearthquake Imperceptible	+600,000
2.0 to 2.9	Generally not felt but recorded	300,000
3.0 to 3.9	Felt by most people if nearby	49,000
4.0 to 4.9	Minor shock Damage slight and localized	6,000
5.0 to 5.9	Moderate shock Energy released equivilant to atomic bomb	1,000
6.0 to 6.9	Large shock can be destructive in populous regions	120
7.0 to 7.9	Major earthquake Inflicts serious damage. Recorded over whole world	14
8.0 to 8.9	Great earthquake Produces total destruction to nearby communities Energy released is millions times first atomic bomb	Once every 5-10 years
9.0 and up	Largest earthquakes	One or two per century

Note: The Richter scale is logarithmic; an increase of 1 magnitude signifies 10 times the ground motion and the release of roughly 30 times the energy.

as they travel from the hypocenter to the seismograph station and calculates back to the original amount of released energy. Although many widely scattered stations should get the same results, in practice, the magnitudes do vary slightly so an average magnitude is calculated from all reporting stations.

The Richter scale is logarithmic. Each step up the scale corresponds to an exponentially larger event than the step below. An increase of 1 magnitude signifies a 10-fold increase in ground motion, and, for all practical purposes, an increase of roughly 30 times the energy. Therefore, an earthquake with a magnitude of 7.5 releases 30 times more energy than one with a magnitude of 6.5, and roughly 900 times that of a 5.5 magnitude earthquake.

Almost a billion times more energy is released by a major earthquake of 8.5 magnitude than the smallest earth tremors felt by humans. This fact should dispell the notion that moderate earthquakes, such as those that often occur along the San Andreas fault, decreases the chances for the occurrence of a major earthquake in the same region. This is because it would take thousands of Earth tremors to release the same amount of energy equal to one great earthquake.

The problem with any scale that attempts to determine the magnitude of an earthquake is that the energy released from an earthquake is not a point source, like a single light bulb in a flashy Las Vegas casino sign, but extends along the entire length of the fault. This complicates matters considerably. As the rupture propagates over the surface of the fault, the point from which seismic radiation is being emitted moves and causes the seismic waves from one portion of the fault to interfere with waves from another portion. The shorter the period and consequently the larger the earthquake the more important this interference becomes.

In this century, about 60 earthquakes have been observed with magnitudes ranging between 8.0 and 8.7, and yet those earthquakes near the upper end of the spectrum might radiate vastly different amounts of seismic energy. What happens is that, for large earthquakes, the magnitude scale becomes saturated. This happens because the faults for large earthquakes are very long, and it takes much longer for the wave emitted from the farther end of the fault to reach the station than the nearer end. This makes for an underestimation of the actual size of some major earthquakes. This is why, in 1977, the 1964 Good Friday Alaskan earthquake was upgraded from 8.5 magnitude to 9.2, and the 1906 San Francisco earthquake was downgraded from 8.3 magnitude to 7.9.

GROUND MOTIONS

Generally, the most destructive earthquakes produce seismic wavelengths smaller than the dimensions of their faults. Ground motions are also strongly influenced by the rupture processes such as the speed the rupture travels over the fault surface, the frictional strength of the fault, and the drop in stress across the fault. The drop in stress during a large earthquake appears to be a constant, and is independent of the magnitude of the earthquake. This consistency probably arises from the similarity of physical properties of the rock materials within the fault zone, and the forces driving the lithospheric plates.

Because seismographs located near faults are highly disrupted or even destroyed during a large earthquake, short-period seismic waves that are responsible for most of the earthquake damage were not as well understood as long-period ones that can be studied from a safe distance. Rugged seismic instruments called accelerographs (FIG. 11-9) have been planted near many earthquake faults in California and elsewhere to measure the shorter earthquake wavelengths. The study of these wavelengths can help engineers design earthquake proof structures for those areas prone to large earthquakes.

The total amount of slippage accumulated from a number of earthquakes over a period of time allows scientists to estimate the velocity at which the tectonic plates bounding the fault are moving past each other. By comparing that velocity with the velocity computed by independent geological, magnetic, and geodetic evidence, it is possible to determine how much of the relative motion of the plates causes earthquakes and how much causes aseismic slip. It seems that in some areas such as Chile, which is noted for some of the worlds largest earthquakes, all the motion between plates is accomplished by earthquake slippage. In other regions such as the Marianas arc in the western Pacific, the motion is accomplished by long-term, steady aseismic slip.

EARTHQUAKE ZONES

Roughly 95 percent of the energy released by earthquakes is concentrated in a few narrow zones that wind around the globe (FIG. 11-10). The greatest amount of energy is released along a path located near the outer edge of the Pacific Ocean, and a belt that runs through the folded mountainous regions that flank the Mediterranean Sea and continues on through Iran and past the Himalayan Mountains into China. A continuous belt extends for thousands of miles through the worlds oceans and coincides with the mid-ocean rift systems. Earthquakes are also associated with landbound rift zones such as the 3,600 mile East African Rift.

At the eastern end of the Himalayan range lies perhaps the most seismically active part of the world. Here an immense seismic belt some 2500 miles long stretches across Tibet and much of China. For centuries, this area has been shaken by catastrophic earthquakes responsible for the deaths of millions. Since the turn of this century, more than a dozen earthquakes of 8.0 magnitude or greater have been recorded.

West of this belt, in the Hindu Kush range of North Afganistan and the nearby Russian Republic of Tadzhikstan, is the seat of many earthquakes of intermediate depth (100–150 miles). Three earthquakes in this century have had magnitudes of 8.0 or over. This is a notoriously active seismic belt with two thousand minor earthquakes registered annually, and in 1977, there were no less than six thousand.

From there, the Persian arc spreads in a wide

FIG. 11-9. A strong motion accelerograph. (Courtesy of USGS.)

sweep through the Pamir and Caucasus Mountains to Turkey. The eastern end of the Mediterranean is a jumbled region of plates in collision, providing rich ground for earthquakes. The whole of the Near East is inherently unstable attesting to the many earthquakes reported in Biblical times. The remaining regions surrounding the Mediterranean have been devastated by earthquakes since historic times.

Certain areas of the Earth are referred to as stable zones. Earthquakes can and do happen in these zones, although less frequently than the earthquake-prone areas. Principally, the stable zones are associated with shields composed of ancient rocks in the interior of continents. These stable zones include Scandinavia, Greenland, Eastern Canada, parts of northwestern Siberia and Russia, Arabia, the lower portions of the India subcontinent, the Indo-China peninsula, almost all of South America except the Andes Mountain region, the whole of Africa except the Rift Valley and northwestern Africa, and much of Australia. When earthquakes do occur in these regions, it might be because the underlying crust was weakened by

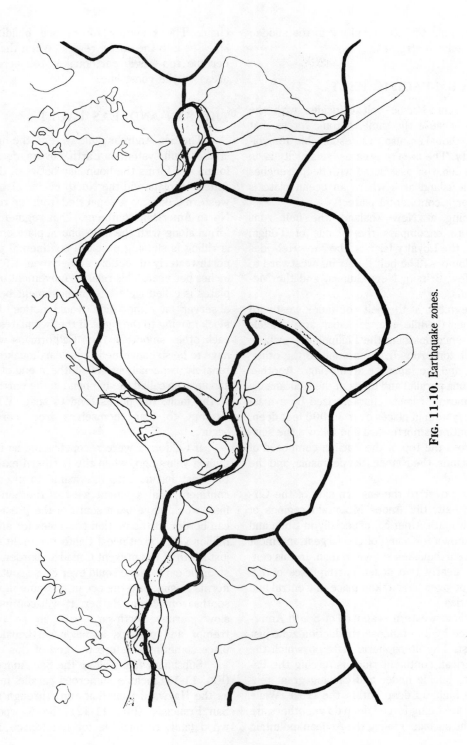

Fig. 11-10. Earthquake zones.

previous volcanic activity, resulting in the sudden release of pent-up stresses.

THE CIRCUM-PACIFIC BELT

The Circum-Pacific belt coincides with the ring of fire because the same tectonic forces that produce earthquakes also are responsible for volcanic activity. The area of greatest seismicity is on the plate boundaries associated with deep trenches and volcanic island arcs where an ocean plate is thrust under a continental plate.

Beginning at New Zealand, the belt runs northward to encompass the islands of Tonga, Samoa, Fiji, the Loyalty Islands, the New Hebrides and the Solomons. The belt then runs westward to embrace New Britain, New Guinea, and the Moluccas islands.

One segment of the belt continues westward over Indonesia while the principal arm travels northward, encompassing the Philippines — where a large fault zone runs from one end to the other — Taiwan, and the Japanese archipelago. Another inner belt runs parallel and takes in the Marianas, a string of volcanic islands characterized by a massive trench system in places over 30,000 feet deep. The belt continues northward and follows the seismic arc across the top of the Pacific, composed of the Kuril Islands, the Kamchatka peninsula, and the Aleutian Islands.

Crossing over to the eastern side of the Circum-Pacific belt, the Andes Mountain regions of Central and South America, especially in Chile and Peru, are known for some of the largest and most destructive earthquakes known to man. In this century alone, nearly two dozen earthquakes of 7.5 magnitude or over have taken place in Central and South America.

The whole western seaboard of South America is affected by an immense subduction zone just off the coast. The lithospheric plate on which the South American continent rides is forcing the Pacific plate to buckle under and causing great tensions to be built up deep within the crust. While some rocks are being forced deep down, others are pushed to the surface, raising the Andean mountain chain. The resulting forces are building great stresses into the entire region. When the stresses become too large, earthquakes roll across large areas on the coast line.

THE SAN ANDREAS FAULT

The San Andreas fault system, the most well-studied fault system on Earth, covers much of California and forms the boundary between the North American plate and the North Pacific plate. Southwestern California is separated from the rest of the North American continent. That segment of California along with the lithospheric plate on which it is riding is slipping past the continental plate in a northwesterly direction at between 1.5 and 2.5 inches per year. This relative movement of the two plates is called right-lateral movement because an observer on either side would notice the other block moving to the right. If the two plates slid past each other smoothly, then Californians would not have to be so concerned about earthquakes. Unfortunately, especially in the southern end of the fault and an area called the big bend in the northern part of the fault, the plates tend to snag. When they attempt to tear themselves free, earthquakes occur.

If California were reconstructed as it was 30 million years ago, when the northern extension of the East Pacific Rise first came to intercept the continent, that segment west of the San Andreas fault would have been south of the present Mexican border. If the motion continues for another 30 million years, southwest California might find itself just south of the present Canadian border. No catastrophic earthquake could ever cause southern California to sink into the ocean, as some modern-day soothsayers claim. Rather, it will continue on its slow journey northward with an an occasional tremor and perhaps a major earthquake taking place sometimes before the end of this century.

Subsidiary faults along the San Andreas Fault (FIG. 11-11) include numerous parallel faults such as the Hayward fault that runs through suburban San Francisco (FIG. 11-12), the Newport-Inglewood fault, responsible for the March 10, 1933

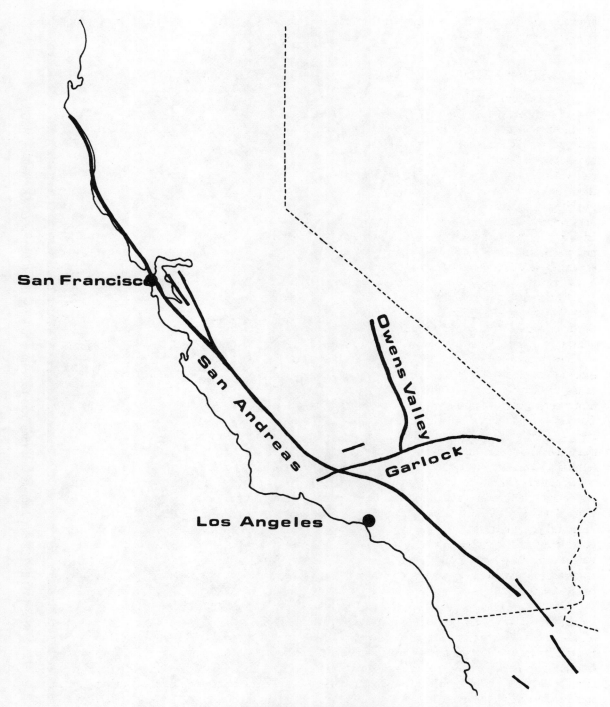

FIG. 11-11. The San Andreas and associative faults.

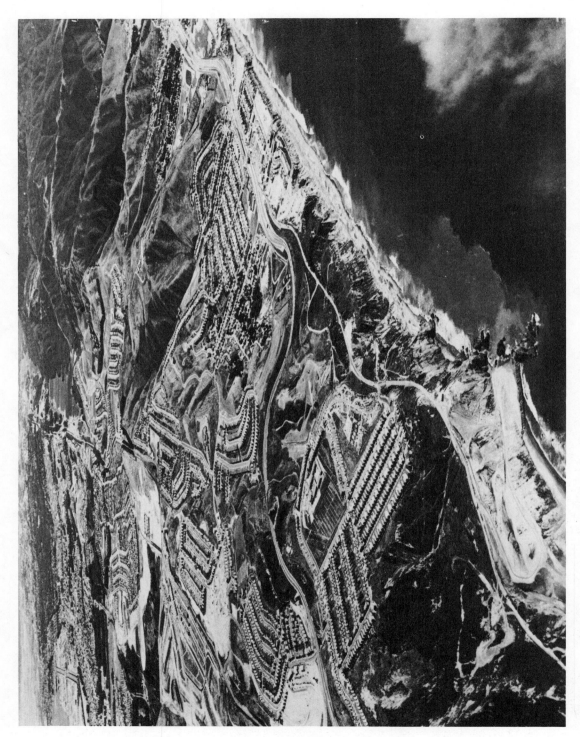

FIG. 11-12. The San Andreas fault runs from top center to lower left. (Courtesy of R.E. Wallace, USGS.)

FIG. 11-13. Early twentieth century California earthquakes. (Courtesy of NOAA/EDIS and USGS.)

FIG. 11-13. Early twentieth century California earthquakes. (Courtesy of W.L. Huber, NOAA/EDIS and USGS.)

Long Beach earthquake, and transverse faults such as an obscure fault that caused the 1971 San Fernando Valley earthquake of 6.6 magnitude northwest of Los Angeles. The Garlock fault, a major east-trending fault, was responsible for the July 21, 1952 Kern County earthquake of 7.7 magnitude.

Movement along this fault is left-lateral and combined with the right-lateral movement of the San Andreas fault is causing the Mojave Desert, to the south, to move eastward with respect to the rest of California.

The complex crustal movements associated

FIG. 11-14. The geologic provinces of the western U.S.

Fig. 11-15. The Wasatch Mountains of Utah. (Courtesy of R.R. Wooley, USGS.)

with these faults are responsible for most of the tectonic and geological features of California such as the Sierra Nevada and Coastal Ranges. Because a good many of the earthquakes are produced by these faults, California is indeed on shaky ground (Fig. 11-13).

OTHER CONTINENTAL FAULTS

The rest of the country is criss-crossed with faults mostly associated with mountain ranges, and 39 states lie in regions that are classified as having moderate to major seismic risk. The Basin and Range Province (Fig. 11-14) — including southern Oregon, Nevada, western Utah, southeastern California, and southern Arizona and New Mexico — is composed of numerous fault-block mountain ranges that are bounded by high-angle normal faults. The crust is broken into hundreds of pieces that have been tilted, rising 3000 to 5000 feet above the basin, to form nearly parallel mountain ranges 50 miles long.

The Wasatch Range of north-central Utah and south Idaho (Fig. 11-15) is an example of a north trending series of normal faults, one below the other, extending for 80 miles, with a probable net slip along the west side of 18,000 feet. The Tetons of western Wyoming, one of the most spectacular mountain ranges, were upfaulted along the eastern flank and downfaulted to the west.

The Rocky Mountains, stretching from Mexico into Canada, were created by the same mechanism of upthrusting connected with plate collision as the Andes of Central and South America. The upper Mississippi and Ohio River Valleys suffer frequent earthquakes, and the northeast trending New Madrid fault and its associative faults are responsible for two major earthquakes and numerous tremors. The Appalachian Mountains were produced by folding, faulting, and upwarping of sediments and have been the home of many earthquakes past and present. Finally, along the eastern seaboard, major earthquakes have hit Boston, New York, Charleston and other areas since Colonial days.

12

The Big Wave

SINCE ancient times, men have written accounts of the effects of earthquakes. The Roman philosopher Seneca (4 B.C.?–A.D. 65) wrote that the manner of shaking the Earth is of three types. Either it shakes from side to side, up and down, or a combination of the two, and at the same instance both rocks and lifts up the earth together. Man often thinks the ground beneath his feet is solid, and yet descriptions of the ground motion arising from major earthquakes should dispell any notions of the sort.

According to reports, the ground literally rolls like a swelling sea or shakes like a dog after a swim. Animals stand sideways to the motion with their legs spread wide apart. People are thrown to the ground where they lay spreadeagled to prevent themselves from being tumbled about while the earth heaves and tosses. People have a sensation of loosing their balance as if they were trying to stand up in a small boat during rough seas. The ground and buildings are heaved up and settle back down again. Trees sway from side to side. The earth opens up and closes again. Strange eerie lights glow from the ground. Loud roars are heard.

GROUND SHAKING

Ground shaking is a term used to describe the vibration of the ground during an earthquake. It is caused by surface waves and P and S waves, also known as body waves because they penetrate the body of the earth. The P and S waves vibrate fast but with small movement; therefore, they cause only minor damage to structures. P waves travel about 15,000 miles per hour and are the first waves to cause a building to vibrate in an up and down motion. S waves, traveling about 10,000 miles per hour, arrive next and cause the structure to vibrate from side to side. S waves are more damaging than P waves because buildings are more easily damaged from horizontal motion than vertical motion.

The majority of damage by earthquakes is caused by surface waves. Surface waves travel around the surface of the Earth with velocities that are slower than body waves and are the last to arrive (FIG. 12-1). There are two general types of surface waves. Rayleigh waves, named for the British physicist Lord Rayleigh who first described them in 1900, have motions in the vertical plane aligned in the direction of travel like waves caused by a pebble tossed into a pond. The other type of wave is Love waves, named for the British mathematician A.E.H. Love. Love waves, also called (L) or longitudinal waves, are transverse shear waves that vibrate the ground horizontally at right angles to the direction of the wave (FIG. 12-2). L waves produce the largest ground motions and make the most vivid scribbles on seismograph recordings. Some have been known to travel the Earth from end to end with such persistence that they were still recorded on seismographs after four or more days following a major earthquake.

Surface waves have much larger amplitudes and lower frequencies than body waves and are the cause of most of the direct damage done by earthquakes. Generally, the severity of the ground shaking increases as the magnitude of the earthquake

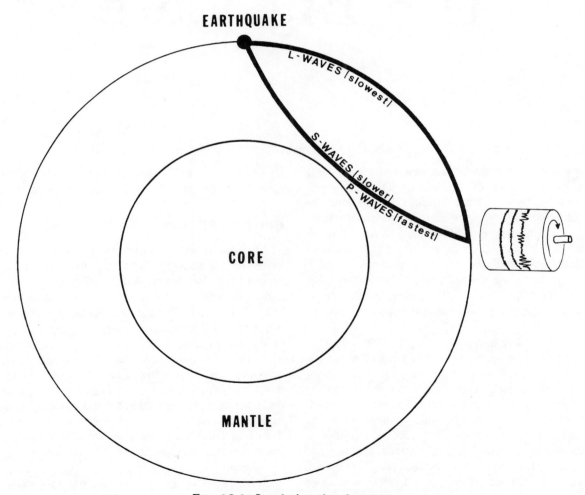

FIG. 12-1. Speed of earthquake waves.

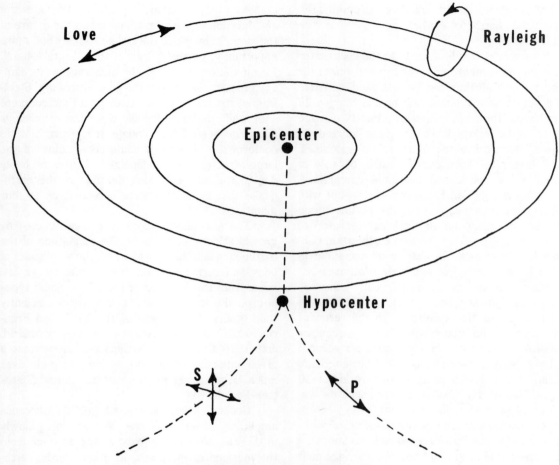

FIG. 12-2. Types of earthquake waves.

increases and decreases with distance from the hypocenter. Body and surface waves cause the ground and consequently a building to vibrate in a complex manner. If one part of the building is moved several inches in one direction while another part moves in a different direction, the building is easily damaged.

The building site will greatly affect the amount of movement that a structure experiences. Generally, structures built on bedrock will be damaged less severely than those built on less consolidated, easily deformed material such as natural and artificial fills. Therefore, it is the type of ground

that supports the structure that affects the amount of movement where soft sediments generally absorb the high-frequency vibrations and amplify the low-frequency vibrations. This only applies to earthquake wave damage and does not include the sometimes total destruction arising from an actual break in the ground or permanent displacement on the surface.

Earthquakes can also trigger landslides that are particularly damaging, especially on the coast. If there is an inactive volcano in the vicinity, it too could come alive. In addition, the length of time that the ground is in motion greatly affects the amount of damage done to buildings; generally, the longer the earthquake the more severe the damage.

Aftershocks, readjustments in the rocks after the main movement, and subsequent minor or moderate earthquakes can be just as destructive and finish off what the main earthquake started. In urban areas, the main causes of property damage due to major earthquakes are fires started by crossed electrical wires and broken gas lines. These fires often burn out of control because of broken water mains and disrupted communications. This is why San Francisco was rebuilt with duplicate water mains. If a rupture occurs in one line, the water can be shut off and rerouted to another. Since the San Francisco earthquake, California has been lucky in that most major earthquakes have occurred in relatively rural areas.

Man-made structures are particularly susceptible to earthquakes because the seismic waves have frequencies that coincide with the resonant frequencies of the structures. These frequencies range from a tenth of a Hertz (cycles per second) for large structures such as the Chicago Sears Building, the tallest building in the world, to 30 Hertz or higher for small structures such as systems of pipes in an industrial plant.

All buildings are inherently capable of withstanding large vertical forces of one or more gs (the acceleration of gravity) because they are built against the force of gravity, and their structural strength could well exceed the acceleration of gravity. But because the largest ground motions are usually in the horizontal plane, special precautions must be followed in "earthquake country" to ensure adequate resistance to large horizontal forces.

The study of the 1964 Alaskan earthquake gave scientists new insights into the role of ground shaking as a destructive force. As the energy released by an earthquake travels along the Earth's surface, it causes the ground to vibrate in a complex manner, moving up and down, similar to the motion of water in ocean swells, as well as side to side, similar to the way wave energy travels down a cracked whip. The amount of destruction attrib-

utable to the vibrations depends on the intensity and duration of the vibrations and on the nature of the material on which the structure rests but, more importantly, on the design of the structure itself. All multi-story buildings in Anchorage were damaged to some degree by the ground shaking. Steel-framed structures fared better than rigid concrete ones while the more flexible wood frame buildings fared the best. Even thought they were built to conform to California building codes, most of the large structures were damaged. This is probably due to the unusually long duration of the earthquake that lasted, by some accounts, up to four minutes.

The size of the geographic area affected by ground shaking depends on the magnitude of the earthquake and the rate at which the amplitudes of body and surface seismic waves diminish as distance from the hypocenter increases. Some types of ground transmit seismic energy more efficiently than others. Comparison of the 1906 San Francisco, 1971 San Fernando, 1811–12 New Madrid, and 1886 Charleston earthquakes shows that a given intensity of ground shaking extends over much larger areas in the Eastern United States (see FIG. 12-3).

Ground shaking affects a larger area because amplitudes of seismic waves decrease more slowly in the East than in the West as the distance from the hypocenter increases. In other words, earthquakes are felt over longer distances in the East than in the West. This indicates a substantial difference in the crustal composition and structure of the two regions. The East is composed of older sedimentary structures. In the West, the rocks are relatively young igneous and sedimentary rocks.

EARTHQUAKE SPECIAL EFFECTS

Earthquake lights have frequently been reported associated with earthquakes, and the luminosity often occurs in a dome-shaped pattern in the air close to the ground. Principally, they occur during the earthquakes, but they have also been observed before and after them. Sightings have been made on both land and sea and have been

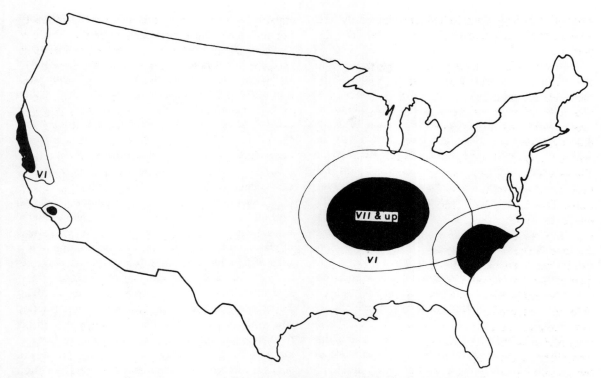

FIG. 12-3. Comparison between western and eastern U.S. earthquakes.

reported as far away as 275 miles. Earlier historic accounts attributed these ghostly lights to meteors or to the ignition of flammable vapors arising from fissures. Numerous accounts tell of fireballs rising from the ground and falling into the sea. The lights are associated with peculiar electric effects, and sheet lightning has often been seen shooting through the thick dust clouds produced by earthquakes.

There have been numerous reports of strange electrical activity before and during an earthquake. Some of the electrical arcs in modern times could also be attributed to crossed overhead electrical wires. There have also been reports of radio and magnetic disturbances. The lights apparently occur when friction at the fault line heats up a thin strip of rock that vaporizes water that forms an insulating barrier around the slipped section of the fault. The combination of rock shearing and water vapor-

ization generates an electric field responsible for the discharge of electricity. Scientists have been studying the electrical phenomenon with an eye on using them for predicting earthquakes.

The low grumbling noise caused by earthquakes is generally more often heard on hard ground rather than soft ground. In the cities, it is oftentimes difficult to distinguish ground noise from that of crumbling buildings. Sometimes, this noise takes the form of short explosions or a succession of bangs that has been mistaken for artillery fire. The noise can be a loud crackling sound like throwing gravel on a tin roof. Sometimes, there is a loud rushing sound like a strong wind blowing through trees. Other times there is a booming sound resembling thunder. Earthquake noises have been described preceding the tremor by as much as two weeks; such is the case of the 1976 earthquake in Turkey that killed 4000. More often than not, the earthquake is heard at the same time it is felt. The duration of these rumblings is generally short. The sound lasts only as long as the earthquake itself.

Atmospheric pressure waves produced by earthquakes can make a booming sound like thunder and can be heard for great distances. Sometimes, the pressure waves reach into the upper atmosphere. Scientists have shown that the 1968 Japan earthquake and the 1969 Kuril Island earthquake produced detectable effects on the Earth's ionosphere. Seismic surface waves traveling across the Pacific Ocean launched acoustic pressure waves that apparently traveled almost vertically upward through the atmosphere. These earthquakes correlated precisely when the ionosphere 210 miles above the Earth was observed to fluctuate vertically by about a mile. It seems reasonable to assume that large earthquakes release so much energy that their geophysical effects are felt globally.

Other effects indicative of underground disturbances near an earthquake include the rise or fall of water levels in wells. Some springs and fountains stop flowing altogether while others gush yellow or red water, having a sulfurous smell and a foul taste. The emission of sulfurous fumes and other odors during the 1835 Concepcion, Chile earthquake was so great that it blackened the water in the harbor. Steam, water, mud, and sand spouts have been reported ejecting material as high as the tops of trees. Earthquakes have been reported to temporarily dry up river beds such as when the River Thames dried up in the 1158 London earthquake. Lakes have overflowed their banks like sloshing water out of a bowl.

SEISMIC SEA WAVES

A wave of a different sort is produced when an earthquake occurs underwater. This creates what is known as a seismic sea wave or tsunami, a name given by the Japanese who have suffered a great deal from these waves. Actually, tsunami means tidal wave in Japanese, but the waves really have nothing to do with the tides. Most tsunamis are caused by the vertical displacement of the ocean floor, but many others arise from inland earthquakes, coastal and oceanic landslides, and volcanic eruptions, such as the 1883 explosive eruption of Krakatoa. This sets up ripples on the ocean much like those formed by tossing a pebble into a pond —only much greater. In the open ocean, the wave crests are up to 300 miles long and usually less than 3 feet high. The distance between crests is between 60 and 120 miles. Because of this, a tsunami has a very gentle slope and passes by practically undetected by ships or aircraft.

Tsunamis travel at speeds between 300 and 600 miles per hour. Upon entering shallow coastal waters, they have been known to grow into a wall of water up to 200 feet high. Most are only a few tens of feet high. As they touch bottom upon entering shallow water, especially in a harbor or narrow inlet, their speed decreases rapidly to about 100 miles per hour. This sudden breaking action causes the water to pile up, and the wave height is magnified tremendously. The destructive force is immense, and the damage it causes as it crashes to shore is awsome. Large houses and buildings often are crushed with ease, and sizable ships are sometimes cast up high and carried well inland.

JAPANESE TSUNAMIS

Japan is renowned for its tsunamis (FIG. 12-4) which, since time immemorial, have ravaged its coastline. In 1896, a tsunami was reported to have killed over 27,000 people. Over 1000 lost their lives to a tsunami in 1933. Devastating tsunamis have struck Japan at least 15 times in the last 300 years. Because earthquakes on the bottom of the ocean previously went undetected, the only warning of a tsunami was a rapid withdrawal of water away from the shore. Residents of coastal areas that have been hit by numerous tsunamis have learned to heed this warning and take to higher ground.

A few minutes after the retreat of water, there is a huge surge capable of extending hundreds of feet inland. In succession, each surge is followed by a rapid retreat back to the ocean.

FIG. 12-4. Japanese tsunami. June 16, 1964 in Niigata, Japan. (Courtesy of NOAA/EDIS.)

These waves, separated by intervals from 10 to 20 minutes, are able to traverse large stretches of the ocean before their energy is totally disipated.

THE LISBON TSUNAMI

The tsunami that followed the great Lisbon earthquake of 1755 was felt on both sides of the Atlantic Ocean. At Antigua in the West Indies 3,500 miles away, a wave of 12 feet was reported. Further west, on the Island of Saba, the sea rose 21 feet, and elsewhere in the West Indies, tides of 15 feet and more were reported from a number of places.

At Kinsale, on the southern coast of Ireland, 1000 miles from Lisbon, a large mass of water suddenly, without warning, poured into the harbor and swept away everything in its path. Up and down the south and west coasts of England and ports in Europe experienced waves 6 to 9 feet high. At the Spanish coastal town of Cadiz, 260 miles from Lisbon, a wave 60 feet high hurled itself upon the town. Over the lower parts of Lisbon, a wave 20 feet high swept over houses, destroyed bridges, and drowned hundreds of people. On the Island of Madeira in the Azores, great quantities of fish were left high and dry when the sea retreated. Many deaths were associated with this phenomenon when unwary villagers attempted to reap this unexpected bounty — only to lose their lives in the next wave.

THE HILO TSUNAMI

On coasts and islands where the sea floor rises gradually or are protected by shallow water reefs, much of the energy of the tsunami is spent before it reaches the shore. Hawaii is surrounded by very deep water, and submarine trenches lie immediately outside principal harbors. With the water shallowing rapidly, an oncoming tsunami builds to a prodigious height and pounds down on the unprotected shores of the Island.

Since 1819, more than 100 locally and distantly generated tsunamis have been recorded in Hawaii, 16 of which caused significant damage. In the aftermath of the great Aleutian Islands earthquake on April 1, 1946, a gigantic wave 100 feet high swept down on the lighthouse at Scotch Cap on the island of Unimak. Four hours later, the wave struck Hawaii 2000 miles away. The 4-foot wave grew suddenly to 55 feet and crashed down on the resort town of Hilo on the east side of the Island. The wave swept into the harbor, crushing everything in its path, and left behind a trail of destruction and 173 dead. It was the worst disaster in the Island's history and prompted research into the causes and methods of forecasting tsunamis.

Two years after the Hilo tsunami, the Seismic Sea Wave Warning System was established. This was the forerunner of an international network. Centered at Honolulu this network spans the entire Pacific to give warning of oncoming tsunamis.

THE CHILEAN TSUNAMI

The coasts of Chile have frequently been inundated with tsunamis throughout history (FIG. 12-5). The tsunami from the great Chilean earthquake of 1960 destroyed villages along a 500 mile stretch of coastal South America. Fifteen hours later it struck Hawaii. In Hilo, 15 to 35 foot waves caused $23 million in property damages and killed 61 people. The death toll could have been much greater had there been no warning. The tsunamis traveled over 10,000 miles across the Pacific to Japan. About 22 hours after the earthquake, considerable destruction was inflicted upon the coastal villages of Honshu and Okinawa, leaving 180 people dead or missing. In the Philippines, 20 people were killed, and coastal areas of the United States and New Zealand were damaged. For several days afterwards, tidal gauges, located in Hilo, were able to detect the waves as they bounced about the Pacific.

THE ALASKAN TSUNAMI

The 1964 Alaskan earthquake generated a tsunami that inflicted heavy damage to communities in the vicinity of the Gulf of Alaska (FIG. 12-6), completely destroying the town of Chenega. Kodiak was also heavily damaged and most of its fishing fleet destroyed when the tsunami carried

FIG. 12-5. The 1868 Chilean tsunami. (Courtesy of Rear Admiral Billings, US Navy, NOAA/EDIS.)

FIG. 12-6. The 1964 Alaskan tsunami, Valdez, AL. (Courtesy of R.W. Lemke, USGS.)

FIG. 12-6. The 1964 Alaskan tsunami, Valdez, AL. (Courtesy USGS.)

many vessels into the business district. The tsunami killed 107 people, while only 9 people died directly from the earthquake damage in Anchorage. The tsunami destruction extended along much of the West Coast of North America, causing more than $100 million in damage.

In spite of one hour's warning, 11 people perished in Crescent City, California. The first wave to hit the city was about 13 feet high and was followed by three progressively smaller waves. People thinking that the tsunami was over returned to the shore to begin cleaning up. They were met by the fifth and most devastating wave, which crested about 20 feet high and caused $7.5 million in property damage.

This was not the first time a great tsunami has hit the California shores. The 1812 earthquake off of Santa Cruz Island was associated with the largest tsunami ever reported in California. The wave was reported to have reached as much as 50 feet high at Gaviota, California, 30 to 35 feet high at Santa Barbara, and 15 or more feet high at Ventura. The 1927 Point Arguello earthquake produced waves of about 7 feet high in the nearby coastal area.

TSUNAMI WATCH

Seismic sea wave reporting stations, administered by the National Weather Service, are stationed in various parts of the Pacific. The Pacific region is responsible for about 90 percent of all recorded tsunamis in the world. When an earthquake of 7.5 magnitude or over occurs in the Pacific area, the epicenter is ploted and the magnitude is calculated. A tsunami watch is then put out to all stations in the network. Also notified are the military and civilian authorities (FIG. 12-7).

Each station in the network detects and reports the sea waves as they pass in order to monitor the progress of the tsunami. From this data, it is possible to calculate when the wave is likely to reach the many populated areas at risk around the Pacific. A tsunami produced by an earthquake in Alaska would reach Hawaii in six hours, Japan in nine hours, and the Philippines in 14 hours (Fig. 12-7). A tsunami originating off the coast of Chile

FIG. 12-7. The August 16, 1976 tsunami on Mindinao Island, Philippines. (Courtesy of R.E. Wallace, USGS.)

would reach Hawaii in 15 hours and Japan in 21 hours. Such warning is plenty of time to take necessary precautions.

Unfortunately, the unpredictable nature of tsunamis causes many false warnings that result in areas being evacuated unnecessarily or residents ignoring the warnings altogether. This happened on May 7, 1986 when a tsunami predicted for the West Coast from the 7.7 magnitude Adak earthquake in the Aleutians, for some reason, failed to arrive. People ignored a similar tsunami warning in Hilo in 1960 at the cost of their lives.

There is not much that can be done to prevent damage from tsunamis, but given the advance warning time, coastal regions can be evacuated successfully with minimal loss of life. This is not so with ground shaking that often strikes like a thief

FIG. 12-8. Earthquake building damage. (Courtesy NOAA/EDIS and USGS.)

in the night. Evacuation in most cases might be impractical, even if a warning is given, and might result in more deaths from traffic jams than the earthquake itself. The only other practical alternative is to construct earthquake-proof structures that can withstand minor earthquakes with little or no damage, moderate earthquakes with only minor damage, and provide a degree of safety in large earthquakes — even though the building is heavily damaged.

EARTHQUAKE PROOF CONSTRUCTION

In earlier times, houses of simple construction, that looked as though the wind could blow them over, survived the most powerful earthquakes. Ancient civilizations living in earthquake-prone areas learned how to protect themselves by constructing simple dwellings.

Ancient Japanese houses consisted of a light framework put together without struts or ties, with all the timbers crossing at right angles. The beams were filled inside with interwoven bamboo plastered with mud and rested on large square rocks buried on the ground. When an earthquake struck, the effect on the buildings was like shaking a giant wicker basket.

In South American communities, buildings were constructed with a solid lower story built of stone and an upper story of light wood and walled with rushes or cane. These structures were able to stand the test of time, but as man's accommodations have become more sophisticated and materials used more complex, earthquake damage has become a serious and expensive problem (FIG. 12-8).

Most large urban centers of today are a combination of the old and the new. Modern structures blend in with hundred-year-or-older buildings, some whose foundations have weakened through time. As space becomes a premium, architects and engineers are forced to reach upward with towering blocks of masonry that dominate the skyline. Economics becomes a major factor and, to save money, designs and materials might not always strictly conform with building codes.

Certain buildings must be able to withstand a major earthquake. Structures such as physical plants, hospitals, and schools are vital to the community. The ability of buildings to withstand ground shaking depends on the type of ground it is sited on, its design, its orientation with respect to the shock wave, the type of materials used, the quality of workmanship, and above all, the nature of the shock.

A short, sharp high-frequency shock, lasting for only a few seconds is comparatively easy for an engineer to combat. Two- to four-story buildings are most vulnerable to this type of shock while taller buildings might escape unscathed. A longer, lower frequency shock, lasting for a fraction of a minute or longer, is a different matter entirely. If a multi-story building is not engineered right, the whole structure could come tumbling down to the ground while lower buildings are practically untouched.

For many years seismologists, engineers, and scientists from other disciplines have put forth theories on earthquake-resistant construction and design. Their theories were put to the test during the early morning 1971 San Fernando earthquake of 6.6 magnitude and 60 second duration (FIG. 12-9). One-story houses performed better than those of two or more stories. Whether floors were constructed of wood or concrete slabs made little difference. Braced or reinforced brick chimneys survived consistantly better than unbraced ones. Newer houses survived, on the whole, better than older ones, and flimsy built mobile homes often suffered damage.

Schools failed to stand up to the tremors, but luckily classes had not yet started. The freeways were twisted and contorted, and newly constructed overpasses collapsed. Had the Lower Van Norman Dam, badly damaged during the earthquake, actually given way, many of the 80,000 people asleep below could have drown. This could have become the most catastrophic event in the history of the United States.

Before the 1971 San Fernando earthquake, building codes were calculated on the premise of a probable maximum acceleration of 10 percent of

FIG. 12-9. The February 9, 1971 San Fernando, California earthquake. (Courtesy NOAA/EDIS.)

gravity for a moderate-size earthquake. When it was discovered that accelerographs in the San Fernando Valley showed that some buildings were exposed to accelerations equal or greater than the force of gravity, it became obvious that the codes were inadequate.

If an earthquake, even a moderate one, struck, then buildings would be subjected to forces five to ten times stronger than those allowed for in the original specifications. Another problem is that the longer the duration, the more likely the tall buildings would resonate and start to swing. Therefore, a building designed for a short-duration earthquake could be devastated. Luckily, geologists know where most of the active faults are located. Engineers will know at least in what direction the seismic waves are likely to come from and structures can be orientated accordingly with the long axis parallel to the expected ground motion.

The type of building construction determines a great deal how well a structure survives an earthquake. Steel-framed buildings, having strength combined with a degree of flexibility, and are light in mass are likely to suffer little damage. Concrete buildings with few door or window openings that tend to weaken the structure are also likely to survive well.

Unreinforced hollow concrete block structures and ancient brick buildings generally are heavily damaged. Overweight roofs might cause the building to become top-heavy. Balconies and parapets are very dangerous to people in the streets below. For this reason, experts suggest that people remain indoors during an earthquake rather than rush into the streets. To make room for packed cars underneath, many modern buildings are propped up on concrete pillars with little or inadequate cross-bracing. Such a structure is doomed to fail in all but the slightest tremor.

Working in cooperation, Japan and the United

States in 1979 set up a program to validate the integrity of structures designed for earthquake-prone areas. Full-scale experiments were carried out at the Building Research Institute in Tsukuba, Japan with tests simulating the lateral displacement, or shaking, that might occur with ground acceleration motions similar to those measured in actual earthquakes.

Lateral movement, usually greatest in the top floors, was achieved by pushing against a seven story test structure with hydraulic jacks, simulating the inertial forces experienced in a 15-second earthquake. The worst damage was caused by a sway of more than 13 inches. This caused severe cracking on major load-bearing walls. The worst damage was successfully repaired by injecting epoxy resin into cracks and buttressing or replacing damaged steel bars in the concrete. When the tests were repeated, the repairs appeared to have restored much of the building's original integrity.

Earthquake-proof construction is still a relatively new technology, but certain basic rules have been known for some time. Unreinforced concrete or masonry buildings are among the most vulnerable structures and wood-framed, single-story houses are among the safest.

There are two schools of thought concerning multi-story steel-framed buildings. Many American engineers believe that the buildings should be designed as flexible as possible. Japanese engineers prefer the buildings to be as rigid as possible. The Japanese point to a major earthquake that hit Sendai, Japan in 1978. This earthquake left most rigid buildings unscathed. Skyscrapers with flexible skeletons, while they might remain standing through an earthquake, have the added hazard of wrenching violently out of plumb, and furniture, and other loose objects are sent crashing against walls, windows, and people.

One innovative design to maximize safety during an earthquake has the building resting on giant shock absorbers. This type of construction is not new. The giant Minuteman missile silos and command centers rest on springs to prevent damage due to a near-miss in a nuclear attack.

Unfortunately, 80 percent of California's new high-tech firms, with billions of dollars worth of equipment and materials at risk, are housed in so-called "tilt up" buildings. With this design, concrete walls are poured in forms flat on the ground and are then tilted up like playing cards — a disaster just waiting to happen. The Japanese, showing much more awareness of the problem, spend $3 billion annually on earthquake protection the United States budgets only about $7 million.

When the next big earthquake comes, and it surely will within the lifetimes of most Americans alive today, it will take its measure in death and destruction. It is not the earthquake itself that kills and mames, but the buildings that fall on people. Therefore, an earthquake is a man-made disaster.

13

Future Shock

THE forecasting of impending catastrophy is an ancient and respected art as old as man himself. Earthquake prediction was a constant preoccupation for early soothsayers, astrologers, and prophets. Indeed, there are many instances recorded in history of destructive earthquakes having been forecast. Many of the predictions of natural phenomenon came true probably because those making them were highly attuned to their environments and made their predictions based on past experience. Also, animals became frightened, excited, or acted strangely just before an earthquake.

Many predictions are ineffective because people are strangely reluctant to believe in empending disaster. The 1042 earthquake in Tabriz, Iran was predicted by the chief astrologer. No matter how hard he tried to convince the townspeople to leave they simply would not listen. As a result, 40,000 people lost their lives when the earthquake did strike. Little is different today. Although scientists point out the hazards of building on active faults, buildings are still going up on dangerous ground.

AREAS AT RISK

FIGURE 13-1 shows the locations of some of the world's major earthquakes. At present, there are hundreds of geologists, geophysicists, and seismologists — mainly in the United States, Soviet Union, Japan, and China — actively engaged in research into earthquake prediction. Most of these investigators believe that such a goal is attainable; others are more skeptical.

There are even those who feel that the side effects of prediction might be worse than the benefits and that efforts should be abandoned altogether. There is also the "cry wolf" syndrome. If a prediction proves to be false, people might ignore any further warnings. The economic, social, and political factors involved complicate matters so that decisions are not entirely based on scientific studies. This exemplifies many of the problems that face modern society.

Nevertheless, earthquake prediction is still a highly desirable goal in light of a major earthquake

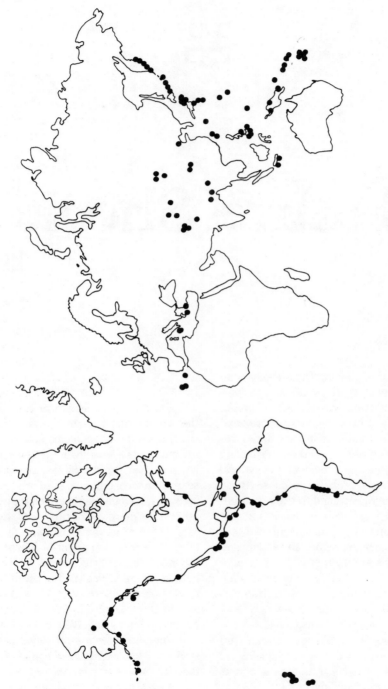

FIG. 13-1. World map showing the locations of some of the major earthquakes.

occurring in an urban area, costing the lives of tens of thousands of people and billions of dollars in property damage. If Japan, which is now a prosperous world economic leader, should suffer an earthquake similar to the one that destroyed Tokyo and Yokohama in 1923, it could cause a collapse of its economy and throw the country into bankruptcy from which it might not recover for some time.

The United States has been much more fortunate because most of the earthquakes have occurred in the sparsely populated West (FIG. 13-2). California is an exception. The third largest state has the highest population of any state in the Union. California also has the distinction of being the most earthquake-prone area in the continental United States. The center for many of the nation's crucial high-tech industries, California has some 10 percent of the nation's human and industrial resources. Some 85 percent of these are in a strip of 21 counties along the continental margin that are well within the seismic domain of the San Andreas fault.

"Silicon Valley" in Santa Clara County in Northern California manufactures one-forth of all the nation's semiconductors used in electronic equipment. During the 1906 San Francisco earthquake, Santa Clara County suffered severely.

The northeastern United States is even more heavily populated and has a substantial portion of the nation's manufacturing facilities. Based on occurrences of earthquakes in the past, the Northeast is also a seismic-risk area. This places one third of the nation's population and much of its industry in two regions of highest risk (FIG. 13-3).

Scientific investigations indicate that predictions of strong earthquakes could be made many years in advance, and methods for making short-term predictions of weeks, or even days, could also be developed. It should then become possible to devise a remedial policy that could greatly reduce casualties and lower property damage. The long-range prediction could encourage the strengthening of existing structures in the threatened area as well as motivate authorities to revise and enforce building and land-use regulations.

The short-term predictions could mobilize disaster relief operations and set in motion procedures for the evacuation of weak or flammable structures, such as older buildings, and other hazardous areas. The shutdown of hazardous facilities, such as nuclear power plants, petroleum distillation plants, and natural gas pumping stations — along with the evacuation of areas below dams and low-lying coastal areas subject to floods and tsunamis — could also follow a short-term prediction.

EARTHQUAKE FORECASTING

What is needed is earthquake prediction similar to weather forecasting. Generally, severe earthquakes cause more damage to urban areas than hurricanes, tornadoes, or floods. In this endeavor, it is important that a number of earthquake precursors are found, with each based on a different physical measurement. Confidence in prediction is enhanced when it is based on several independent lines of evidence.

In the late 1960s, the Soviet scientists A.N. Semenov and I.L. Nerseov startled the seismological world by announcing their discovery of variations in the velocity of seismic waves, changes in electrical resistivity of rocks in the fault zone, and an increase in the content of the radioactive gas radon in deep water wells just before earthquakes occurred in the Tadzhikistan, Tashkent, and Kamchatka regions. Therefore, physical parameters of the rocks in faults, such as electrical resistivity, seismic wave velocity, and the amount of deformation could be monitored just as temperature, pressure, and cloud formation are monitored to predict the weather.

Changes in the volume of crustal rock in the focal region can be observed on tiltmeters, sea-level gauges, and repeated ground surveying over the fault line. In parts of Japan and China, historic records dating back hundreds of years indicate changes in the water level of lakes, rivers, or the ocean that might be related to the same phenomenon. Changes in water level, turbidity, and temperature in deep wells can be observed both visually and with instruments.

Observing the radon gas content of well

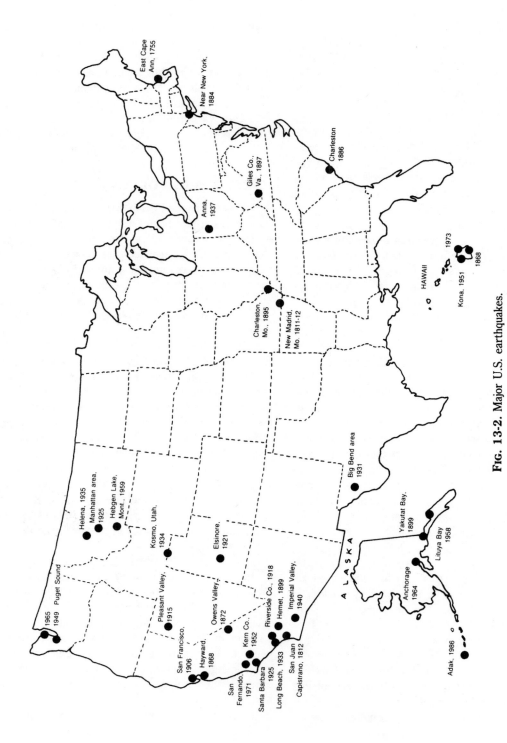

FIG. 13-2. Major U.S. earthquakes.

Major U.S. earthquakes:

East Cape Ann, 1755
Near New York, 1884
Charleston 1886
Giles Co., Va., 1897
Anna, 1937
1973
1868
Kona, 1951
HAWAII
Charleston, Mo., 1895
New Madrid, Mo. 1811-12
Big Bend area 1931
Helena, 1935
Manhattan area, 1925
Hebgen Lake, Mont. 1959
Kosmo, Utah, 1934
Elsinore, 1921
Pleasant Valley, 1915
Owens Valley, 1872
Riverside Co. 1918
Hemet, 1899
Imperial Valley, 1940
Kern Co., 1952
Long Beach, 1933
San Juan Capistrano, 1812
Santa Barbara 1925
San Fernando, 1971
Hayward, 1868
San Francisco, 1906
Puget Sound
1965
1949
ALASKA
Yakutat Bay, 1899
Lituya Bay 1958
Anchorage 1964
Adak, 1986

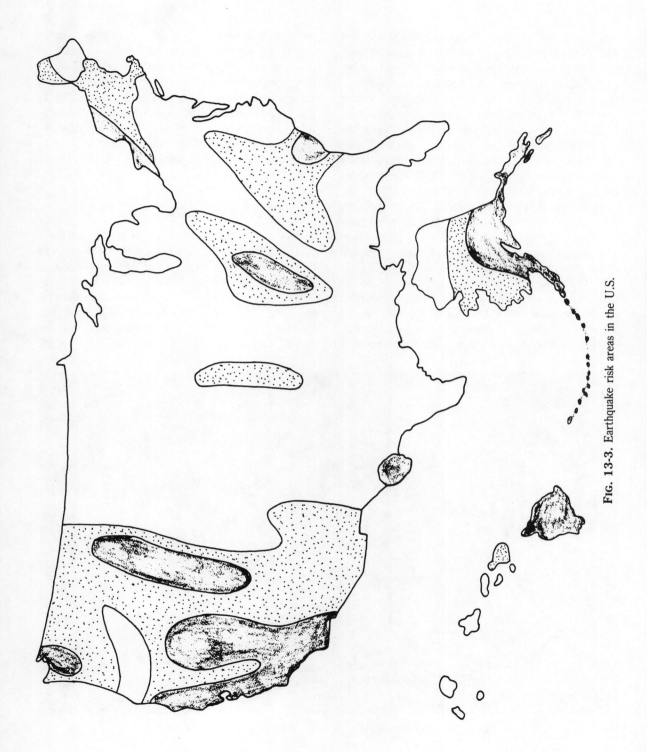

FIG. 13-3. Earthquake risk areas in the U.S.

water, a technique used extensively by the Soviet Union and China, also seems to be a sensitive indicator of forthcoming seismic activities. This is because as rocks begin to rupture, they release trapped radon gas, that is a radioactive daughter product of uranium, into the water table. Other indicators include changes in resistivity along the fault that is measured by feeding an electrical current into the ground at two points several miles apart. Voltage changes between two intermediate points can be observed if the resistivity of the intervening crustal rocks changes. Magnetometers on the earth's surface (FIG. 13-4) can detect minute changes in the magnetic field in the focal region and gravity meters (FIG. 13-5) can detect upward movements of the crust.

The plate-tectonics model explains the occurrence of major earthquakes along faults consisting of the boundaries of the Earth's great crustal plates. Combining this information with earthquake statistics makes it possible to predict earthquakes by identifying particularly dangerous areas, establishing an earthquake record for an earthquake prone area, and estimating the relative danger. Averaged over a sufficiently long period of time, the sum of the various slippages or displacements along faults such as aseismic slip, fault displacement accompanying earthquakes, and inelastic deformation such as crustal folding must equal the total amount of displacement between the two plates.

EARTHQUAKE CYCLES

Geologic fingerprints are left by previous earthquakes in the strata around the San Andreas fault, dating back as long as 20 million years ago. As a result of past earthquakes, old stream channels on one side of the fault can be found offset on the other side (FIG. 13-6). By measuring the amount of displacement and radiocarbon dating the strata, a relative magnitude and date can be ob-

FIG. 13-4. Magnetometer. (Courtesy of E.F. Patterson, USGS.)

FIG. 13-5. Gravimeter. (Courtesy of USGS.)

estimated to be between 2 and 5 percent per year, or about 50 percent in the next 20 to 30 years.

Seismically active regions have many more small-to-moderate earthquakes than large ones. In California, large earthquakes—such as the great quake of 1857 along the southern San Andreas fault—have occurred in the past on the average every 150 years or so. Moderate earthquakes occur about every 22 years and numerous small earthquakes occur yearly. Periods of calm before a strong shock are frequently observed. Seismic activity is at a minimum and then increases dramatically just before the main shock. The pattern of radiation of seismic waves, as shown on seismographs strategically placed around faults, reflects the stress field building up in the crust.

In central Asia, Soviet investigators have found that the stress pattern shown by the small tremors is random during the calm period, but becomes highly organized beginning three to four months before the main shock. Also, the compressional stresses become aligned in the same direction as that of the forthcoming shock. The best evidence of this phenomenon are the swarms of small earthquakes, or foreshocks, preceding the 1975 Haicheng earthquake in China. The swarms began two months before the main shock, and the positions of the tremors seemed to move along a belt several hundred miles long. Geodetic (ground survey) measurements also indicated that strain was accumulating along the fault.

EARTHQUAKE MODELS

Two principal models have been proposed to explain the geophysical observations prior to an earthquake. The dilatancy-diffusion theory is supported by most American scientists and the dilatancy-instability theory is supported by the Soviets and Chinese, with a few American and Japanese adherents. When a rock is squeezed, it deforms and eventually breaks. Just before it breaks it swells, owing to the opening and extension of tiny cracks. The increase in the volume of a rock due to stress is a property known as dilatancy, and begins when the stress reaches about half the breaking strength

tained. This produces a 1400 year record in which 12 large earthquakes occurred. The interval between earthquakes is between 50 and 300 years, and the average interval is roughly 150 years.

It has been nearly 130 years since the last great earthquake on the southern end of the San Andreas fault. Moreover, the rate at which strain accumulates along the fault is roughly 1.5 inches per year; thus, the total strain is about 15 feet and this could generate an earthquake of 7.5 or greater magnitude anytime. This information was incorporated into a prediction of the Geological Survey prepared for the National Security council. In that analysis, the probability of an earthquake of magnitude 8.3 along the southern San Andreas fault is

FIG. 13-6. Stream offset over the San Andreas fault. (Courtesy of R.E. Wallace, USGS.)

of the rock.

Both models begin with a stage in which elastic strain builds up in a fault. In the next stage, small cracks open in the rocks of the strained portion of the fault and the volume increases. This stage marks the real beginning in earthquake precursory phenomenon because the open cracks change the physical properties of the rock. There is a drop in seismic velocity (the ratio of velocities between P and S waves) and an increase in electrical resistivity if the rock is dry and a decrease if the rock is wet. Water flow through the rock increases. Therefore more radon gas enters the water table.

In the American model, the number of small tremors decreases prior to an earthquake because the cracks, as they increase in number, causes the rocks to squeeze out water in the fault zone and the rocks for a short while become less slippery. Consequently, sliding friction increases and actually inhibits faulting.

In the third stage, the two models differ markedly. In the American model, water diffuses back into the dilatant region and raises the pore pressure in the cracks, weakening the rock to the point where small tremors increase in number with the main shock soon to follow. In the Soviet model, water plays no role at all. Instead, a avalanchelike growth of cracks leads to instability and rapid deformation of the rocks. The stresses partially drop in the region surrounding the zone of unstable deformation, cracks partially close, and the rock recovers some of its original characteristics. This sequence of events accounts for the increased seismic velocity, the decrease in volume, and other changes in the physical properties of the rocks. The developing instability finally gives way to faulting and the main shock ensues. In both American and Soviet models, stress is released by the earthquake and the rock recovers most of its original properties.

It appears that large earthquakes could provide warning times on the order of 10 years or more. The magnitude of the predicted earthquake is dependent on the duration of the precursor anomalies. For instance, an event with a magnitude of 5.0 on the Richter scale has an anomaly lasting for about four months. A major earthquake of 7.0, which has about a thousand times more energy, could be preceded by an anomaly beginning several years before the event. The discovery that the size of an earthquake, as well as its location and timing is predictable, should be important for land-use planning. Also, the larger the magnitude of the forthcoming earthquake the longer the lead time available for making plans to combat its effects. Unfortunately, nature does not always act according to plan. Although there might appear to be plenty of time to make preparations, the earthquake could still strike when it was totally unexpected.

So far only a handful of earthquakes have been successfully predicted before the fact. Several times that many have been "predicted" after the fact by going back over the data and finding the precursory signals. It is difficult to know how many formal predictions, based on the methods described have failed, because studies have only been made in the last couple of decades and the science is not yet perfected. Therefore, it might be too early to base a worldwide earthquake watch on the rudimentary knowledge scientists have gained thus far. Although the major earthquake belts extend for tens of thousands of miles, only a small fraction of that distance is adequately instrumented to test prediction methods. With the pooling of data being gathered in various parts of the world, tests of the validity of prediction methods are constantly being evaluated.

INSTRUMENTATION

The leading agency for earthquake prediction in the United States is the Geological Survey. In central California, the Geological Survey has installed a network of stations equipped with seismometers and tiltmeters in the region of the San Andreas fault. Magnetic and electrical observations are also conducted but to a much lesser degree.

In Southern California, a large number of instruments were installed in a joint effort between the Geological Survey and Cal Tech. Data from these arrays are telemetered into Menlo Park and Pasadena on telephone lines and microwave transmitters. In 1984, these instruments registered no less than 10,000 tremors. This ability to pinpoint earthquake locations and monitor precursory velocity changes, tilts in the crust, magnetic fluctuations, and changes in electrical resistivity is paying off. In 1974, a 5.0 magnitude earthquake struck 10 miles north of Hollister in central California. The tremor was preceded by distinct tilt changes, magnetic fluctuations, and seismic velocity changes. Even though the earthquake was successfully predicted, it was not made public prior to the fact — much to the seismologists' chagrin. Moreover, the most damaging California earthquake of 1984, registering 6.2, occurred at the right place with the right magnetude as forecast, but it struck totally without giving warning signs.

The instrumentation also includes several networks of laser distance-ranging devices. A change in the length down the sides of a triangle yields a measure of the crustal stress along a line, and a change in the area enclosed yields a volumetric measure of the crustal strain. These distance measurements are accurate within about half an inch over a line of about 20 miles long. Vertical strain in the crust corresponds to changes in the elevation of the land, as measured directly by standard survey methods and indirectly by determining the local strength of the Earth's gravitational field.

Geodetic measurements from satellites (FIG. 13-7) might also offer measurements of horizontal movement of crustal blocks precisely enough for earthquake prediction. A considerable effort has been spent to develop reliable, inexpensive instruments that will measure strain continuously at a single point on the Earth. Unfortunately, the near surface is so noisy — caused by seasonal variations in temperature, rainfall, fluctuations in barometric pressure, and fluctuations in the water table — that a widely deployed strain instrumentation might not be feasible.

One instrument that is capable of continuous measurement of strain is called a creep meter.

Another is called a bore-hole strain meter (FIG. 13-8). What these instruments show is that parts of Southern California are rising by as much as 4 inches yearly. This displacement of that large a volume of crust suggests a great earthquake might be imminent.

EARTHQUAKE RESEARCH PROGRAMS

Substantial research programs investigating the prediction of earthquakes are under way in China, Japan, and the Soviet Union. The United

FIG. 13-7. Satellites could one day help predict earthquakes. (Courtesy of U.S. Air Force.)

FIG. 13-8. Borehole seismometer. (Courtesy of USGS.)

interpret the signals of strain accumulating in the Earth with an eye to understanding the earthquake process.

Many potentially important methods — such as arrays of wells that monitor water level and radon gas content, networks of resistivity sensors, magnetometers, and gravity meters, sea-level gauges, and advance surveying techniques — are being tested. In addition, a few studies are being conducted in other earthquake prone areas outside of California. It seems that with thousands of lives and billions of dollars worth of property at stake, a program such as this would be highly cost-effective.

In the Soviet Union, the earthquake prediction program is centered at the Institute of Physics of the Earth in Moscow. Their program involves laboratory and field measurements comparable to that in the United States. The Soviet field experiments are the longest running thus far, dating back 30 years. The impressive discovery of anomalous precursors stems from these efforts. The strategy of the Soviet investigators is somewhat different from that of the United States. Several experimental sites are being monitored in central Asia and Kamchatka with a number of instruments spread over a wider area. The United States has a high density of instruments mostly located in the San Andreas fault region.

The Soviet Union is exploring other prediction methods and new techniques. Whether their concepts work any better remains to be seen. What is important is that a lively exchange of ideas pertaining to earthquake prediction is taking place between the two countries. This provides a wider base of study that neither country could accomplish on its own.

Since the turn of the century, Japanese earth scientists have been devoted to earthquake prediction, for obvious reasons (FIG. 13-9). Nevertheless, a formal research program did not get under way until 1965. For years, reports of anomalous changes in tilt and sea level prior to earthquakes have come out of Japan. Unfortunately, the data was so sparse and of low quality that Western scientists mostly ignored it. Now it seems that

States currently spends some $17 million annually on earthquake prediction and another $43 million on research programs including work on earthquake-hazard assessment, engineering of buildings to resist earthquakes, and studies of the fundamental nature of earthquakes. Progress on short-term prediction has been slow. On the other hand, progress in long-term prediction and the understanding of how earthquakes occur has been substantial. Now more than ever, the aim is to learn to

FIG. 13-9. The June 16, 1964 Niigata, Japan earthquake. (Courtesy of NOAA/EDIS.)

some of these reports must have described actual precursory phenomenon.

The Japanese program emphasises surveys every five years, extending over 12,000 miles. Observatories are equipped with strain detectors and tiltmeters. Observations of the levels of seismicity, changes in seismic velocity, and magnetic and electrical phenomenon are also under way. Cooperation between Japan and the United States in this field is also quite close.

Following the 1966 destructive Hsingtai earthquake in the province of Liaoning, China has embarked on a highly aggressive earthquake prediction program. Over 10,000 scientists, engineers, and technicians are actively engaged in the program. In addition, over 300,000 volunteer helpers watch for earthquake precursors. Many of these amateur earthquake watchers build their own equipment as well as operate professional instruments in remote areas. Animals have also been observed for peculiar behavior patterns, but the Chinese admit that their animal data are questionable and might be worthless. China also has an extensive educational program.

The Chinese have made successful predictions involving the evacuation of people from their homes. In 1975, removing people from the area of the Haicheng earthquake in Liaoning province saved countless lives. Unfortunately, an evacuation did not take place prior to the earthquake that struck at Tangshan a year later and killed a reported 650,000 people. This earthquake was not preceded by any known precursory phenomenon and goes to show that earthquake prediction in China, as elsewhere, is still not a certitude. Nevertheless, progress is being made in China on a more intense level, involving more people and equipment. This amount of effort will eventually pay dividends in lives saved. China could easily become a world leader in earthquake prediction. It is through international cooperation that the rest of the world could benefit as well.

DAMAGE PREVENTION

No matter how you make them predictions cannot prevent earthquakes. What is needed is a comprehensive program to reduce the vulnerability of society to destructive earthquakes. Unlike earthquake prediction, about which there is a good deal of optimism, but so far no guarantee of success, research and development in other areas such as earthquake engineering, risk analysis, land-use regulation, stricter building codes, and disaster preparedness is bound to result in reduced casualties and lowered economic losses. Earthquake engineering deals with the efficient and economic design of structures that might be subjected to ground shaking. Included is the alteration of existing structures to improve their performance in an earthquake. Residences, commercial buildings, schools, hospitals, dams, bridges, and power plants should be closely examined for weaknesses that could prove fatal to the community in the event of an earthquake.

Even if structures could withstand the ground shaking, there is also the added hazard of foundation failure causing buildings to topple over due to the ground giving way underneath them. This was dramatized in Anchorage during the 1964 Alaskan earthquake where a layer of clay below the city liquified, causing the ground to slide towards the sea. Severe ground shaking can cause certain types of soils to settle or liquify, thereby losing their ability to support structures. This phenomenon is poorly understood, but it is an important aspect of earthquake engineering. When it is better understood, it might be possible to take countermeasures such as draining the effected area or institute land-use regulations that would limit construction on vulnerable soils, along active faults, in potential landslide areas, or in coastal zones that are subject to tsunamis.

Risk assessment is a new and important part of earthquake research. It asks the question, to what degree — in an area given a probability of strong earthquakes — are the added costs of safer construction offset by the potential saving of life, property, and productivity. Experience has shown that people cling to an area for various reasons no matter how hazardous it is. More often than not, cities are located where they are for their climate, economic importance, strategic defense, and recreational facilities.

When cities are destroyed by natural or man-made disasters, they are rebuilt on the same site for the exact same reasons they were built there in the first place or simply because it is home. Forcing people to move off their land is not always a good practice and generally causes more problems than it solves. Taking all these factors into consideration, including the hazards of fire and flooding, they are combined in an overall assessment of the risk on which decisions are based on land-use and construction practices in earthquake-prone cities.

As a result of state legislation and state and federal funding, an experimental effort called the Southern California Earthquake Preparedness Project, or SCEPP, was established in 1980. The purpose of the project was to develop plans for using predictions effectively to reduce the social and economic impact of earthquakes, for responding to unpredicted earthquakes, and for guiding recovery from an earthquake.

Mechanisms for distributing information about the likelihood of earthquakes were developed. Panels of earth scientists from the Geological Survey and the California Division of Mines and Geology will assist in judging the scientific validity of a prediction. The responsibility for carrying out emergency plans for impending danger or a destructive earthquake rests with the Federal Emergency Management Agency, FEMA, and the State Office of Emergency Services. The Geological Survey put out two earthquake "watches" similar in scope to tornado watches in the Midwest. One was for a large magnitude earthquake in Southern California and the other for a moderate earthquake in the Mammoth Lakes region of eastern California. The latter warning was actually followed by a series of earthquakes of magnitudes 5 and 6.

Earth scientists are gaining confidence in their ability to make long-term predictions of earthquakes. The next steps will be the development of integrated systems of measurement and rapid, automated data collection and analysis, and to apply this analysis to the complexities of crustal deformation. The conversion of long-term predictions into short-term predictions, and thence into warnings will pose difficult problems.

The long-term evidence indicates that a major earthquake is imminent, yet the short-term geophysical parameters remain essentially unexplained and confusing. They could be precursors of an earthquake or they could be normal fluctuations in the crust; scientists do not have enough experience to say for sure. In China some predictions have been correct, but there have also been many failures. Like weather forecasting, earthquake forecasting might not be an exact science, but at least it is better than nothing at all — or is it?

One of the most serious objections is that

FIG. 13-10. Nuclear bomb crater. (Courtesy of U.S. Department of Energy.)

mass panic might occur as a result of a warning of an impending earthquake and, especially in the big American cities, more people could die from traffic jams trying to flee the danger than the actual earthquake. China was successful in evacuating Haicheng, in 1975, simply because their society is more rigidly controlled and regimented, and the evacuation was conducted in an orderly manner without loss of life or undue hardships. Such an evacuation would be difficult, if not impossible, in the United States because of the independent nature of the American people. Studies have shown many weaknesses in evacuation programs for nuclear war.

If a city was evacuated following an earthquake warning, and the earthquake failed to appear, officials would be subject to accusations and recriminations and many lawsuits would result from such action. The public might not listen to another warning and fail to take precautions such as shutting down hazardous industrial plants which could prove fatal if an earthquake did strike.

CONTROLLING EARTHQUAKES

The possibility of controlling or modifying earthquakes came about quite by accident. Between 1962 and 1966, studies of seismic activity were conducted at the Rocky Mountain Arsenal. The Arsenal produces materials for nuclear and chemical weapons outside of Denver, Colorado. For a period of 80 years prior to 1962, the U.S. Coast and Geodetic Survey reported that no significant earthquake activity was located in the Denver region. In 1962, the arsenal started to dispose of wastes from its chemical warfare production into a 12,000-foot well. During the period of fluid waste injection from April 1962 to September 1965, about 700 microearthquakes were reported, with 75 intense enough to be felt.

It was believed that the injection water under pressure lubricated a nearby fault that had been building up strain over the years. This lubrication effect is not one of making rocks along the fault zone slippery. Instead, the water exerts an outward force directed perpendicular to the fault plane. The induced outward force opposes the natural inward force caused by the weight of the overlying rocks and the fault slips. When the injection was halted for about a year, there was a marked drop in seismic activity. As pumping resumed again, so did the tremors.

Other earthquakes caused by human activity have occurred in regions adjacent to large reservoirs like Lake Mead on the Arizona-Nevada border. Ever since the lake was filled in 1936, hundreds of small tremors have been recorded. They are thought to have been caused by the added weight of the lake, which causes the crust to bulge slightly. Fault slip might also be aided by the lubricating effect as water percolates into the substratum. A large reservoir in India is believed responsible for triggering a disastrous earthquake in which 200 people lost their lives. Underground nuclear explosions (FIG. 13-10) have also been responsible for initiating numerous small aftershocks. None has been as great as the explosion itself.

Laboratory and field experiments have shown that injection of fluid into a fault zone reduces frictional resistance by decreasing the effective normal stress across the fault. In a sense, fluid injection serves to weaken the fault; fluid withdrawal could strengthen it. If a preexisting stress is present, an earthquake could result if a fault was unlocked by fluid injection. In a remarkable field test of these ideas, workers from the Geological Survey injected and withdrew fluids in a water injection well in the Rangely oil fields in northwestern Colorado. It was found that they could switch seismic activity on and off at will. These results could be extended to include control of major faults such as the San Andreas in Southern California. This could reduce the threat of a major earthquake by triggering numerous small earthquakes by fluid injection or small nuclear explosions. Such methods would slowly and continually release the elastic strain that might otherwise build up and be released as a high-magnitude earthquake.

The problems with earthquake control are numerous. It takes thousands of minor tremors to equal the energy released by a single, strong earthquake. To the citizens living in the area, this constant, artificially induced shaking of the ground could become quite unnerving. Not all faults are shallow and accessible by present-day drilling technology, as most are in California. Also, drilling in fault zones is difficult and precarious where the fractured rock causes numerous cave-ins and loss of drill rod (making the venture highly expensive). The worst problem is that tampering with dangerous faults might just cause the very same earthquake that the scientists were trying to prevent in the first place.

14

Losing Ground

WHEN Mount St. Helens erupted in 1980, a wall of earth slid down the mountain in what was called the greatest landslide in modern history. The valley below was filled with debris measuring 5 miles by 4 miles.

A wall of mud from the flanks of the Nevado del Ruiz volcano swept through Armero, Columbia in 1985, burying 22,000 people. Soil-flow failures caused by the 1920 Kansu, China earthquake killed an estimated 180,000 people. As the tremor rumbled through the region, immense slides rushed out of the hills, burying and carrying away entire villages, damming streams, and turning valleys into instant lakes.

In the 1964 Alaskan earthquake, landslides and ground subsidence caused the greatest damage to man-made structures. The ground beneath Valdez and Seward gave way and both waterfronts floated toward the sea, taking with them the lives of 31 people. In Anchorage, landslides caused $50 million in damage and houses were destroyed when 200 acres were carried toward the ocean. The destruction was so complete that the area was bulldozed over and made into a park, appropriately named "Earthquake Park."

The 1971 San Fernando earthquake unleashed nearly 1000 landslides, distributed over a 100-square-mile area of remote hilly and mountainous terrain.

In Italy, on the night of October 9, 1963, a torrent of water, mud, and rocks lunged down a narrow gorge, shot across the wide bed of the Piave River and up the mountain slope on the opposite side, completely demolishing the town of Longarone and killing 2000 of its inhabitants. This was a nonearthquake produced landslide and it was called history's greatest dam disaster. Yet, when it was all over, the Vaiont Dam was still intact.

One side of the dam was supported by Mounte Toc, nicknamed by the local inhabitants "the mountain that walks." Regardless of assurances by engineers concerning its safety and expensive efforts to stabilize the slopes, the mountain not only walked that night — it galloped. About 600 million tons of the mountainside slid instantaneously into the new reservoir that was only half filled with water. The water was forced 800 feet above its previous level, and one great wave rose 300 feet above the dam and dropped into the gorge below. Constricted by the narrowness of the gorge, the water increased its speed tremendously and snatched up tons of mud and rocks as it raced on its destructive journey.

LAHARS

Kelut Volcano on Java has a deep crater lake that has been blown out from time to time by volcanic eruptions. In 1919, such an outburst created a large mudflow that killed 5000 people. In November 1985, a similar eruption of Nevado del Ruiz killed some 26,000 people in Columbia.

Lahars is an Indonesian term for mudflows arising from volcanic eruptions (FIG. 14-1). They are masses of water-saturated rock debris that move down the slopes of the volcano in a manner resembling the flowage of wet concrete. The debris is commonly derived from masses of loose unstable rock deposited on the flanks of a volcano by explosive eruptions.

The water is provided by rain, melting snow, a crater lake, or a lake or reservoir adjacent to the volcano. Lahars can also be induced by a pyroclastic or lava flow moving across snow causing it to rapidly melt. Lahars can be either hot or cold, depending on whether hot rock debris is present. The speed of the lahars depends mostly on their fluidity and the slope of the terrain and sometimes move distances of 50 miles or more down valley floors at speeds exceeding 20 miles per hour. Lahars might even travel greater distances than pyroclastic flows, and can run as far as 60 miles from their sources.

Losses from lahars decrease rapidly as the

FIG. 14-1. Lahar from 1980 Mount St. Helens eruption. (Courtesy of J. Cummans, USGS.)

height above the valley floor increases and gradually as distance from the volcano increases. Human beings and structures can be swept away by the vast carrying power of the lahars. Lava flows that extend into areas of snow or glacial ice might induce melting and cause floods as well as lahars. Flood-hazard zones extend considerable distances down some valleys. For some volcanoes in the western Cascade Range, these zones can reach as far as the Pacific Ocean.

LIQUEFACTION

The term used to describe the physical process that produces ground failure during earthquakes and violent volcanic eruptions, is called liquefaction. This phenomenon is restricted to certain geologic and hydrologic environments, mainly areas where sands and silts were deposited within the last 10,000 years and where groundwater is within 30 feet of the surface. Generally, the younger and looser the sediments and the higher the water table, the more susceptible the soil.

Liquefaction causes clay-free soils, primarily sands and silts, to temporarily lose strength and behave as viscous fluids rather than solid material. It takes place when seismic shear waves pass through a saturated granular soil layer that distorts its structure and causes some of the void spaces to collapse in loosely packed sediments. Each collapse transfers stress to the pore water surrounding the grains.

Disruptions to the soil generated by these collapses increases pressure in the pore water and causes drainage to occur. If drainage is restricted, then there is a buildup of pore-water pressure. When the pore-water pressure reaches the pressure exerted by the weight of the overlying soil, grain contact stress is temporarily lost and the granular soil layer flows like a fluid for a short time.

There are three types of ground failure associated with liquefaction, lateral spreads, flow failures, and loss of bearing strength. In addition, liquefaction enhances ground settlement or subsidence. Sometimes there are sand boils that are fountains of water and sediment that spout

from the pressurized liquefied zone and can reach several tens of feet high. Sand boils are caused by water laden with sediment that is vented to the surface by artesianlike water pressures develop during the liquefaction process. Sand boils could also cause local flooding and the accumulation of large amounts of silt and sand in the most unlikely areas.

Lateral spreads involve the lateral movement of large blocks of soil as a result of liquefaction in a subsurface layer and takes place in response to ground shaking (FIG. 14-2). Lateral spreads generally develop on gentle slopes, most commonly less than 6 percent. Horizontal movements on lateral spreads commonly are as much as 10 to 15 feet, but where slopes are particularly favorable and the duration of the ground shaking is long, lateral movement might be as much as ten times greater. Lateral spreads usually break up internally. Numerous fissures and scarps are formed and damage is seldom catastrophic.

During the 1964 Alaskan earthquake, more than 200 bridges were damaged or destroyed by lateral spreading of flood plane deposits near river channels. These spreading deposits compressed bridges over the channels, buckled decks, thrust sedimentary beds over abutments, and shifted and tilted abutments and piers.

Lateral spreads are also destructive to pipelines. In the 1906 San Francisco earthquake, a number of major pipeline breaks occurred that hampered firefighting efforts. Therefore, it was the inconspicuous ground-failure displacements, as much as 7 feet, that were largely responsible for the destruction of San Francisco.

The most catastrophic type of ground failure due to liquefaction are flow failures, consisting of liquefied soil or blocks of intact material riding on a layer of liquefied soil. These failures commonly move several tens of feet and — under certain geographical conditions — they can travel tens of miles at speeds as great as many tens of miles per hour.

Flow failures usually form in loose saturated sands or silts on slopes greater than 6 percent and originate on both land and underwater. The 1920 Kansu, China earthquake induced several flow fail-

TABLE 14-1. Summary of Soil Types

Climate	Temperate (humid) >160 in. rainfall	Temperate (dry) <160 in. rainfall	Tropical (heavy rainfall)	Arctic or desert
Vegetation	Forest	Grass and brush	Grass and trees	Almost none, no humus development
Typical area	Eastern U.S.	Western U.S.		
Soil type	Pedalfer	Pedocal	Laterite	
Topsoil	Sandy, light colored; acid	Enriched in calcite; white color	Enriched in iron and aluminum, brick red color	No real soil forms because no organic material; chemical weathering very low
Subsoil	Enriched in aluminum, iron, and clay; brown color	Enriched in calcite; white color	All other elements removed by leaching	
Remarks	Extreme development in conifer forest abundant humus makes groundwater acid; soil light gray due to lack of iron	Caliche: name applied to accumulation of calcite	Apparently bacteria destroy humus, no acid available to remove iron	

ures as much as 1 mile in length and breadth, killing as many as 180,000 people. Many of the largest and most damaging flow failures have taken place underwater in coastal areas. Submarine flow failures carried away large sections of port facilities at Seward, Whitter, and Valdez during the 1964 Alaskan earthquake. These flow failures generated large tsunamis that overran parts of the coastal area, causing additional damage and casualties. Submarine slides following earthquakes also move down continental slopes. Undersea telephone cables have been known to break after an earthquake and repair ships have found cables buried under thick debris.

When the soil supporting a building or some other structure liquefies and loses strength, large deformations could occur within the soil, allowing the structure to settle and tip over. Soils that liquify beneath buildings distort the general subsurface geometry causing bearing failures and subsequent subsidence and tilting of the building. Normally these deformations occur when a layer of

Fig. 14-2. Lateral spread following the March 27, 1964 Alaskan earthquake. (Courtesy of R.D. Miller, USGS.)

saturated, cohesionless sand or silt extends from near the surface to a depth of about the width of the building. The most spectacular example of this type of ground failure took place during the June 16, 1964 Niigata, Japan earthquake where several four-story apartment buildings tilted as much as 60 degrees. Most of the buildings were later jacked back into an upright position, underpinned with piles, and reoccupied.

Most clays lose their strength when they are disturbed by ground shaking. If the loss of strength is large, some clays, called quick clays, might fail. Quick clay is composed primarily of flakes of clay minerals arranged in very fine layers and has a water content which often exceeds 50 percent. Quick clay has a most amazing and treacherous quality and, ordinarily, it is a solid capable of supporting over a ton per square foot of surface area;

but the slightest jarring motion can immediately turn it into a liquid.

The five large landslides that affected parts of Anchorage during the 1964 Alaskan earthquake are examples of spectacular failures of clays sensitive to ground shaking (FIG. 14-3). The failure zones of these slides pass through layers of quick clay as well as other layers composed of saturated sand and silt. Because of the severe ground shaking, loss of strength took place in the clay layers and liquefaction took place in the sand and silt layers. These were the major contributing factors to the landsliding attributed by liquefaction.

LANDSLIDES

Landslides not associated with liquefaction are rapid slides of overburden with or without its underlying bedrock (FIG. 14-4). Slides involving overburden alone are called debris slides. Two types involving bedrock are called rockslides and slump. Rockslides develop when a mass of bedrock is broken into many fragments during the fall, and this material behaves as a fluid, spreading out in the valley below (FIG. 14 – 5). It might even flow some distance uphill on the opposite side of the valley. Such landslides are commonly called avalanches, but this term is more accurately used to describe snow slides. Rockslides are generally large and destructive, involving millions of tons of rock. Rockslides are apt to develop if planes of weakness, such as bedding planes or jointing, are parallel to a slope. This is especially true if the slope has been undercut by a river, a glacier, or construction work.

Slumps develop in cases where a strong, resistant rock overlies weak rocks. Material slides down in a curved plane, tilting up the resistant unit while the weaker rock flows out to form a heap.

FIG. 14-3. Landslide in Anchorage, Alaska, following March 27, 1964 earthquake. (Courtesy of W.R. Hansen, USGS.)

FIG. 14-4. The June 23, 1925 Gros Ventre, Wyoming landslide. (Courtesy of W.C. Alden, USGS.)

Unlike rock slides, slumps develop new cliffs nearly as high as those previous to the slump, setting the stage for a new slump. Thus slumping is a continuous process, and generally, many previous generations of slumping can be seen far in front of the present cliffs.

Residents of California are all too familiar with landslides in their state. Just within the last 10 years there have been 4000 landslides in the Los Angeles basin alone, causing considerable property damage. In the 1950s, repeated heavy rains and floods devastated the hillsides of Los Angeles, setting off landslides that destroyed or seriously damaged hundreds of homes. In response to this year-round destruction, city and county officials began to deal with the nonearthquake geologic hazards of the mountainous and hilly seaside region. Landslide-control legislation required new building sites to be inspected by an accredited geologist for landslide potential. Unfortunately, crafty land developers find their way around the law, and homes are still sliding down mountain sides or into the ocean.

One of the most spectacular examples of an avalanche occurred during the May 31, 1970 Peruvian earthquake of 7.7 magnitude that killed more than 18,000 people. It began when a sliding mass of glacial ice and rock, 3000 feet wide and about a mile long, rushed downslope with a deafening noise. Everywhere, it was accompanied or proceeded by a strong turbulent air blast. The ice was partially melted by frictional heat that made the slopes more slippery. By some accounts, the avalanche traveled 9 miles to the town of Yungay in two to four minutes (FIG. 14-6). The trajectories of thousands of boulders, weighing up to 3 tons each and hurled more than 2,000 feet across the valley, indicated that the velocity of the slide reached upwards of 250 miles per hour. The volume and velocity of this enormous plunging mass enabled it to ride over obstacles such as a 600-foot ridge between the valley and the town of Yungay, which was buried by the avalanche. The avalanche continued on across the valley and as much as 175 feet up the opposite bank where it partly destroyed

FIG. 14-5. The August 24, 1964 Rockslide on Sherman Glacier, Alaska. (Courtesy of USGS.)

another village. Flash flooding from broken mountain lake basins and from the avalanche-swollen waters of the Rio Santa River created a wave as much as 45 feet high that contributed to the earthquake's death and destruction.

A similar, but less spectacular, landslide was triggered by the 1959 Hebgen Lake, Montana earthquake that resulted in 26 deaths. The slide moved from north to south and resulted in a large scar in the mountainside. The debris traveled uphill on the south side of the valley and dammed the Madison River, creating a large lake. In the spring of 1983, a slide buried a highway and railroad tracks in the Wasatch Range of Utah. The slide created a dam that formed a lake, threatening residents below with flooding and forcing the evacuation of 500 people.

The Alaskan earthquake of 1958 caused an enormous rockslide to fall into Lituya Bay and generated a wave of water surging 1,720 feet up the mountainside (FIG. 14-7). Trees were bowled over and everywhere the shores in the bay were inundated with water.

Soil avalanches occur in weakly cemented, fine-grained materials that form steep stable slopes under ordinary conditions. Many slopes failed during the New Madrid, Missouri earthquake of 1811–12. The size of the area affected by earthquake-induced landslides depends on the magnitude and focal depth of the earthquake, the topography and geology of the ground near the fault, and the amplitude and duration of the ground shaking. In past earthquakes, landslides have been abundant in some areas having intensities of ground shaking

Fig. 14-6. The May 31, 1970 Yungay, Peru avalanche. (Courtesy of USGS.)

as low as VI on the Modified Mercalli Scale (which would only be 3 to 5 on the magnitude scale).

ROCKFALLS

Material that drops at nearly the velocity of free fall from a near vertical mountain face is called a rockfall or soilfall, depending on its composition.

Rockfalls can range in size from the dropping of individual blocks on a mountain slope to the failure of masses weighing hundreds of thousands of tons that avalanche nearly straight down a mountain face.

Individual blocks commonly come to rest in a loose pile of angular blocks, or talas, at the base of a cliff. Should large blocks of rock drop into a

FIG. 14-7. The August 29, 1958 Lituya Bay, Alaska rockslide. (Courtesy of D.J. Miller, USGS.)

standing body of water, such as a lake or fjord, immensely destructive waves might be set in motion with no warning. This is a hazard particularly feared in Norway where small deltas might provide the only available flat land at sea level. Should such a rock-fall-induced wave burst through the village streets and houses, destruction is likely to be as complete as it is sudden. These waves might range anywhere from 20 to 300 feet high.

The most impressive rockfall recorded occurred at Gohna, India in 1893. A stupendous mass of rock, loosened by the driving monsoon rains, dropped 4000 feet into one of the narrow Himalayan Mountain gorges. A great natural dam was formed 900 feet high and 3000 feet across the gorge at the crest and extended for 11,000 feet up and down stream. This pile of broken rock, involving about 5 billion cubic yards, impounded a lake 770 feet deep. When the dam burst two years later, it set a world record. About 10 billion cubic feet of water discharged in a matter of hours, with the flood cresting at 240 feet high.

The most celebrated example of a rockfall in North America occurred in Alberta, Canada in 1903. A mass of strongly jointed limestone blocks at the crest of Turtle Mountain — which was possibly undercut by coal mining carried on below the base — broke loose and plunged down the deep escarpment. Some 40 million cubic yards fell and washed through the small coal-mining town of Frank in one gigantic wave, killing 70 people on the way. The rockfall then swept up the opposite slope 400 feet above the valley floor.

MASS WASTING

Not all earth movements are caused by ground shaking. Mass wasting is the mass transfer of material down slopes under the direct influence of gravity. Slipping, sliding, and creeping occur down even the gentlest slope. Creep is the slow downslope movement of overburden and, in some cases, bedrock (FIG. 14-8). It is recognized by down-hill tilted poles and fence posts that show a more rapid movement of near-surface soil material than that below.

In such cases, trees would be unable to root themselves and only grass and shrubs would grow on the slope. In other cases where the creep is slower, the trunks of trees would be bent. After the tree is tilted, new growth would try to straighten it. If the creep is continuous, the tree would lean downhill in its lower part and be progressively straighter higher up. Creep might be very rapid where frost action is prominent. After a freeze-thaw sequence, material would move down the slope due to the expansion and contraction of the ground.

If the amount of water in the overburden increases, it increases the weight and drastically reduces stability by lowering the resistance to shear and an earthflow results (FIG. 14-9). This is a transition between the slow and rapid varieties of mass wasting. It is a more visible form of movement than creep, but slower than a mudflow or landslide. Earthflows are characterized by grass-covered, soil-blanketed hills. Although commonly they are minor features, some might be quite large and cover many acres. Earthflows usually have a spoon-shaped sliding surface, whereupon a tongue of overburden breaks away and flows a short distance. An earthflow differs from creep in that a distinct, curved scarp is formed at the breakaway point.

With increasing water content, an earthflow might grade into a mudflow (FIG. 14-10). The behavior of mudflows is similar to that of fluids. Such a viscous mass very often carries along in it a tumbling mass of rocks and boulders (some as large as automobiles).

Rain falling on loose, pyroclastic material on the sides of certain types of inactive volcanoes also produces mudflows. Mudflows are the most impressive feature of many of the world's deserts (FIG. 14-11). In this case, a heavy thunderstorm produces large amounts of runoff in the drainage area of a stream. The runoff takes the form of rapidly moving sheets of water that pick up much of the loose material. Because these sheet floods flow into the main stream, all of this muddy material is suddenly concentrated in the main stream channel. As a result, a dry stream bed is transformed very rapidly into a flash flood. This flood of muddy material moves very swiftly. In some cases, there is a steep, wall-like front. Such a mudflow could cause much damage as it flows out of the mountains.

Eventually, loss of water thickens the mudflow to the point that it no longer flows. Mudflows often carry large blocks and boulders onto the floor

FIG. 14-8. Railroad damaged by creep. (Courtesy of W. Atwood, USGS.)

FIG. 14-9. Earthflow in Washington County, Pennsylvania. (Courtesy of J.S. Pomeroy, USGS.)

FIG. 14-10. The September 22, 1905 Slumgullion mudflow in Colorado. (Courtesy of W. Cross, USGS.)

FIG. 14-11. Alluvial fans from the Sierra Nevada Mountains, California. (Courtesy of H.E. Malde, USGS.)

of the desert basins far beyond the base of the bordering mountain range. This produces strange monoliths out in the middle of nowhere that linger long after the erosion of the enclosing mud that rafted them out beyond the mountains.

Another type of mudflow occurs in colder climates and is called solifluction. When frozen ground melts from the top down, as during warm spring days in the temperate regions or during the summer in areas of permafrost, it causes surface mud to move downslope over a frozen base on whose surface it easily slides. This creates many problems in construction in the far north permafrost areas. Foundations must extend down to the permanently frozen layers or otherwise whole buildings could be damaged by loss of support or simply carried away.

The most common triggering mechanisms for mass wasting include vibrations from earthtremors or explosions that break the bond holding the slope together, overloading the slope so that it can no longer support its new weight, undercutting at the base of the slope, and oversaturation with water. The addition of water is generally seasonal and newly made road cuts stand until the following spring when motorists find their way barred by massive rock and soil material piled up on the highway.

The effect of the water is twofold: it adds to the weight of the slope, and it lessens the internal cohesion of the overburden. Although its effect as a lubricant is commonly considered to be its main role, this effect is actually very slight. The main effect of water is the lessening of the cohesion of the material by filling the spaces between soil grains with water.

Children building sand castles on the beach are familiar with the cohesive property of water that allows them to build their structures to prestigious size. This is because small amounts of moisture between the grains holds the grains together by surface tension. Any additional water completely fills the intergrain voids. The consequent loss of surface tension means that the sand flows outward like a fluid.

If large amounts of fluid such as water or oil is pumped out of a porous substratum without being replaced, just the opposite occurs and surface tension is lost causing a complete collapse of the grains. This causes subsidence of the ground in places such as Mexico City.

Another form of subsidence occurs when acidic meteoric water percolates into the ground and dissolves limestone or the lime cement of sandstone layers. The ground looses its support and a sinkhole results. If this occurs in a residential area, as sinkholes often do in Florida, houses disappear (FIG. 14-12).

Another type of movement of soil material is called frost heaving and it is associated with freezing and thawing mainly in the temperate climates. The expansion of water as it freezes pushes rocks upward through the soil. In northern regions, farmers find a new crop of rocks each spring. In the Middle Ages, peasants thought that the stones actually grew in the soil just as crops do.

The mechanism for frost heaving is complex.

The small expansion of water during freezing is not enough to account for the several inches of uplift of rocks or fence posts that is a common occurrence in areas prone to frost heaving. Most of the soil water is in the pore spaces of fine material. When this water freezes, it expands, pushing nearby rocks upward. During freezing, soil moisture migrates to pockets of fine material and forms layers of ice. This additional volume of ice causes several inches of uplift. When melting occurs, the surface tension of the water in the fine sediments pulls the sediments together, leaving the rocks at the height where they were pushed up.

The Arctic has a bizarre manifestation of frost heaving that consists of regular polygonal-patterned ground looking much like a giant tiled floor. This is produced when frost heaving is applied repetitively over many years to a soil of mixed composition. The coarse material, such as gravel and boulders, is gradually shoved radially outward from the central area, and the finer materials lag behind.

SOIL EROSION

Soil erosion causes the most wide-spread degradation of the land surface, even more so than earthquakes or mass wasting. Falling rain erodes

FIG. 14-12. A collapse sinkhole under a house in Florida. (Courtesy of USGS.)

FIG. 14-13. Cropland erosion near Pierre, South Dakota. (Courtesy of USDA.)

surface material in two ways: by impact and runoff. The impact of raindrops that hit the ground with a velocity of about 32 feet per second loosens material and splashes it into the air. On hillsides, some of this material falls back at a point lower down the hill. One-tenth of an inch of rain amounts to about 11 tons of water per acre, and the energy of this water is about 55,000 foot-pounds per second. Ninety percent of this great amount of energy is dissipated in the impact. Most of the impact splashes are to a height of 1 foot or less, and the lateral splash movement is about four times the height.

Impact erosion is most effective in regions that have little or no grass or forest cover such as desert areas or newly plowed fields that are subjected to sudden downpours. Splash erosion accounts for the puzzling removal of soil from hilltops where there is little runoff. It could also ruin soil by splashing up the light clay particles that are then carried away by the runoff, leaving infertile silt and sand behind. The rainwater that does not infiltrate into the ground runs down the hillside and erodes in the same manner as that of a swift-flowing stream. This water might gather in lower places and cut deep gullies. The amount of erosion depends on the steepness of the slope and the type and amount of vegetative cover.

The most disastrous effects of soil erosion are man-induced (FIG. 14-13). Before man began farming, sometime after the last Ice Age, erosion was probably no more than 10 billion tons of topsoil yearly, slow enough to be replaced by the generation of new soil. Estimates of recent soil erosion rates are as much as 25 billion tons a year. In other words, we are losing the ground beneath our feet much faster than nature is putting it back. In order to feed a hungry world, new forests must be felled to provide new farmland to replace the land ruined by erosion. This occurred on a grand scale in this country when cotton was "king," and growers were forced to move ever further westward, cutting down great forests in their path and leaving devastated land behind.

Tropical rain forests are in danger of becoming extinct as they are forced to make way for agriculture and cattle grazing. The fragile soil that allows such prestigious growth of vegetation is being eroded by logging and slash-and-burn clearing of millions of acres yearly. One hundred years ago, worldwide rain forests covered an area equal to twice the size of Europe. Now that area is cut in half. Once the fragile soil has been exposed to the elements of weather and man's activities, it can never support new growth and the rain forest is lost for all time. As the world population explosion continues and as the land is continually being destroyed on a grand scale, mankind's greatest natural catastrophy might soon be upon us.

15

Volcanic Treasure Troves

THE California gold rush all started in early 1848 with the discovery of gold at John Sutter's sawmill near present-day Sacramento. Word spread quickly and, before long, Californians dropped everything, bought pickaxes and shovels, and headed for the hills to mine gold. They were later joined by other get-rich-quick men from other parts of the country as 25,000 people came by ship from the East Coast. They began arriving at the overcrowded port of San Francisco which, by the beginning of 1849, was rapidly swelling into a boomtown. Over twice that number came overland in wagons, storming into California from various directions. Several thousand poorly equipped fortune hunters died en route, mostly from disease, famine, and cold weather.

Mining camps quickly grew into shantytowns where miners lived under extremely primitive conditions, and claim disputes and drunken brawls were a common occurrence. Everything was paid for in gold dust and prices were exorbitant. Out of the many thousands who went into the mountains

to dig for gold, only a few actually got rich. Most of those who got rich did so through the trafficking of gold and the selling of high-priced commodities the miners needed to sustain themselves. Goldfever brought so many Americans into California that it quickly surpassed the population requirement for statehood. The California legislature hastily drew up a constitution, and California came into the Union as the 31st state on September 9, 1850. By 1852, the population reached a quarter of a million, and its mines yielded over $80 million in gold.

GOLD

The gold-bearing veins of the foot hills of the western Sierra Nevada Range in California are usually steeply inclined ledges dipping down into the granite roots of the range. The hydrothermal veins of the Mother Lode system trend north-south covering a distance of some 200 miles. The veins are composed of a hard, milky-white quartz, generally no more than 3 feet wide, and have a few specks of gold and pyrite (fools gold) sprinkled throughout. Seldom did stringers of pure gold shoot through the veins, and most miners had to be satisfied with panning for gold out of sands and gravels washed down from the mountains.

Gold has a specific gravity of about 19, making it eight times heavier than ordinary sands and gravels. Therefore, if sands and gravels are placed into suspension with water by vigorous swirling or sleucing, the gold will fall out of the mixture and end up on the bottom of the container. This is known as placer mining (FIG. 15-1). For this type of mine to be profitable, many tons of sand and gravel, along with plenty of water, must be processed. Finding enough water in the desert climate becomes a special problem. After the spring runoff, many mines run dry and are shut down. An individual panning for gold might find enough to pay for his provisions, but little or nothing else.

The gold rush did not end in California but headed eastward into the western states of Nevada, Wyoming, Colorado, and New Mexico. Per-

haps the most unusual mining episodes and mines with the most colorful names were in Colorado (FIG. 15-2). The Colorado Mountains are peppered with old, abandoned mining camps attesting to the many thousands who had more gold in their eyes than they found in the ground. Small mining towns sprang up with names like Cripple Creek, Telluride, Durango, Silvertown and many others (FIG. 15-3). When the underground mines played out, gold dredging techniques were developed. Some of the old mining towns became ski resorts and tourist attractions while many more became ghost towns with only a few remnants to mark their past.

The gold at Cripple Creek was discovered around 1890 and existed in a complex mass of basaltic breccia, a rock composed of angular pyroclastic fragments of basalt. All mines were in an area of about 2.5 miles wide and were excavated out of nine separate volcanic necks, tapering downward in carrot-shaped pipes that once formed the feeders to an ancient volcano.

The present surface level of the mines is a

FIG. 15-1. Gold placer mining in La Plata County, Colorado, 1875. (Courtesy of W.H. Jackson, USGS.)

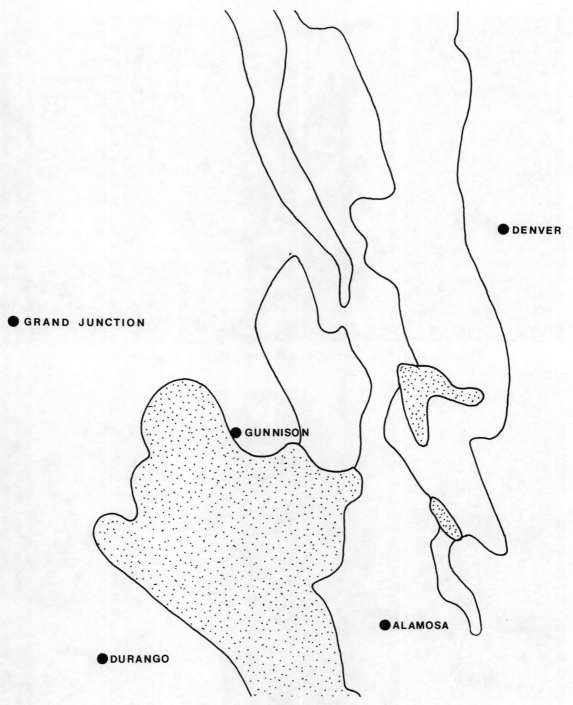

FIG. 15-2. Gold mining in Colorado.

Miner's camp on King Solomon Mountain, Colorado, 1875. (Courtesy of USGS.)

Durango, Colorado in 1901. (Courtesy of USGS.)

Gold dredge on Lay Creek, Colorado. (Courtesy of H.S. Gale, USGS.)

FIG. 15-3. Cripple Creek mining district, Colorado, 1903. (Courtesy of Ransome, USGS.)

little less than 10,000 feet above sea level. At least 2000 feet of the original volcano has been eroded to reveal its richly mineralized core. The ore occurs in irregular sheets and veins cutting across the basaltic breccia. Individual veins range in size from hair-line cracks to complex zones 40 feet or more across. Because the volcanic pipes taper off downward, the mine workings do not extend much over 3000 feet below the surface.

SILVER

Silver is often associated with gold, and the Comstock Load in Nevada was the scene of one of the largest mining booms in the history of the opening of the American West. Originally discovered in 1859, production did not reach its peak until the 1870s. Many mines were scattered along a 3-mile mineralized fault zone that separated young volcanic rocks from older rocks. The lode forms a slab, inclined about 40 degrees to the horizontal, and reaches a thickness of 400 feet and a depth of 3000 feet below the surface. The mines were plagued with hot water flooding the workings. Many a miner lost his life to scalding water or heat exhaustion. This implies that there was a large mass of hot rock below the lode that might have been responsible for producing the mineral wealth. The silver combines with sulfur to make simple silver minerals with a nearly 3 percent gold content. Therefore, the mines are even more economical.

The silver and gold mines in South America were responsible in large part for the Spanish settlement there shortly after Columbus reached America. Natives of the Inca Empire, which stretched half way down the Andes Mountains from Ecquador to near Santiago, Chile mined silver and gold out of eroded stumps of ancient volcanoes. The Spaniards heard rumors of streets paved with gold and the Inca people bedecked with it. When the Spanish Conquistadors landed in Peru in 1532, they found an Empire torn apart by a terrible civil war. The Spaniards easily captured the Inca Emperor and demanded a ransom paid with a room full of gold and silver. The Incas had no problem complying with this demand. In addition, the Spaniards melted down masterpieces of Inca goldsmiths into bullion and sent it back to Spain.

The Spaniards discovered a new silver mine called Cerro Rico (hill of silver) in Bolivia. The ancient volcano was 3 miles high and shot through with veins of rich silver ore. Some veins were more than 12 feet thick and provided a variety of silver minerals including native or metallic silver. Spanish galleons loaded their precious cargos from docks pilled high with gold and silver. Some of the ships were lost at sea due to storms or pirates, but most of the ships made it to Spain. So much cheap gold and silver flooded the Spanish economy that it brought down the empire.

COPPER

The Andes Mountains have an abundance of other metals, especially copper. An observant army officer discovered a strange looking, greenish rock 50 miles south-east of Santiago, Chile. When the rock was assayed, it was found to be rich in copper. The El Teniente (The Lieutenant) mine, named in honor of the officer, is one of the largest underground mines in the world. Nearly 9000 feet above sea level, the mine is associated with a volcanic breccia pipe that probably brought mineralized fluids into the surrounding rocks composed of old andesite lavas and igneous intrusives. These country rocks, as geologists call them, are mineralized throughout with a variety of copper minerals with an average copper content of 2 percent and reserves estimated at a quarter of a billion tons of ore.

The Keweenaw peninsula extends into Lake Superior from Canada and contains a 100-mile-long and 3-mile-wide belt of very old basalt lavas that contains abundant native copper. There were originally about 400 individual basalt flows, totaling 20,000 feet thick, no less than 2 billion years old. The copper is concentrated in the tops of the lava flows where it fills the open spaces with small bits of copper metal. Hydrothermal fluids containing copper sulfide came up from intrusive rocks underlying the basalts and found their way into the intervening layers of the basalt flows. Oxygen derived from iron oxides within the basalt combined with sulfur of the copper minerals and reduced them to metallic copper. The copper was originally worked by Canadian Indians and rediscovered by the Jesuits in the seventeenth century. Large-scale mining began in 1845 and was developed into the largest copper mining district in North America until the late 1880s. Then the porphyry copper deposits of the Southwestern United States were developed.

IRON

Basalt is generally composed of about 5 percent iron, but iron is such a common element that ores have to be extremely rich (most over 30 percent iron) before they are economically workable. This is why oxidized lavas are not usually mined for their iron content. Oxidation of basaltic lavas occurs when steam or other gases pass through them when they are still in a highly fluid state, producing iron minerals such as hematite and magnetite. The El Laco mine on the border between Chile and Argentina is a rarity among iron mines. The ore body is a large lava flow consisting almost entirely of the iron minerals hemitite and magnitite. It began with a large mass of andesite that was completely oxidized while still underground. The iron was concentrated in a homogeneous fluid saturated with water vapor, and this mixture erupted at the surface as an iron lava.

HOT WATER ORES

Copper, tin, lead, and zinc (FIG. 15-4) ores are also concentrated directly by volcanic action (especially by the intrusion of magma bodies into the earth's crust). These concentrations are formed as hydrothermal vein deposits formed from mineral fillings precipitated from hot waters percolating along underground fractures. A gigantic underground still is supplied with heat and some of the ingredients from the magmatic roots of volcanoes.

As the magma cools, silicate minerals (such as quartz) crystallize first and leave behind a concentration of other elements in a residual melt. Further cooling of the magma causes the rocks to shrink and crack, allowing the residual magmatic

fluids to escape toward the surface and invade the surrounding rocks where they form veins. Certain minerals precipitate over a wide range of temperatures and pressures. This is why they are commonly found together with one or two of the minerals predominating in high enough concentrations to make their mining profitable.

Two metals that are on opposite extremes of the hydrothermal spectrum are mercury and tungsten. Mercury is the only metal that is a liquid at room temperatures. Because it is a good thermal and electrical conductor, it is useful in thermometers and thermostats. Because it forms a gas at low temperatures and pressures, much of the Earth's mercury is lost to the surface from volcanic steam vents and hot springs. Near many active volcanoes, the concentration of mercury in the air even exceeds the health standards established by the Environmental Protection Agency.

Tungsten, on the other hand, is one of the hardest metals on Earth and it is used for hardening steel and for filaments in light bulbs. Tungsten precipitates at very high temperatures and pressures and often occurs at the contact between a chilling magma body and the rocks it invades. It is common for tungsten enriched fluids to invade limestone, forming a calcium tungstenate called scheelite. This mineral has the unusual property of becoming brightly florescent under a black light (ultraviolet light). This greatly aids in prospecting outcrops for tungsten at night. The prospector shines his black light on an outcrop, and if it glows, he has hit pay dirt.

SULFUR

Volcanoes have been called the gateways to hell or the forge of Volcan, the Roman god of weapons, because of their fire and brimstone. When volcanoes erupt, they expel huge amounts of vapors and gases, many of which are sulfur compounds. Hence the smell of brimstone. Sulfur is one of the most important nonmetallic minerals on Earth. In industry, sulfur is converted to sulfuric acid and used, among other things, in the manufacture of automobile batteries and the extraction of metals from ores. Because sulfur exists in abun-

FIG. 15-4. Relative positions of tin belts.

dance in other geologic settings, volcanoes only contribute a small proportion of the world's economic requirements for sulfur.

The largest volcanic sulfur mines are in northern Chile. The open pit mine atop Aucanquilcha Volcano has the distinction of being the highest mine in the world; it is some 20,000 feet in elevation. The mine is situated in the core of a complex andesite volcano, and the entire central part contains ore with 30 percent sulfur. The only people who can work at such high altitude are the barrel chested Indians from the Bolivian high plateau. Because of the extremely difficult and hazardous working conditions, their life expectancy was very short.

Toward the turn of this century, geologists found that hot springs at Sulfur Bank, California and Steamboat Springs, Nevada were depositing some of the same metal-sulfide compounds that occurred in ore veins. Therefore, if the hot springs are depositing ore minerals at the surface, then it stands to reason that hot spring water might be filling up cracks with an ore deposit on its way to the surface.

The American mining geologist Waldemar Lindgren, by digging a few hundred yards from Steamboat Springs, discovered rocks with the texture and mineralogy of typical ore veins. He proved that many ore veins formed by circulating hot water. This concept vastly improved mineral exploration because any evidence of hydrothermal alteration of rocks on the surface, even though metals might not be found at first, was enough to focus attention on the area. However, only a small percentage of the hydrothermal areas contain workable ore deposits. Therefore, some other processes must be at work.

Because most of the metals are found as sulfides, presumably, a source of sulfur and the chemistry that makes metal sulfides stable is needed. But the most puzzling part concerns how the hot water can carry enough metal to its place of deposition. Obviously, people who drink mineral water from hot springs do not drop dead from lead or mercury poisoning; therefore, the concentrations of these and other metals must be quite low. Either

an ore deposit requires a huge amount of water over a very long time, or some hot waters can carry more metal than is seen at the surface.

Another reason might be that the rocks surrounding the magma chamber are the true source of the minerals found in hydrothermal veins. In this case the volcanic rocks only act as a heat source that pumps ground water into a giant circulating system. Heavier, cold waters move down and into the cooling volcanic rocks carrying trace quantities of valuable elements leached from the surrounding rocks. When heated by the cooling magma body, the waters become less dense and rise into the fractured rocks above. After cooling and losing pressure, they precipitate their mineral load into veins and move down again to pick up another load of minerals.

OIL AND GAS

The theory of plate tectonics provides some of the answers for why certain ore bodies exist at certain locations. Hydrothermal activity is a reflection of high heat flow and high heat flow is associated with plate boundaries. The Salton Sea of Southern California and the Red Sea have shown evidence of recently transported metals at extensional plate boundaries. Another area of high heat flow is associated with the igneous activity at converging plate margins. Many hydrothermal ore deposits have been found in new and ancient converging margins and doubtless many more future ore deposits will be found thanks to plate tectonics.

Plate tectonics has also aided in the exploration for oil. The continental drift theory helps to explain why oil reserves are located where they are and might suggest new sites to explore for oil. It is commonly believed that oil and natural gas is formed out of the remains of abundant plant and animal life that lived in tropical regions tens or even hundreds of millions of years ago. It is also the same for coal in which plant fossils are actually found between coal layers. Deep burial and heat provided by the Earth's interior created a gigantic pressure cooker that through geologic time has baked the organic materials into hydrocarbons

(FIG. 15-5). Eventual drifting of the continents and erosion of the surface has brought the oil and gas deposits where they are today.

DIAMONDS

Diamonds and pencil leads made of graphite have one very important thing in common. They are both different forms of pure carbon. In graphite, the carbon atoms are arranged in layers like sheets of mica and the loose bonding between layers permits the sheets to easily break off and slide past one another. This gives graphite a soft, greasy feeling and allows a writer to make squiggles on a piece of paper. Graphite is one of the softest minerals on Earth. Diamonds are the hardest known minerals. The reason for this difference is that, in diamonds, the atoms of carbon are compressed into a tight network that interlocks in all directions. In order to obtain this close packing of carbon atoms, extremely high temperatures and pressures are needed. The only place this occurs naturally is deep in the bowels of the Earth some

125 miles below the surface. The only way diamonds can make it to the surface is through volcanic pipes.

Diamonds have been discovered in many different localities, but only in a few are they found in notable amounts. Most commonly, diamonds are found in alluvial deposits, or placers, from eroded volcanic mountains. They accumulate because of their inert chemical nature, great hardness, and fairly high density. Diamonds were first found in India. The earliest diamonds came from stream gravels in the southern and central portions of the country. It is estimated that 12 million carats (a carat is a unit of weight for gemstones equal to 0.2 grams) were produced from Indian mines. Today, the production is only a few hundred carats a year. India was virtually the only source of diamonds until they were discovered in Brazil in 1725. East-central Brazil produces about 160,000 carats annually, chiefly from stream gravels near the city of Diamantina, Minas Gerais. Extensive upland deposits of diamond-bearing gravels and clays are also worked. In 1866, diamonds were discovered in

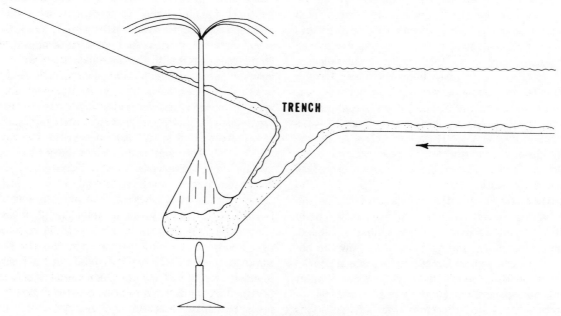

TRENCH

FIG. 15-5. Origin of oil and gas.

the gravels of the Vaal River in South Africa, and, in 1871, in the "yellow ground" of several volcanic pipes located near the city of Kimberley.

On the desert coast just south of the mouth of the Orange River in Cape Province, South Africa, terrace deposits containing high-quality stones were discovered in 1927. Later, similar deposits were found along the coast north of the Orange River in South-West Africa, extending 50 to 60 miles up the coast. Elsewhere in Africa, alluvial diamonds have been found in the Congo, Angola, Ghana, and Sierra Leone.

About 95 percent of the world's output of diamonds comes from the African continent. The Congo is by far the largest producer and supplies from placer deposits over 50 percent of the world's demand. These Congo diamonds are mostly of industrial grade and therefore represent only about 13 percent of the world's total value of diamonds produced. Industrial diamonds are also produced synthetically. These diamonds are unsuitable for cutting into gems because of their small size, but several million carats are manufactured yearly by subjecting pure carbon to extreme temperatures and pressures similar to those found deep within the Earth.

KIMBERLITE PIPES

Although some gem-quality diamonds are still recovered from gravels, the principal South African production is from kimberlite pipes (named for the town of Kimberley, South Africa). They are composed of jumbled fragments of coal and peridotite rocks believed to be derived from deep within the mantle. The intrusive bodies vary in size and shape, although many are roughly circular and pipe-shaped. Prospecting in South Africa for diamonds has uncovered over 700 kimberlite pipes and other intrusive bodies—most of which are barren.

The kimberlite deposits were originally worked as open pits. As the mines got deeper, underground methods had to be employed. At the Kimberley mine, the world's deepest diamond mine, the diameter of the pipe at the surface is about 1000 feet and decreases with depth. Mining stopped in 1908 at a depth of 3500 feet even though the pipe continued downward. At the surface of the mine, the kimberlite is weathered to a soft yellow rock and at depth the rock gives way to a harder blue rock. The ratio of diamonds to barren rock varies from pipe to pipe. In the Kimberley mine, the ratio was 1 to 8 million by weight. In some mines it might be as high as 1 to 30 million.

The world's largest and most productive diamond mine is the Premier mine, located 24 miles east of Pretoria, South Africa. Since mining began there in 1903, over 30 million carats—or 6 tons—of diamonds have been produced. The world's largest diamond, the Cullinan, weighting 3024 carats (21 ounces), was found at the Premier mine in 1905. The most notable kimberlite pipe outside of South Africa is the Williamson Diamond Mine in Tanzania. The mine was discovered in 1940 and has made this country a major diamond producer.

The method of extraction from the blue rock is to crush the rock fine enough to permit concentration. The diamonds are then separated on tables coated with grease, to which the diamonds adhere while the rest of the material is washed away.

Diamonds have been found sparingly in other parts of the world—including Guyana, Venezuela, and Australia, and various parts of the United States. Small stones have occasionally been discovered in stream sands along the eastern slope of the Appalachian Mountains from Virginia to Georgia. Diamonds have also been reported from the gold sands of Northern California and Southern Oregon. Sporadic occurrences have been noted in the glacial till in Wisconsin, Michigan, and Ohio.

In 1906, diamonds were discovered in a kimberlite pipe near Murfreesboro, Arkansas (FIG. 15-6). This locality resembles the diamond pipes of South Africa, and became the only active diamond mine in the country (yielding about 40,000 stones). It is now a tourist attraction where diamond hunters pay a small fee to sift through the black soil in search of that allusive gem. The diamond field is plowed regularly and, generally, after a rainstorm is the best time to search because the surface of the freshly turned soil is washed exposing what

FIG. 15-6. Arkansas diamond mine. (Courtesy of H.D. Miser, USGS.)

might otherwise look like bits of glass. This sort of diamond mining seems like child's play. Indeed, babies have been found sucking on a sizable diamond while playing in the dirt as parents frantically search in vain.

The diamond is the most important of the gem stones. Its value depends upon its hardness, its brilliance—resulting from its high index of refraction—and its "fire" resulting from its strong dispersion of light. The value of a cut diamond depends upon its color, purity, size, as well as the skill with which it has been cut. In general, the most valuable are those flawless stones that are colorless or possess a blue-white color. A faint straw-yellow color that diamonds often show detracts from their value.

Diamonds colored deep shades of yellow, red, green, or blue—known as fancy stones—are greatly prized and bring very high prices. Diamonds can be colored deep shades of green by irradiation with high-energy nuclear particles or blue by exposing them to fast-moving electrons. A stone colored green by irradiation can be made deep yellow by heat treatment. These artificially colored stones are difficult to distinguish from those of natural color.

Volcanic and hydrothermal processes are important in producing the wealth of the Earth. Ore deposits form very slowly, and it takes millions upon millions of years to create an ore with high enough mineral concentrations to be suitable for a mine that then can be depleted in less than a generation. Modern man's insatiable demand for ores and fossil fuels make for the depletion of readily available ore deposits occurring sometime in the not too distant future. Then, low grade deposits will have to be worked. Unless there is a revolution in mining technology, the cost of mining will rise dramatically and this will raise the prices for goods and commodities. Conservation of natural resources and recycling metals such as aluminum and iron is the only sure way of preserving the wealth of the Earth for future generations.

16

Volcano Weather

ACCORDING to the Roman scholar Virgil, when Caesar died, in 44 B.C., the Sun felt pity for Rome and therefore covered its beaming face with darkness. Pliny the Elder writes that one of the largest volcanic eruptions in the Northern Hemisphere (since the last Ice Age) occurred during the year of Julius Caesar's death. The Sun shone feebly for nearly a year. Pliny the Elder lost his life to the A.D. 79 Vesuvius eruption that destroyed Pompeii. Pliny the Younger gave the most vivid description of the eruption.

Probably the first to suspect a connection between volcanic eruptions and their effects on the weather was Benjamin Franklin. In 1784, Franklin was living in Paris as the first diplomatic representative of the newly formed United States of America. While in France, Franklin reported that, during the summer months, a constant dry fog existed over all of Europe (and parts of North America). The winter of 1783–84 was more severe than any for many years. Franklin attributed the strange weather phenomenon to vast quantities of dust from the eruptions of Laki in Iceland and Asama in Japan that spread across the Northern Hemisphere during the summer of 1783.

THE DUST VEIL INDEX

Climatologists have little doubt that the severe winter Benjamin Franklin described was caused by the eruptions in Iceland and Japan. With over 200 years of observations of volcanoes and weather since 1784, the correlation is quite close. However, volcanoes alone cannot explain all the ups and downs of the climate. The English meteorologist Hubert H. Lamb carried out an extensive historical survey of all volcanic eruptions from 1500 to 1970 and related their impact on the atmosphere to a standard scale using the 1883 eruption of Krakatoa as 1000 units on the dust veil index. Actually the 1815 eruption of Tambora in Indonesia blasted three times as much dust into the upper atmosphere as did Krakatoa. Therefore, its dust veil index would be 3000.

FIG. 16-1A. Extent of Pleistocene glaciation in the Continental U.S.

FIG. 16-1B. Alpine Glacier on Jack Mountain, Colorado. (Courtesy of A. Post, USGS.)

Because Tambora was proceeded and followed by other eruptions around the world between 1811 and 1818, taken together the total veil was 4200—the largest in modern history. Had Napolean known about the effects of the volcanic eruptions on the weather, he might have stayed home instead of marching into Russia in the summer of 1812. A few months later, he not only had to face Russian bullets, but also one of the worst Russian winters on record.

THE YEAR WITHOUT SUMMER

Following the eruption of Tambora in 1816, Europe and North America suffered what Europeans called "the year without summer," and what Americans called "eighteen hundred and froze to death." Average June temperatures in New England were as much as 4 degrees centigrade (7 degrees Fahrenheit) below normal. New England and eastern Canada received widespread snow that month and frost every month that year.

In some parts of England, the temperature was 3 degrees centigrade below normal, and certain regions had rain on all but three or four days from May to October. Crops were either killed by frost, failed to ripen, or rotted in the field. The potato crop failed in Ireland, and there were food riots in Wales. Throughout the rest of Europe, there was widespread famine and thousands of lives lost from starvation and disease. Although not much of a compensation for all the havoc it caused, the Tambora eruption produced some of the most beautiful sunsets ever seen.

THE EFFECTS OF VOLCANOES

By blocking out the heat from the sun, volcanic dust could have caused the glacial ice cover to increase, bringing on the "little ice age" that occurred between 550 and 125 years ago. Some climatologists argue that many volcanic eruptions occurring around the world in a short space of time throw so much dust into the upper atmosphere that this alone could cause the onset of an ice age (FIG. 16-1). Their argument is supported by geological evidence of thin layers of volcanic dust buried in sediments that correlate reasonably well with times of increased ice cover. Some scientists have turned the argument around by saying that ice ages cause volcanoes to erupt. This idea is not so far-fetched as it might seem, and there are those who seriously believe that the weight of the ice, pressing down on the rocks of the continents, cause an increase in volcanic activity by squeezing magma out of volcanic reservoirs like squeezing toothpaste from a tube. It remains to be seen how well this idea fits in with the plate tectonics theory.

Since the 1883 eruption of Krakatoa occurred at a time of improved communications, sophisticated instrumentation, and no long-running wars to distract people's attention, its effects on the climate were better observed than that of Tambora, nearly 70 years earlier (FIG. 16-2).

Scientists and nonscientists alike marveled over the changes in the atmosphere produced by the eruption. Ordinary people could not help but notice the spectacular green-tinged sunsets and the appearance of a blue moon. It was estimated that 7 cubic miles of rock, ash, and dust were thrown into the atmosphere, much of which reached upwards of 50 miles into the stratosphere where it spread throughout the world and lingered for years. Scientists at the Montellier Observatory in southern France noticed with astonishment a drop in the direct solar radiation from 30 percent above normal for that time of the year to 20 percent below normal, and it remained 10 percent below normal for three years after the eruption.

Only part of the incoming solar radiation that is lost is scattered back into space by the dust (FIG. 16-3). Some of the radiation goes to warm the dust itself and some is scattered sideways. Radiation still reaches the ground, but at an indirect angle. This sideways scattering of sunlight is responsible for making the sky blue and is the reason for spectacular sunrises and sunsets. Therefore, scattered solar radiation does not reach the surface directly from the Sun's disk (which is what measurements of direct solar radiation record).

If the total output of the Sun actually did fluctuate by as much as 10 percent, as it might have done in its early history, this would play havoc

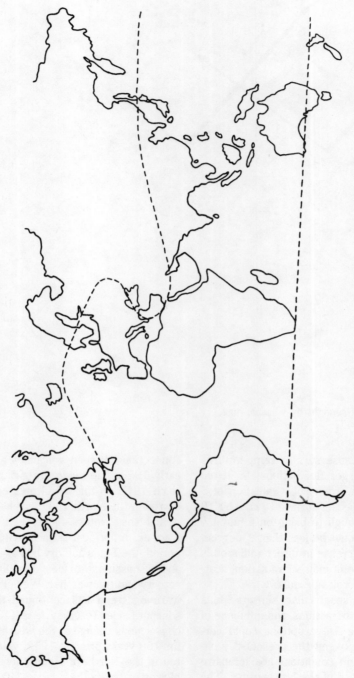

FIG. 16-2. World-wide spread of dust cloud from the 1883 eruption of Krakatoa.

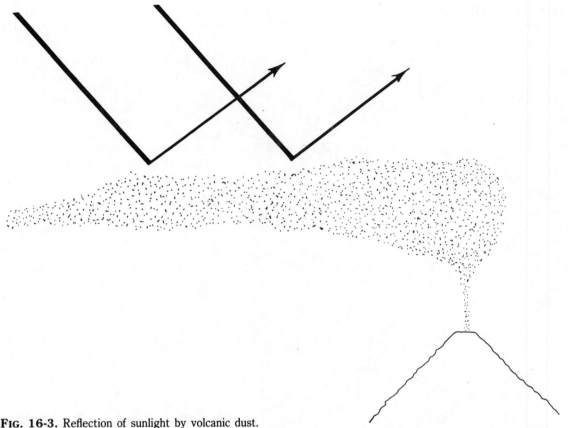

Fig. 16-3. Reflection of sunlight by volcanic dust.

with life on Earth because surface temperatures would reflect much larger fluctuations. In actual practice, a decrease in direct solar radiation of 5 percent would not cause the surface to cool by 10 degrees — which is enough to bring on a new ice age — but rather, it would be less than 1 degree. This is because the decrease in direct radiation is matched by an increase in indirect radiation, scattered sideways by the volcanic dust.

Apart from the spectacular sunsets, blue moons, and other side attractions, the influence of one or more Krakatoa-size eruptions could certainly tip the scales between the present-day climate conditions. Current conditions are comparatively warmer than those of the last century. The American meteorologist Harry Wexler made the connection between volcanoes and climate in the early 1950s. He made the striking discovery that since 1912 no major volcanic eruptions have occurred in the Northern hemisphere and during this period the winters have been growing steadily warmer. Ignoring the fact that during this same period, the Sun's activity had also been increasing, and dismissing the idea of a link between solar activity and the weather, Wexler indicated that the warming trend has continued through three full sunspot cycles (each cycle is 11 years). The most conspicuous change in the weather patterns is that for 150 years prior to 1912, volcanoes have erupted in the Northern Hemisphere in one great explosion after another. Since 1912 they have been comparatively quiet.

ATMOSPHERIC DUST

The effect of dust in the atmosphere on the climate depends on the nature of the dust and its location in the atmosphere. Krakatoa was a less significant eruption than Tambora in terms of the effects on climate even though the volcano sent an impressive amount of dust into the atmosphere. Eruptions that throw dust into the atmosphere are divided into the following two categories: those that create dust layers in the troposphere and lower stratosphere up to about 20 miles altitude, and those that reach altitudes of about 30 miles or more. It is the first group that has the greatest influence on the climate because such eruptions produce dense, long-lived dust clouds.

Atmospheric scientists agree that it might not be the dust alone that blocks out heat from the Sun. Volcanoes also produce vast quantities of water vapor and gases, including sulfur dioxide, that reacts with water to produce sulfuric acid. These aerosols might also penetrate the stratosphere like a fine mist and obscure sunlight. With the combination of both dust and aerosols being tossed up into the atmosphere, the large volcanic eruptions make the most important contributions affecting the climate.

Many of the coldest, wettest summers, like those of 1784 and 1816, have been termed "volcanic dust years." It might be that volcanic dust played an important part in all the very worst summers and some of the coldest winters from the seventeenth century to the twentieth century. But the dust veil alone could not be responsible for all the climatic changes over the past three or four centuries. Although volcanic dust is an important contributor to climatic change, this alone might not be the only cause, nor even the main cause, of some climatic variations over the centuries. A combination of changing volcanic influence and the changing solar influence, measured by sunspot activity, might best explain the pattern of climatic change over the past 500 years. But the long-term effects on the climate by volcanic eruptions might still overshadow those of sunspot activity.

The albedo is a measurement of the amount of sunlight reflected back into space, and is influenced by the amount of atmospheric dust, cloud cover, snow and ice cover, and other light-colored areas on the ground (TABLE 16-1). Changes in the albedo of the Earth caused by snow and ice fluctuations could be affected by solar variations caused by increased sunspot activity. Taking all factors into consideration, including a buildup of carbon dioxide in the atmosphere, it appears that volcanic dust and aerosols still account for the largest influence on the climate and coincides with the record of temperature changes since 1600. Sunspot variations do not provide such a good agreement.

CLIMATIC CYCLES

A former student of Harry Lamb's, P.M. Kelly — and his colleagues at the University of East Anglia in England — looked for regular variations in the dust veil index and climate, and found

TABLE 16-1. Albedo of Various Surfaces

SURFACE	PERCENT REFLECTED
Clouds, stratus	
<500 feet thick	25-63
500-1000 feet thick	45-75
1000-2000 feet thick	59-84
Average all types and thicknesses	50-55
Snow, fresh-fallen	80-90
Snow, old	45-70
White sand	30-60
light soil (or desert)	25-30
Concrete	17-27
Plowed field, moist	14-17
Crops, green	5-25
Meadows, green	5-10
Forests, green	5-10
Dark soil	5-15
Road, blacktop	5-10
Water, depending upon sun angle	5-60

that both show a 7 to 8 year cycle. It is highly unlikely that the two cycles kept in step from 1725 to 1950 simply by coincidence. This discovery supports the idea that changing volcanic activity alone influences the climate. The volcanic cycle could also be related to a similar known fluctuation in the Earth's rotation, over which the length of day first increases and then decreases by a fraction of a second. These slight wobbles in the Earth could trigger volcanic eruptions, thereby affecting the weather.

The scientists made an even more startling discovery of a 180-year rhythm in volcanic activity resulting from changing tidal stresses acting on the Earth. This cycle is similar to a 180-year weather cycle and a 180-year rhythm in solar activity. The changes in tidal stresses are related to the gravitational forces caused by the alignment of the planets. This so-called Jupiter effect last occurred in 1984. Some scientists have even suggested that the solar rhythm is affected by the tidal influences of the planets which, in turn, seems to influence the weather on Earth. Sunspot variations and changes in volcanic activity and climate might also be produced independently, and the cycles could just be coincidental.

In the cores taken from the Greenland ice sheet are found detectable traces of volcanic eruptions dating back 10,000 years (near the end of the last ice age). Direct temperature measurements are made by comparing the changing proportions of oxygen isotopes in the ice. Because volcanic eruptions eject huge quantities of acid gases into the atmosphere, periods of great volcanic activity are followed by periods of acid rainfall or acid snowfall. The traces of acid in the ice sheet conduct electricity more easily than does ice made of pure water. The acid can be detected by observing the drop in electrical current through the ice core at various points along its length.

A comparison of the top layers of the ice with the historic record of volcanic eruptions shows that the "acid test" is a very good indicator of volcanic activity in latitudes north of 20 degrees south. These latitudes are the only ones of interest to those of us in the Northern Hemisphere. The acid-ity changes match up well with other indicators such as tree rings where narrow bands of growth indicate colder seasons, rings in mudstones caused by alternating wet and dry seasons, and historic records of climate.

GLOBAL COOLING

Until the 1980 eruption of Mount St. Helens, the best documented evidence of how dust from volcanoes affects the transmission of solar radiation through the atmosphere was the 1963 eruption of Mount Agung in Bali. Mount Agung has a geographical position much like that of Tambora. After the eruption, the temperature of the troposphere between 30 degrees south and 30 degrees north latitudes fell by almost half a degree centigrade by late 1964. By end of 1966, the temperature had recovered to about its preeruption average. The effect was more intense in the northern latitudes, where it amounted to a decrease of 0.6 degrees C. Further studies indicated, however, that the volcano's effects on the climate were twice as much as they should have been. Until the Limited Test Ban Treaty was ratified in 1963, countries — mainly the United States and the Soviet Union — tested their nuclear weapons in the atmosphere. These nuclear explosions lofted huge amounts of radioactive debris and oxides of nitrogen into the stratosphere. Besides the radioactive fallout having a worldwide health effect, the lingering nuclear dust clouds cooled the atmosphere by the same degree as the Agung eruption.

If Mount St. Helens had erupted differently than it did in the spring of 1980, that summer could well have been cool and wet for the United States (FIG. 16-4). Instead, most of the blast was directed laterally and little of the rock and ash was directed upward into the stratosphere. There was no global high-altitude dust cloud. Although there were measurable effects on the stratosphere, the loss of the solar radiation reaching the ground and the effects on the weather during 1981 were minimal.

Further studies indicated, however, that had the dust from the volcano been blasted vertically into the atmosphere, the worldwide effects would

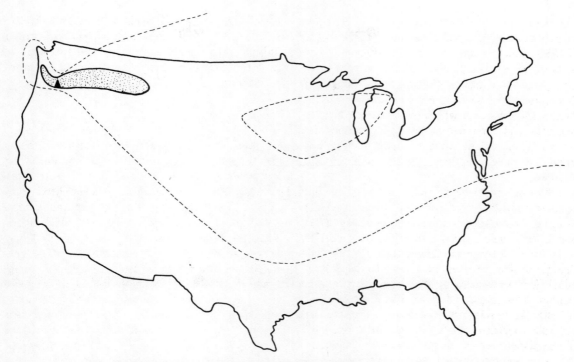

FIG. 16-4. Distribution of ash cloud from the 1980 eruption of Mount St. Helens.

probably have been noticeable, but not too severe. Dust injected into the stratosphere in the temperate zones tends to spread less and has a lesser effect than dust injected by volcanoes in the tropics. The dust from volcanic eruptions in the tropics is carried poleward by a high-altitude flow of air originating from the tropics and concentrated in the higher latitudes where sunlight strikes the Earth from a steep angle and therefore has a longer path through the dust. All six eruptions of Mount St. Helens during 1980 together blasted out a mass of dust estimated to be more than the dust from the single eruption of Krakatoa. Perhaps it was a lucky accident that the dust blasted sideways instead of upward. Even the high latitude might not have saved us from bad weather and ruined crops.

To understand what the world missed by the manner in which Mount St. Helens erupted, it is necessary to relive the events of 1816. As the dust from the Tambora eruption spread to the Northern Hemisphere, the temperate zone experienced waves of bitter cold that first killed the crops in the fields and then ruined repeated efforts of the farmers to salvage something from the wreckage.

In New England, farmers complained, as they usually do when spring is late, and there were hard frosts even in May. In June, things seemed to be back to normal. Then on June 6, a wave of cold air moved out of the Arctic and flowed into New England. Winter conditions returned and lasted for five days, leaving several inches of snow on the ground (FIG. 16-5). In July, a second cold wave swept over the region and ice and frost killed crops between July 5 and 9.

Summer weather did not return until July 12, and it remained reasonably warm until August 20, at which time the harvest was about to begin. Then came the worst of it all. Frost killed crops from Maine to Pennsylvania and the mountains in Vermont were covered with snow. In Canada, condi-

FIG. 16-5. The June 1816 snow line in New England.

tions were much worse. While wheat survived reasonably well in the United States, Canadian wheat perished from the onslaught of cold weather.

Europe, devastated by the last stages of the Napoleonic Wars which ended in 1815, was further wrecked by the weather of 1816. In France, all food reserves went to feed Napolean's army. There was no food left to tide the civilians over even in an ordinary bad summer, and many regions were affected by famine and rioting. The cold summer of 1816 set many records in Europe. July was the coldest in the English Lancashire plain in 192 years. In Geneva, Switzerland, the mean summer temperature was the lowest since 1753. Throughout Europe, many regions were afflicted with shortfalls in the harvest, and there was widespread starvation and riots. The failure of the potato crop in Ireland caused widespread famine that led to a

typhus epidemic in 1817 to 1819 that killed 65,000 people. The typhus spread all over Europe and only added to the havoc caused by the war and bad weather.

It is amazing that no one made the connection between the eruption of Tambora and the unseasonably cold summer weather of 1816. Some nineteenth-century scientists blamed the bad weather on an unusual amount of sunspots that were clearly visible to the naked eye that year. It is possible that the sunspots were more visible than normal because of the slight darkening of the Sun due to the volcanic dust in the atmosphere.

Others attributed the cold weather to a breakup of icebergs from the Arctic. Ice drifted south and cooled the North Atlantic. Perhaps the most bizarre explanation had to do with electrical fluids circulating within the Earth. Earthquakes that occurred during 1815 interrupted these currents, and the interior resistive heating was reduced. Some even claimed that lightning rods introduced by Benjamin Franklin had disrupted the natural flow of the internal electricity and thereby disrupted the weather.

WARMING TRENDS

Since the end of the nineteenth century, the world first warmed up slightly by about half a degree centigrade, and then it cooled down after 1940. The lofting of dust and soot from man's activities has had a profound and lasting effect on the weather. During World War II, the bombing and burning of cities on such a grand scale could have had a major effect on the lowering of the temperature.

By the 1970s the cooling reached 0.4 degrees below the peak low of the early 1940s. To some extent, this pattern might be related to changes in solar activity. Another factor that must have played some part is the changing pattern of volcanic activity in which the middle of the twentieth century was relatively free from the cooling effects of volcanic dust.

After several eruptions in the late nineteenth and early twentieth centuries, there were relatively few great volcanic outbursts for several decades. It could be that the gradual warming of the world up to the 1940s corresponds to the time it took for volcanic dust to settle out of the stratosphere. In the second half of the twentieth century, volcanic activity has been on the rise after a period of relative quiet.

Besides increasing volcanic activity in the second half of this century, there has been an increase of human activity such as air pollution from factories and automobiles, contrails from jet aircraft, windblown soil from freshly plowed or barren farmland, and smoke from slash-and-burn agriculture. The clearing of great forests to make way for new farmland has also increased the Earth's albedo, causing more sunlight to be reflected back into space instead of warming the Earth.

All this activity is equivalent to a continuously erupting "human volcano," adding its burden, along with the real thing, into the atmosphere. The amount of dust suspended in the atmosphere at any one time, as the result of human activity alone, is estimated at 15 million tons. This is believed to have a large influence on the climate today, producing a continuing global cooling. On the other hand, there are those who believe that increasing human activity also releases large amounts of carbon dioxide into the atmosphere, causing a greenhouse effect and global warming. There appears then to be a tug of war between the two forces because volcanoes also inject large amounts of carbon dioxide — one of the volatiles in the magma — into the atmosphere.

As in volcanic eruptions, a lot is dependent on the type of pollutants being released into the atmosphere by mankind, including the size of the dust particles and where they are concentrated in the atmosphere. Large dust particles in the troposphere could actually trap heat from the ground that would otherwise escape into space, and could thereby warm the Earth. It is the smaller particles, or aerosols, that tend to allow the heat from the ground to escape out into space while stopping heat from the Sun from reaching the ground.

Human activities are responsible for about 30 percent of the atmospheric loading of aerosols out of a total of about 40 million tons. If the dust overlies light-colored surfaces, such as snow-packed areas, it absorbs more incoming solar heat than the surface would be able to (so there is a net warming of the world). If instead, the dust overlies a dark colored surface, such as a forest, it absorbs less heat than the surface would be able to (so there is a net cooling of the ground). It appears, however, that the human volcano effect is unlikely to cause a net warming influence on the globe, but just the opposite, and it is not yet as important as volcanic eruptions.

This century's answer to Krakatoa, as far as the effects on the climate are concerned, was the 1982 explosive eruption of El Chichon in southern Mexico, almost exactly 100 years after Krakatoa. The volcanic cloud might have cooled the Northern Hemisphere by as much as any volcanic eruption in the past 100 years. A dense cloud of sulfurous gases and dust was shot into the stratosphere with the highest concentration, measured above Hawaii, at approximately 16 miles altitude. The immense cloud was still detectable at least one month after the eruption. It took 10 days to reach Asia, two weeks to reach Africa, and completely circumnavigated the globe in three weeks.

In 1983, the average temperature in the Northern Hemisphere dropped about half a degree centigrade. This translates into swimmers shivering on the beaches in the summertime, which was also unusually wet, and one of the coldest winters in quite a long while. Part of this climatic disturbance was caused by the reawakening of the El Niño current in the Pacific ocean from 1982 to 1983, which destroyed the anchovy crop and appeared to have been connected with the El Chichon eruption. The effects on the climate by the El Chichon eruption were not nearly as great as those of Tambora or Krakatoa. More intense effects, in combination with the human volcano, could have been devastating to a world where three-quarters of the human population goes to bed hungry.

EXTINCTION OF THE DINOSAURS

Many scientists hold to the belief that the massive die out of the dinosaurs and large numbers of other species at the end of the Cretacious, 65 million years ago, was due to large-scale volcanic eruptions taking place in a short time span. The lofting of so much volcanic dust and aerosols into the atmosphere could have brought on rapid cooling. Because the large reptiles are thought to be cold blooded, the loss of body heat under these frigid conditions would surely cause their demise. Another explanation for the die out could be the result of a magnetic pole reversal during which time the Earth's magnetic field dies away to nothing for a short period. This would allow a torrent of cosmic radiation, normally repelled by the magnetic field, to flood over the Earth (FIG. 16-6). Land animals are particularly susceptible to this form of radiation. There might also have been climatic changes due to the high influx of cosmic

FIG. 16-6. Aurora borealis. (Courtesy of NOAA.)

radiation causing a worldwide ionic cloud cover that could effectively block out the Sun.

One of the most fascinating theories proposed for the extinction of the dinosaurs was put forward by the American physicist Luis Alvarez and his son, the geologist Walter Alvarez. They suggested that the Earth might have been struck by a 6-mile-wide asteroid. The giant impact not only disintegrated the asteroid, but also threw up enormous amounts of fine dust from the impact into the atmosphere. The dust might have been so thick that it kept sunlight from reaching the ground for months, causing starvation and death for three-quarters of all life on Earth. Part of their evidence for such a disaster was a thin, worldwide layer of clay—probably formed when the dust settled out of the atmosphere—which had a high concentration of iridium (a rare isotope of platinum). Iridium is normally found in only trace amounts on Earth, but it is several thousand times more abundant on asteroids and meteors. The thin mud deposits with iridium concentrations over a hundred times greater than normal were located at the Cretacious-Tertiary boundary — the exact time when the die-out occurred. Some scientists refute the theory, and suggest that the iridium could have been expelled by a large number of erupting volcanoes.

Taking Alvarez's theory one step further, the American astronomer Carl Sagan and his colleagues proposed a scenario for nuclear war called "nuclear winter." It began with observations of the Martian dust storm that completely encircled the planet during the 1971 *Mariner 9* mission. Dust storms on Earth never reach such proportions, but volcano eruptions can send up vast quantities of dust and aerosols into the atmosphere, where the particles encircle the Earth.

Fine volcanic particles shot up into the stratosphere are not washed out by rain as they are in the troposphere; they might linger for years. If thousands of nuclear weapons (present arsenal on both sides is about 55,000 warheads) were to go off simultaneously, they would cast up huge volumes of radioactive dust into the stratosphere. Burning cities and forests would clog the troposphere below. This could effectively block out the Sun for months, and there would be darkness at noon and subzero temperatures in the summertime. What happened to the dinosaurs and other animals 65 million years ago could very well happen again in this age, only this time the results would be man-made.

Volcanoes and earthquakes are tremendous natural forces capable of wreaking havoc on mankind and his environment. The effects of earthquakes are felt over wide areas, and their ability to destroy whole cities has been well documented over the ages. Although their destruction is fairly mild and localized by comparison, volcanoes have the distinction of being able to affect the climate over large parts of the world. Volcanic eruptions and earthquakes can now be predicted with some degree of certainty, although one might slip by every once and a while. This allows people some time to make decisions concerning their property and welfare — not so with nuclear war.

Taken together, all the destruction to man and his environment caused by volcanoes and earthquakes since time immortal could not begin to approach that of our present-day nuclear stockpiles. Earthquakes might level great cities and start huge firestorms, as do nuclear weapons, but they are not accompanied by a huge blast wave that kills and maims in tragically large numbers. Earthquakes do not leave behind large doses of deadly radioactive poisons that linger thousands of years. Major volcanic eruptions have been spread out over long periods of time, but nuclear war would be equivalent to 1000 Mount St. Helens going off all at once.

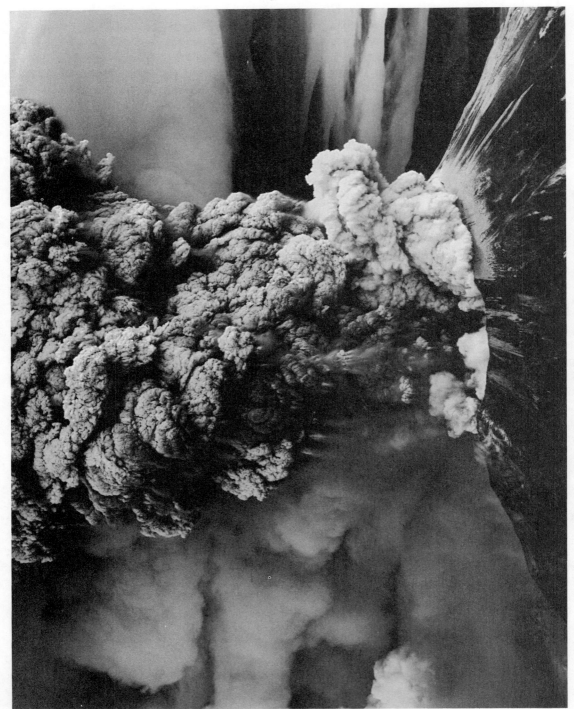

FIG. 16-7. Mount St. Helens. (Courtesy of Austin Post, USGS.)

APPENDIX

⚜

Dating Geological Events

EARLY geologists tried a number of methods to date the Earth. One such method dealt with the sedimentation rates of deposits and gave various ages depending upon the region. Another method attempted to measure the salinity of rivers and compare it with the salinity of the oceans. The oceans were believed to have started with fresh water and acquired saltiness through time. Yet, another method was to determine how long it would take the Earth to cool down to its present temperature from a molten state. The Sun was also thought to burn conventional fuels that would allow it to burn for only a few tens of millions of years.

Today, scientists know that the Sun's power is derived from fusion. This produces copious amounts of energy and makes the Sun shine for billions of years. Scientists also know that the half-lifes of certain radioactive elements found on the Earth, the Moon, and meteorites have placed the age of the Earth at 4.6 billion years.

ABSOLUTE TIME

In 1896, the French physicist Henri Becquerel, looking for new sources of X rays, accidentally stumbled across similar rays, called gamma rays, radiating from uranium. He mistakenly placed a rock sample containing uranium in a drawer with some photographic paper. When the photographic paper was developed, Becquerel discovered that it was exposed as it would be with X rays. The source for these mysterious rays could only have come from the rock. Uranium and other elements were discovered to be radioactive by Marie and Pierre Curie in 1898. Two English scientists, physicist Ernest Rutherford and chemist Federick Soddy, discovered in 1902 that radiation produced heat and that the emissions transformed the original parent element to a new daughter element that was totally different in chemical composition. By the end of the first decade of this century, the

American chemist B.B. Boltwood, using the rate of decay, calculated the half-lives of several radioactive elements. This gave geologists their first tool for the absolute dating of rocks.

The half-life is the time it takes for one-half of a radioactive element to decay to a stable daughter product. If one pound of a hypothetical radioactive element had a half-life of 1 million years, then after a period of 1 million years there would be half a pound of original parent material and half a pound of daughter product. The ratio of parent element to its daughter product is determined by chemical analysis of a sample rock. When the quantities of parent and daughter is equal, then their ratio is 1 to 1, and one half-life has expired, meaning that the specimen is 1 million years old. After 2 million years, three-quarters of the parent element has decayed into its daughter product and after 4 million years, only one-sixteenth of the original parent element remains. In other words, if the chemical analysis of a rock showed a ratio of parent and daughter of 1 to 15, then that sample is 4 million years old. Generally, radioactive elements are usable for age dating up to about 10 half-lifes. After that, the amount of parent material is reduced by about one thousandth of its original mass.

Of all the radioactive elements that exist in nature, only four have been proven useful in dating ancient rocks (TABLE A–1). The others are either very rare or have half-lives that are too short or too long. Rubidium-87 has a half-life of 47 billion years. Uranium-238 has a half-life of 4.5 billion years. And uranium-235 has a half-life of .7 billion years. These are only used for dating rocks that are millions or even billions of years old. Potassium-40 is more versatile for dating younger rocks. Although the half-life of potassium-40 is 1.3 billion years, recent analytical techniques have made it possible to detect minute amounts of its stable daughter product, argon-40, in rocks as young as 50,000 years. The two uranium isotopes are important in dating igneous and metamorphic rocks. Both species of uranium occur together. Therefore, they could be used to cross-check each other. If the dates from the two different decay series agree, then it is fairly certain that the dates are correct.

Dating sedimentary rocks is another problem because their material was derived from weathering processes. Fortunately, a micalike mineral called glauconite forms in the sedimentary environment and contains both potassium-40 and rubidium-87. As a result, the age of the sedimentary deposit could be established directly by determin-

TABLE A-1. Frequently Used Radioactive Isotopes			
RADIOACTIVE PARENT	HALF-LIFE (YEARS)	DAUGHTER PRODUCT	ROCKS AND MINERALS COMMONLY DATED
Uranium-238	4.5 billion	Lead-206	Zircon, uraninite, pitchblend
Uranium-235	713 million	Lead-207	Zircon, uraninite, pitchblend
Potassium-40	1.3 billion	Argon-40	Muscovite, biotite, hornblend, glauconite, sanidine, volcanic rock
Rubidium-87	47 billion	Strontium-87	Muscovite, biotite, lepidolite, microcline, glauconite, metamorphic rock
Carbon-14	5730	Nitrogen-14	All plant and animal materials

ing the age of the glauconite. Unfortunately, metamorphism, no mater how slight, might reset the radiometric clock by moving the parent and daughter products elsewhere. Therefore, the radiometric measurement only dates the metamorphic event. In order to accurately date these rocks, it is necessary to make what is known as a whole-rock analysis, and large chunks of rock are involved instead of individual minerals.

In order to date more recent events, a radioactive isotope of carbon called carbon-14, or radiocarbon, is used. Carbon-14 is continuously produced in the upper atmosphere by cosmic ray bombardment of gases that then release neutrons. The neutrons are absorbed by the nitrogen in the air, causing its nucleus to emit a proton. This nuclear reaction converts the nitrogen into radioactive carbon-14. In chemical reactions, this element behaves identically to natural carbon-12; therefore, it quickly reacts with oxygen to form carbon dioxide, circulates in the atmosphere, and is absorbed by living matter. As a result, all organisms, including man, contain a small amount of carbon-14 as well as carbon-12.

Carbon-14 decays at a steady rate and has a half-life of 5730 years. When an organism is alive, the decaying radiocarbon is continuously being replaced, and the proportions of carbon-14 and carbon-12 remain constant. However, when a plant or animal dies, it ceases to intake any carbon and the amount of carbon-14 gradually decreases as it decays to stable nitrogen-14. This is accomplished by the emission of a beta particle (free electron) from the nucleus, thus transmuting a neutron of carbon-14 into a proton, and the nitrogen atom is restored to its original state.

Radiocarbon dating was discovered in the late 1940s by the American chemist Willard F. Libby, who received the Nobel Prize for his achievement. By comparing the proportions of carbon-14 and carbon-12 in a sample, radiocarbon dates could be determined by chemical analysis. Until the late 1970s, radiocarbon was useful in dating events only as far back as 40,000 to 50,000 years. However, like potassium-40, the development of improved analytical techniques has increased its usefulness. Carbon-14 can now be used to date events as far back as 75,000 years. This makes it a very valuable tool for geologists who can now date many events taking place in the ice age that began 90,000 years ago. Before this could not be done accurately. Also, paleontologists, anthropologists, archaeologists, and historians, now have a means of accurately dating events taking place in man's distant past.

Since 1945, nuclear explosions in the atmosphere have doubled the amount of carbon-14 found in the atmosphere prior to the nuclear era. To further complicate matters, carbon-12 generated by burning fossil fuels ever since the industrial revolution of the 1850s, has diluted the carbon-14 content in the atmosphere to 98 percent of its preindustrial amount. This tends to throw off the accuracy of radiocarbon dating. Thus, the true dates for events taking place between 5000 B.C. to 400 B.C. are actually older than shown by their carbon-14 content.

For the last 2000 years, there are some minor discrepancies between carbon-14 dates and true dates, but these are insignificant. Generally, the dates are in good agreement. The problem becomes greater when trying to date events older than 2000 years from which time there is a greater divergence of radiocarbon dates from actual recorded dates. The discrepancy indicates that there might have been more carbon-14 available to plants and animals at that time. Even so, radiocarbon dating is the best, and possibly the only reliable method for dating man's activities that took place prior to recorded history.

Although the basic principal of radiometric dating sounds simple enough, the actual procedure is quite complicated because the chemical analysis that determines the amount of parent and daughter product that are present must be painstakingly precise. Not only that, but the quantities of these substances might be on the order of only a few parts per million. There is also a certain amount of naturally occurring daughter material that existed in the rock before the clock began ticking that must be taken into account. Also, many radioactive materials do not decay directly into stable daughter products but take a round-about route going through a whole series of intermediate decay schemes which further complicates the analysis.

In the case of uranium-238, there are thirteen intermediate unstable daughter products formed before the last daughter product, the stable isotope of lead-206, is produced. Each intermediate stage could take minutes, days, or thousands of years before decaying to the next step. This distorts the overall picture, but nevertheless, radiometric dating is sufficiently accurate to make reliable age determinations, especially if two or more methods collaborate with the results.

For instance, the bristlecone pines of the western United States are the oldest known living things on Earth. By counting tree rings, it is possible to establish a 7000-year record. From 7000 to 2000 years ago, radiocarbon ages were found to be too young by as much as 10 percent. Therefore, many dates had to be adjusted upward by the same amount.

Radioactive decay also appears to be constant with time and is unaffected by chemical reactions and the temperatures and pressures generated on Earth. Nor are there any other known conditions or processes that could change the decay rate throughout geologic history. Confirmation that decay rates are steady throughout time is found in certain minerals such as biotite mica. Extremely small zones of discoloration, or haloes, are found surrounding minute inclusions of radioactive particles within the crystal. The haloes consist of a series of concentric rings around the radioactive source. Particles emitted by the radioactive source damage the surrounding biotite minerals. The energy of the particle is determined by how far it travels through the mineral and depends on the type of radioactive element responsible. Because the concentric rings have radii corresponding to the energy of present-day particles, particle energies have not changed. Therefore, it seems reasonable to conclude that the rate of radioactive decay does not change with time.

Radioactive decay is also statistical, and not all individual atoms of a particular radioactive element decay at the very same rate. Some atoms will spontaneously decay faster or slower than others. This is because the emission of a radioactive particle from within the nucleus of an atom is a random event. The majority of the decays cluster around a certain point in time while the rest occur somewhat sooner or later, and this obeys a typical bell curve distribution. Therefore, the radioactive material in a rock is composed of tiny radioactive clocks, each ticking away at its own pace. But taken together as a whole, radioactive elements in a rock can be treated statistically as decaying at the same rate.

In the past, the Earth's magnetic field has reversed itself many times. This discovery gave rise to a new branch of science called paleomagnetism. As iron-rich lavas cool and solidify, the iron molecules face whichever direction the magnetic pole happens to be at that time. The molecules react like miniature bar magnets. Sediments might preserve a similar record as they are being deposited because small magnetic grains settle like tiny compasses, each pointing in the direction of the magnetic pole. The weak magnetic fields are detected by sensitive magnetometers that not only give the direction but also the magnitude of the magnetic field. The pattern of magnetic reversals over the past 100 million years or so, is not regular, but distinctive, like varying widths of tree rings. Therefore, magnetic reversals in rocks throughout the world can be used to supplement other dating methods.

RELATIVE TIME

Relative dating differs from absolute dating in that the latter pinpoints the time in history while the former only places rocks in their proper sequence or order. Relative dating will not tell how long ago an event took place; only that it followed one event and preceded another. Before the development of radiometric dating techniques, geologists had no means of dating events precisely, so relative dating techniques were developed and are still in use today. Absolute dating methods did not replace these techniques but only supplemented them.

The Italian physician Nicolas Steno (1638-1686) was the first to recognize that in a sequence of layered rocks undeformed by folding or faulting, each layer was formed after the one below it and before the one above it. His law of superposition might seem rather obvious to us today, but its discovery was a very important scientific achievement. Steno also put forward his principle of original horizontality, which simply means that sedimentary beds are initially laid down horizontally, and later, folding and faulting inclined them at an angle. If angled rocks are overlain by horizontal ones, there exists a gap in time known as an angular unconformity. If any body of rocks cuts across the boundaries of other units of rocks, it must be younger than those it cuts. This is the principle of cross-cutting relationship whereby granitic intrusions are younger than the rocks they invaded. The sequence of rocks placed in their proper sequence is called a stratigraphic cross-section.

In order to develop a geologic time scale that is applicable to the whole Earth, rocks of similar age are matched up in what is known as correlation. By correlating the rocks from one place to another over a wide area, it is possible to obtain a comprehensive view of the geologic history of a region. A certain bed or a series of beds could be traced from one outcrop to another by recognizing certain distinct features in the rocks. A problem arises, however, if there are two or more rock units at each locality that are identical. Then the question becomes which is which?

To further complicate matters, if there was faulting in the area, one block of a rock sequence might be down-dropped in relation to the other or over-thrusted on top of another. Rocks that occur in repetitive sequences of sandstone, shale, and limestone make correlation even more difficult. Although these methods might be sufficient to trace a rock formation over relatively short distances, they are not adequate for matching up rocks at great distance such as from one continent to another.

If a geologist wants to correlate between widely separated areas or between continents, he has to rely upon fossils. The branch of geology devoted to the study of ancient life based on fossils is called paleontology. A fossil is the remains or traces of organisms preserved from the geologic past. A plant or animal must be buried rapidly in the absence of oxygen or bacteria in order to become a fossil. Given enough time, the remains of an organism is modified. Often fossils become petrified and are literally turned into stone. The original substance, be it wood or bone, is replaced by minerals from circulating solutions or by filling pore spaces with minerals.

The most common petrifying agents carried by the groundwater are calcite and silica. If the groundwater dissolves the remains buried in the sediment, a mold is made. The mold faithfully reflects the shape and surface markings of the organism but does not reveal any information about its internal structure. When the mold is subsequently filled with mineral matter, a cast is created.

Leaves and delicate animal forms are preserved by a type of fossilization called carbonization. It occurs when fine sediment, such as clay, encases the remains of an organism. As time passes, pressure from overlying rocks squeezes out the liquid and gaseous components and leaves behind a thin film of carbon. Black shales deposited as organic-rich mud in oxygen-poor environments, such as swamps, often contain abundant carbonized remains. If the film of carbon is lost from a fossil preserved in fine-grain sediment, a replica of the surface of the plant or animal, called an impression, might still show considerable detail. Other delicate organisms such as insects are difficult to preserve in this manner. Consequently, insects are quite rare in the fossil record. Not only do they need to be protected from decay, but they must not be subjected to any pressure that would crush them. The way many insects are preserved is in amber, the hardened resin of ancient trees. The insect is first trapped in the sticky resin that seals off the insect from the atmosphere and protects the remains from damaging air and water. When the resin hardens, it forms a protective, pressure-resistant case around the insect.

Only a tiny fraction of the organisms that have lived throughout the past have been preserved as fossils. Normally, the remains of a plant or animal are completely destroyed. Only under special circumstances of rapid burial and the possession of hard parts is a fossil made. Usually, when an organism dies, its soft parts are eaten by scavengers or decomposed by bacteria, and the remaining hard parts are then exposed to the elements and turned into dust.

Plants and animals have a better chance of entering into the fossil record if they have hard parts that are buried rapidly. Therefore, shells, bones, teeth, and wood predominate in the record of past life. Unfortunately, because preservation is contingent on these special conditions, the fossil record is well represented by organisms with hard parts and poorly represented or not represented at all by organisms with only soft parts. Also, only a small fraction of all fossils are exposed to the Earth's surface, and most of these are destroyed by weathering processes.

Although the existence of fossils has been known through the ages, it was not until the eighteenth century that their significance as a geologic tool was made evident. The English civil engineer William Smith (1769–1839) discovered that rock formations in canals contained fossils unlike those in the beds either below or above. He also noticed that sedimentary strata in widely separated areas could be identified by their distinctive fossil content. These observations led to one of the most important and basic principles in historic geology. Fossilized organisms succeed one another in a definite and determinable order. Therefore, any time period could be recognized by its fossil content.

When fossils are arranged according to their age, they do not present a random or haphazard picture. Instead, they show progressive changes from simple to complex forms and reveal the advancement of the species through time. This concept became known as the principle of faunal succession. Paleontologists were then able to recognize ages that pertained to groups of organisms that were especially plentiful and characteristic during a particular time period. Within each age, there are many subdivisions based on the occurrence of certain species, and this same succes-

sion is never out of order and is found on every major land mass.

The geologic history has been subdivided into time units of varying magnitudes. The major units were delineated during the nineteenth century, principally by geologists in Great Britain and Western Europe. Because there was no absolute dating during this time, the entire geologic record was created using methods of relative dating. It has only been in this century that absolute dates has been added.

The largest divisions of the geologic record are called eras. The four eras are: the Precambrian, the age of prelife; the Paleozoic, the age of ancient life; the Mesozoic, the age of middle life; and the Cenozoic, the age of new life.

Each era, except the Precambrian, is subdivided into smaller units called periods. The Paleozoic has seven, the Mesozoic has three, and the Cenozoic has two. Each period is characterized by a somewhat less profound change in life forms as compared with the eras which mark boundaries of mass extinctions, proliferations, or rapid transformations of life forms. Finally, the two periods of the Cenozoic have been further subdivided into seven epochs.

The largest era, the Precambrian, lasted for 4 billion years and is not subdivided, owing to the lesser amounts of fossils. It was not until the beginning of the Paleozoic, about 570 million years ago, that there was a proliferation of life. And along with that, abundant fossils.

Since the fairly accurate absolute dates have been applied to the periods of relative time, there has been some difficulty. The basic problem in trying to assign absolute dates to units of relative time is that most radioactive elements are restricted to igneous rock. Even if sedimentary rocks — which comprise most of the rocks on the Earth's surface as well as having all the fossils — did contain a radioactive mineral, most rocks could not be dated accurately because the grains in the rock were derived from rocks that were much older. Therefore, in order to date sedimentary rocks, the geologist must relate them to igneous masses, which of course, cannot contain fossils.

Volcanic ash embedded in a layer above or below the sediments could be dated radiometrically, as well as using cross-cutting features such as a granitic dike that would have to be younger. Therefore, the sedimentary rock formation would be bracketed on both sides with dated materials and its age could be determined fairly close. Today, the Earth's history is dated somewhat satisfactorily for most needs. All that remains, is for future discoveries to adjust the geologic time scale to better perfection.

Glossary

aa lava—A lava that forms large jagged, irregular blocks.

accelerometer—An instrument used to measure large ground movements.

aftershock—A smaller earthquake following the main shock.

albedo—The amount of sunlight reflected from an object.

amplitude—The length of back-and-forth motions.

andesite—An intermediate type of volcanic rock between basalt and rhyolite.

Andromeda Nebula—The nearest large spiral galaxy 2.3 million light years away.

angular momentum—A measure of an object or orbiting body to continue spinning.

antiparticle—A particle with opposite charge and spin of its counterpart.

ash fall—The fallout of small, solid particles from a volcanic eruption cloud.

assimilation—The melting and subsequent combination of solid rock materials, within the molten elements of a magma body.

asthenosphere—A layer of the upper mantle, roughly between 50 and 200 miles below the surface, and is more plastic than the rock above and below and might be in convective motion.

basalt—A volcanic rock which is dark in color and usually quite fluid in the molten state.

batholith—The largest of intrusive igneous bodies, of more than forty square miles on its uppermost surface.

bedrock—Solid layers of rock.

binary stars—Two stars close together and orbiting each other.

black hole—A large gravitationally collapsed body from which nothing, including light, can escape.

blue shift—The shift of spectral lines towards shorter wavelengths, caused by the Doppler effect for an approaching source.

bomb, volcanic—A solidified blob of molten rock ejected from a volcano.

bore hole—A hole drilled into the Earth's crust.

caldera—A large pit-like depression found at the summits of some volcanoes, formed by great explosive activity and collapse.

Cenozoic Era—An age known as recent life, spanning from 65 million years ago to the present.

cepheid variable—A star whose intensity varies periodically and used to determine distances in the universe.

circum-Pacific belt—Active seismic regions around the rim of the Pacific plate, coinciding with the ring of fire.

conduit—A passageway leading from a reservoir of magma to the surface of the Earth through which volcanic products pass.

cone, volcanic—The general term applied to any volcanic mountain with a conical shape.

conservation law—A law that states that a particular quantity does not change, or is conserved in a given physical process.

continent—A slab of light, granitic rock which floats on denser rocks of the upper mantle.

convection—A circular, vertical flow of a fluid medium due to heating from below. As materials are heated they become less dense and rise, while cooler, heavier materials sink.

coral—Any of a large group of shallow-water, bottom-dwelling marine invertebrates which are reef-building colonies common in warm waters.

core—The central part of the Earth with a radius of 2300 miles and consisting of a crystalline inner core and molten outer core composed of iron and nickel.

cosmic rays—High-energy charged particles which enter the Earth's atmosphere from outer space.

crater, volcanic—The inverted conical depression found at the summit of most volcanoes, formed by the explosive emission of volcanic ejecta.

craton—The ancient, stable interior region of a continent, commonly composed of Precambrian rocks.

crust—The outer layers of the Earth's rocks.

density—The amount of any quantity per unit volume.

diapir—Any body, such as a large blob of magma, that pierces the crust.

dilatancy—The growth of pressure fractures in a rock subjected to stress.

disk galaxy—A flat pancake-shaped galaxy with a radius up to 25 times its thickness.

divergent plate boundary—The boundary between crustal plates where the plates move apart. Generally corresponds to the mid-ocean ridges where new crust is formed by the solidification of liquid rock rising from below.

Doppler effect—The effect by which the motion of the source of a wave shifts the frequency of that wave.

earthquake—The sudden breaking of Earth's rocks.

elastic rebound theory—The theory that earthquakes depend on rock elasticity.

electron—A negative particle of small mass orbiting the nucleus and equal in number to the proton.

element—A material consisting of only one type of atom.

elliptical galaxy—A galaxy whose structure is smooth and amorphous, without spiral arms, and ellipsoidal in shape.

engineering seismology—The application of earthquake studies to engineering, and the development of earthquake-resistant construction methods.

epicenter—The point on the Earth's surface directly above the focus of an earthquake.

escarpment—A mountain wall caused by elevation of a block of land.

evolution—The tendency of physical and biological factors to change with time.

extrusive—Any igneous volcanic rock which is ejected onto the surface of the Earth.

fault—A break in the rocks due to an earthquake.

fissure—A large crack in the crust through which magma might escape from a volcano.

focus—The point of origin of an earthquake. Also

called hypocenter.

foreshock—A smaller earthquake preceding the main shock.

fossil—Any remains, impression, or trace in rock of a plant or animal of a previous geologic age.

fractionation—A process by which a subducted slab of crustal rock starts melting on its way down into the mantle, and the lighter components rise back to the surface before the heavier ones.

frequency—The rate at which crests of any wave pass a given point.

fumarole—A hole in the ground through which steam or other hot gases escape from underground, such as a geyser.

galaxy—A large gravitationally bound cluster of stars.

galvanometer—An electric current detector.

gamma rays—Photons of very high energy and short wave length. The most penetrating of electromagnetic radiation.

general relativity—The theory of gravitation developed by Albert Einstein.

geothermal—The generation of hot water or steam by hot rocks in the Earth's interior.

geyser—A spring that ejects intermittent jets of steam and hot water.

gneiss—A banded, coarse-grained metamorphic rock with alternating layers of unlike minerals. It consists of essentially the same components as granite.

Gondwanaland—A southern supercontinent of Paleozoic time, consisting of Africa, South America, India, Australia, and Antarctica. It broke up into present continents during the Mesozoic era.

graben—A valley formed by a down-dropped fault block.

granite—A coarse-grained, silica rich rock consisting primarily of quartz and feldspars. It is the principal constituents of the continents and is believed to be derived from a molten state beneath the Earth's surface.

greenhouse effect—The trapping of heat in the atmosphere by carbon dioxide.

ground shaking—A term used for the motion of the ground due to earthquakes.

ground water—The water derived from the atmosphere which percolates and circulates below the surface of the Earth.

guyot—A submerged flat-topped volcanic seamount.

helium—The second lightest and second most abundant element in the universe composed of two protons and two neutrons.

horst—An elongated, uplifted block of crust bounded by faults.

Hubble age—The approximate age of the universe obtained by extrapolating the observed expansion backward in time. The accepted value of the hubble age is roughly 15 billion years.

hydrocarbon—A molecule consisting of carbon chains with attached hydrogen atoms.

hydrogen—Lightest and most abundant element in the universe composed of one proton and one electron.

hydrothermal deposit—A mineral ore deposit emplaced by hot ground water.

hypocenter—The point of origin of earthquakes. Also called focus.

igneous rocks—All rocks that have solidified from a molten state.

ignimbrite—Volcanic deposits created by ejections of incandescent solid particles.

inertia—inherent resistance to applied force.

infrared—invisible light with a wavelength between red light and radio waves.

insolation—All solar radiation impinging on the Earth.

intensity scale—Scale for rating earthquakes according to their effects.

intrusive—Any igneous body which has solidified in place below the surface of the Earth.

ionization—The process whereby electrons are torn off previously neutral atoms.

iridium—A rare isotope of platinum, relatively abundant on meteorites.

isoseismic map—A map of equal seismic intensity lines.

isostacy—The equilibrium achieved by blocks of crustal rock floating on denser rocks below.

Kelvin—A temperature scale, similar to the centigrade scale with its zero point placed at absolute zero, or −273 degrees C.

lahar—A hot mudflow or ashflow on the slopes of a volcano.

landslide—Rapid downhill movement of Earth materials often triggered by earthquakes.

lapilli—A term interchangable with cinder, which are small, solid pyroclastic fragments.

Laurasia—The northern supercontinent of the Paleozoic, consisting of North America, Europe, and Asia.

lava—Molten magma after it has flowed out onto the surface.

light year—The distance that electromagnetic radiation, principally light waves, can travel in a vacuum in one year or approximately six trillion miles.

limestone—A sedimentary rock composed of calcium carbonate which is secreted from sea water by invertebrates and whose skeletons composed the bulk of deposits.

liquefaction—The loss of strength of certain Earth materials due to seismic waves passing through them, and causing them to flow for a short time.

lithosphere—A rigid outer layer of the mantle, typically about 60 miles thick. It is over ridden by the continental and oceanic crusts and is divided into segments called plates.

loess—A deep deposit of airborne dust.

Love wave—The long, slow transverse earthquake wave first described by A.E.H. Love.

magma—A molten rock material generated within the Earth and is the constituent of igneous rocks, including volcanic eruptions.

magnetic field reversal—A reversal of the north-south polarity of the Earth's magnetic poles. This has occurred intermittantly through-

out geologic time.

magnetite—A dark, iron rich, strongly magnetic mineral, sometimes called a lodestone.

magnetometer—A device used to measure the intensity and direction of the magnetic field.

magnitude scale—A scale for rating earthquake energy.

mantle—The part of the Earth below the crust and above the core, composed of dense iron-magnesium rich rocks.

mass wasting—The downslope movement of rock under the direct influence of gravity.

mesosphere—The rigid part of the Earth's mantle below the asthenosphere and above the core.

Mesozoic—literally the period of middle life, refers to the period between 230 and 65 million years ago.

metamorphic rock—A rock crystallized from previous igneous, metamorphic, or sedimentary rocks created under conditions of intense temperatures and pressures without melting.

meteorite—A metallic or stony body from space that enters the Earth's atmosphere and impacts on the Earth's surface.

microearthquake—A small earth tremor.

microwave radiation—The electromagnetic waves with a wavelength between very-high frequency radio waves and infrared radiation.

mid-ocean ridge—A submarine ridge along a divergent plate boundary where a new ocean floor is created by the upwelling of mantle material.

modified Mercalli scale—A scale for rating earthquakes according to their effects.

Moho—The boundary between the crust and mantle, discovered by Andrija Mohorovicic.

moraine—A ridge of erosional debris deposited by the melting margin of a glacier.

nebula—An extended astronomical object with a cloud-like appearance. Some nebulae are galaxies; others are clouds of dust and gas within our galaxy.

neutrino—A small electrically neutral particle having weak nuclear and gravitational interactions.

neutron—A particle with no electrical charge and

has roughly the the same weight as the positively charged proton both of which are found in the nucleus of an atom.

nova—A star that suddenly brightens during its final stages.

orogeny—An episode of mountain building.

ozone—A molecule consisting of three atoms of oxygen which exists in the upper atmosphere and filters out ultraviolet light from the Sun.

pahoehoe lava—A lava that forms ropy-like structures when cooled.

paleomagnetism—The study of the Earth's magnetic field, including the position and polarity of the poles in the past.

paleontology—The study of ancient life forms, based on the fossil record of plants and animals.

Paleozoic—The period of ancient life, between 570 and 230 million years ago.

Pangaea—An ancient supercontinent that included all the land mass of the Earth.

Panthalassa—The great world ocean that surrounded pangaea.

parallax—The difference in direction of an object as seen from two different points.

photon—A packet of electromagnetic energy, generally viewed as a particle.

photosynthesis—The process by which plants create carbohydrates from carbon dioxide, water, and sunlight.

plasma—A collection of positive and negative charges that are free to to move independently of each other and are usually formed by stripping electrons from their nuclei.

placer—A deposit of rocks left behind from a melting glacier. Also, any ore deposit that is enriched by stream action.

plate tectonics—The theory that accounts for the major features of the Earth's surface in terms of the interaction of lithospheric plates.

pluton—An underground body of igneous rock younger than the rocks that surround it. It is formed where molten rock oozes into a space between older rocks.

precession—The slow change in direction of the Earth's axis of rotation due to gravitational action of the Moon on the Earth.

proton—A large particle with a positive charge in the nucleus of an atom.

pumice—Volcanic ejecta which is full of gas cavities and extremely light in weight.

pyroclastic—The fragmental ejecta released explosively from a volcanic vent.

pyrometer—A device used to measure temperatures of molten rock.

P-wave—A primary or pressure earthquake wave.

radioactivity—An atomic reaction releasing detectable radioactive particles.

radiometric dating—The determination of how long an object has existed by chemical analysis of stable versus unstable radioactive elements.

radio telescope—A large radio antenna designed to listen in on the cosmos.

Rayleigh wave—The earth motion characterized by elliptical particle motions.

red shift—The shift of light towards the lower end of the spectrum indicating that distant galaxies are receding.

rhyolite—A volcanic rock that is highly viscous in the molten state and usually ejected explosively as pyroclastics.

Richter scale—A magnitude scale used for rating earthquake energy.

roots, mountain—The deeper crustal layers under mountains.

St. Elmo's fire—Visible discharges of static electricity in the air, specifically in the masts and rigging of a ship during storms.

sandstone—A sedimentary rock consisting of sand grains cemented together.

scarp—A steep slope formed by earth movements.

schist—A finely layered metamorphic rock that tends to split readily into thin flakes.

sea floor spreading—The theory that the ocean floor is created by the separation of lithospheric plates along the mid-ocean ridges, with new oceanic crust formed from mantle material which rises from the mantle to fill the rift.

sea mount—An undersea volcano.

seiche—oscillation of water in a bay.

seismic sea wave—An ocean wave related to an undersea earthquake.

seismogram—An earthquake wave record.

seismograph—A recording and timing seismometer.

seismology—The study of the Earth from recordings of earthquake waves.

seismometer—A detector of earthquake waves.

shear—A force resulting from side-to-side motion.

shield—Areas of the exposed precambrian nucleus of a continent.

shield volcano—A broad, low lying volcanic cone built up by lava flows of low viscosity.

sial—A lightweight layer of rock that lies below the continents.

sima—A dense rock which composes the ocean floor and on which the sial floats.

solar flare—A short-lived bright event on the Sun's surface which causes greater ionization of the Earth's upper atmosphere due to an increase in ultraviolet light.

spiral galaxy—A galaxy, like our own, with a prominent central bulge embedded in a flat disk of gas, dust and young stars that wind out in spiral arms from the nucleus.

stratosphere—The upper atmosphere above the troposphere, about seven miles above sea level.

strato-volcano—An intermediate volcano characterized by a stratified structure from alternating emissions of lava and fragments.

strong forces—The force responsible for holding particles together in the nucleus.

subduction zone—An area where the oceanic plate dives below a continental plate into the asthenosphere. Ocean trenches are the surface expression of a subduction zone.

sunspot—A region on the Sun's surface which is cooler than surrounding regions and effect radio transmissions on Earth.

supernova—An enormous stellar explosion in which all but the inner core of a star is blown off into interstellar space, producing as much energy in a few days as the Sun does in a billion years.

S-wave—A secondary or shear earthquake wave.

tectonic activity—The formation of the Earth's crust by large scale Earth movements throughout geologic time.

tephra—All clastic material from dust particles to large chunks, expelled from volcanoes during eruptions.

Tethys Sea—The hypothetical mid-latitude area of the oceans separating the northern and southern continents of Gondwanaland and Laurasia some hundreds of million years ago.

tide—A bulge in the ocean produced by the Moon's gravitational forces on the Earth's oceans. The rotation of the Earth beneath this bulge causes the rising and lowering of the sea level.

tilt meter—A device used to observe the amount of swelling within a volcano before eruption.

transform fault—A fracture in the Earth's crust along which lateral movement occurs. They are common features of the mid-ocean ridges, created in the line of sea floor spreading.

tsunami—A seismic sea wave.

tuff—A rock formed of pyroclastic fragments.

ultraviolet—The invisible light with a wavelength shorter than visible light and longer than X-rays.

uniformitarianism—The belief that the slow processes that shape the Earth's surface have acted essentially unchanged throughout geologic time.

viscosity—The resistance of a liquid to flow.

volcano—A fissure or vent in the crust through which molten rock rises to the surface to form a mountain.

volcanism—Any type of volcanic activity.

X-rays—electromagnetic radiation of high-energy wave lengths above the ultraviolet and below gamma rays.

Index

Edited by David Gauthier